End

"It is a great privilege and honor to recommend *God Writes in Blue*, this book of stories, written by a most amazing woman of God, my sister-in-law. I have known Sherri for over 40 years, and cannot think of a more faithful, anointed, servant of God.

As I read *God Writes in Blue*, I became riveted and drawn into these true-life stories which are also testimonies of God's great faithfulness. As you read, you will be inspired and challenged to launch out of your boat onto the sea with Jesus.

Having seen, and in some cases lived out, the stories in the book myself, I wholeheartedly encourage you to get this book and not to put it down until you are finished.

As Chairman of the *United States National Prayer Council*, I have the served side by side with Sherri, who is our Prayer Council's International Director. Her passion for the lost, the nations, and every hurting person is a testament to the love of Christ in her heart.

I pray the body of Christ will embrace this book's message, and that it transforms our hearts for the great commission."

--**Dr. Ted Rose**, Chairman, *United States National Prayer Council*

"Isn't it amazing how God puts beautiful people in our lives to inspire us and help us draw closer to Jesus? My friend, personal prayer warrior, and mentor, Sherri Sumstine is one of those beautiful people. For the last several years, I have had the privilege of getting to know her and hearing her many adventures in the faith. I have been blessed, inspired and challenged to continue with Christ because of this beautiful soul's journey with Christ. Taking a sneak peek at this book, I was again inspired by the word craftsmanship and artistry by which she tells her story of God's unfailing love.

Let the pages of God's investment in Sherri's life lift your spirits and encourage your heart. Friend, it's a must read!"

--**Pastor James Seiler**, Founding Pastor of *Real Life Church of Galt* and *NCN* Church Planting Director

"Some people make an impression from the first meeting. Mike and Sherri were such a couple. God had rescued them, and His hand was upon them in such a distinct way that we all knew it. This book is full of the stories, the adventures, the revelations of the heart written with bravery, transparency and a desire for you to read the story of God as He picked up His pen and wrote in Blue all over their lives.

We have been incredibly blessed to be up-close friends and to have experienced the joy, sorrow, hope, tears and love that comes when you walk that close. We highly recommend this life-changing book."

--Jeff and Cheryl McEachron, *Outreach Ministries International*

"*God Writes in Blue* is written to a generation of people who need to hope again, and to believe again that with God all things are possible.

The author, Sherri Sumstine, writes from her heart; the stories, as she calls them, are testimonies of the amazing things God has done in her life and those she loves. This book is exactly what we need, what *I needed.*

As a prophet, I sense God's hand on this book. It is like He wants people to believe that He still speaks, and that we can hear His Voice. Listen to Him as you read this book, He desires to speak and release faith and hope in you."

--Pastor Julie Sawyer, *A Prophet to the Broken*

"It is my great privilege to recommend this book to everyone, regardless of spiritual or cultural background, including any who are simply curious of its title. Sherri and Mike Sumstine were long time members of *Zion Christian Fellowship,* the church where I was pastor. With a prayer on my lips that this book will be a blessing and an encouragement to all who will read it, I can attest to the accuracy of all the stories that Sherri has shared. If you have never met their wonderful Savior, who can radically change one's heart and life, I invite you to read this book and then invite Him into your heart, too."

--**Pastors Dick and Edie Patterson**, Co-Founders and President of *Outreach Ministries International*

"Sherri has shown that as a result of constant prayer, God will guide and sustain each of us. This book shows that a parent's prayer for their children is not in vain."

--**Bob Sandberg**, National Board Member, *Christian Motorcyclists Association*

"I believe Sherri Sumstine's life story will encourage others to realize that God does intervene in their journey during their most difficult times. Her warm and genuine sharing inspires faith and hope to believe Jesus is waiting to walk with each one who looks to Him for a helping hand, or to His words of hope!"

--**Dr. J. L. Bowers**, Founder of *Grace and Truth Family Restoration Center* in Brownwood, Texas, and Israel National Director, *U.S. National Prayer Council*

"My wife, Judy, and I met Mike and Sherri through the *Christian Motorcyclists Association* (CMA). I believe the first time I met Mike was at a CMA rally in 1985 in Strawberry, California. As years passed and we became more involved in CMA, and biker events, our friendship grew stronger. It was during this time that I learned of Mike's past with hard core bikers, and I saw how the power of God had changed him. Because of his past, Mike had a heart for those who did not know Jesus, especially bikers. It was also during this time, specifically the later years during Mike's illness, knowing this was a difficult time for both, that we witnessed Sherri's deep and loving devotion for Mike.

After Mike went home to be with the Lord it would have been easy for Sherri to quietly disappear, but she didn't. Sherri took up the baton and continued the race. She continues the theme of ministry that was in Mike's heart, reaching people for Jesus. Sherri believes that the most important part of the Christian race is prayer. I believe this book will encourage you, inspire you, and confirm to you that God is not dead; that He hears and answers prayer, and that He is still in the business of changing lives."

--**Joe and Judy Maxwell**, Retired National Evangelist with the *Christian Motorcyclists Association;* Pastor, *Mountain Valley Community Church*, Squaw Valley, California

GOD WRITES
IN BLUE

Powerful short stories of how God writes hope and promise into the stories of our lives

Dear Steve & Lisa —
You both are an amazing part of our story — God always gives us the Best for Now as He writes in blue! I know He does that for you!

Sherri Sumstine

Love,
Sherri Sumstine

2-17-18
2 Cor 3:23

Published in the United States of America

Cover design by Mr. Angel Esqueda. Angel Creative Web Design

 WORLD WIDE

7710-T Cherry Park Dr, Ste 224
Houston, TX 77095
(713) 766-4271

Paperback: 978-1684114153

Contents

Dedication

I dedicate this book to my loving children Michael T. Sumstine, and Stephanie Sumstine Haley. I pray this book will provide you with insight for living as I share, from my perspective, your dad's and my many stories that I know affected yours.

I leave this book as a legacy to our grandchildren and their grandchildren that they might learn not only from our mistakes but also from our milestones.

I also dedicate this book to all who look for hope and the possibility that your life story can become one made anew as it takes on the beautiful color of "God's Blue" writings within it. God longs to step in and rewrite what would have been, changing things for good all the way to the end and beyond.

A special thank you to my Media Advisor, Eileen Hovanesian for her wisdom and tremendous support, and my daughter Stephanie, for her insightful contributions shared with me throughout the writing process.

Foreword

I love the stories in this book, *God Writes In Blue* by Sherri Sumstine, because many of those could have been my story. You see I also had a praying mother. She was a seer, an intercessor, a precious mother full of love, mercy, and grace; but she was also a strong mountain woman who loved Jesus and loved her family, and nothing was gonna come between those two things.

I knew that my mom was different, she went around the house singing all the time, and she talked to herself. Well, that's what I thought when I was little, but as I grew older, I began to realize that mom was praying all the time. She even prayed when she did her work, inside or outside. She "prayed without ceasing."

One of the most beautiful stories that I remember about mom was the time I came in from playing with my toys and found her praying. She was on her knees, on the floor, talking to Jesus. I kinda felt like I shouldn't be there because it was such a personal encounter. But in reality, I was meant to be there. It was a moment in time the Lord wanted me to see. I heard her call out my name to the Lord, asking Him for my soul. She never knew I was there. It truly was a life-changing experience I'll never forget.

Sherri's first story in this book is called "Never Give Up," an amazing account of persevering prayer, regardless of the difficulty or the distance you feel between you and the Lord. We soldier on with faith in Jesus, faith in our calling, and our purpose until the answer comes. I wish the church could see in real time what God does in the heavenly realms when we pray.

John Wesley, the great revivalist, said, "God does nothing but in answer to prayer." The prophet Bob Jones had a vision of thousands of angels with their hands crossed in front of them. Bob asked the Lord, "What are they doing just standing there?"

The Lord replied, "They're waiting for someone to release them through prayer to go and do what I created them for." We have great authority in prayer if we only believe it. Doubt and unbelief are the Achilles heel of prayer.

This book is full of experiences in answered prayer. Sherri didn't try to write a handbook on prayer. This is a record of answered prayer. It's one thing to pray, but it's something else to pray and believe you have what you ask for. Sherri's stories reveal the Father's heart. My prayer is that as you read this book, He will become even more real to you.

--Ricky Skaggs, *Legendary Country/Bluegrass Recording Artist*

Introduction

My prayer is that hope will fill your heart as you read my stories. Hope is what we hold to when we want a new beginning, when we wish for an intervention, or when we are waiting for a miracle. Hope keeps us moving through our life stories. Hope expects something better. Hope helps us persevere.

Whether our story involves chronic illness, a shocking diagnosis, or an inability to conceive a child, hope keeps us moving forward. Whether we are walking a grief journey, our marriage is in trouble, or a deep loneliness that has us in a depression, hope sustains us. Whether our child is missing, or a loved one is caught up in a destructive lifestyle, or addiction, hope says that it is possible our story will end well. Hope is what faith works with to produce confidence that God will come and bring a turn-around in our life or in the life of those we love. I pray this book brings hope!

I coined a saying a few years ago in response to a question that was asked to my late husband, Mike, and me. Someone asked how our ministry was financed. I responded with, "Money doesn't grow on trees, or just come out of the blue. It comes out of God's Blue!" I was referring to God's way of providing the finances we needed. In addition to those faithful monthly partners, we occasionally received "out of the blue" unexpected checks. Mike and I knew both methods came because of God's leading and someone's love and obedience to give into the Kingdom of God. I began to call our "God Money" "Blue Money!"

In writing this book and looking back over all the stories that have shaped my life, I saw one consistent activity that made all the difference time and time again: God's Intervention. I began to call God's Intervention, "Blue Intervention." Blue Intervention came to us not only in financial ways but through His Word strategically sent. We literally felt His loving presence shifting things for our good. It was as if He dipped His pen into His glorious blue ink and wrote into our storyline His whispers of divine wisdom, and clarity into our confusion; and His powerful promises to nullify hopeless situations. He did it all to bring change not only to our story's outcome but most importantly in us! By His involvement, He added an invaluable quality and depth of character into our lives.

I could see how the Father, Son, and Holy Spirit were present and *involved* in our story, all of us in a viable personal relationship. God was investing in our lives directly from His heavenly storehouse. He intervened to show us where to find light in our darkness. He revealed Himself to us as we allowed Him to soften our rebellious and disobedient hearts that had led us to crooked life paths. He made our paths straight. His Royal Blue Pen edited out our wrongs and rewrote our personal storylines to include His great story. When God writes in "blue," it changes everything that would have been!

So, this is a book of stories: Mike's story, my story, and our story. Some of the stories are short, and some are a bit longer. I tried my best to share them as realistic as possible, and true to my perspective. If Mike were telling them, I believe our love, the hope, and the lessons we learned would be the same! I invite you to look for God's "blue" in each one.

As you read this book I hope you will feel as if you are a friend who lived next door, as if we did life together. If by reading this book you become inspired to trust in God with a renewed hope, and ask Him to "write in blue" in your life too, I will have accomplished my purpose and God will have answered my prayer.

Story 1:
Never Give Up

Never give up. Those are powerful words. They are words of courage, hope and perseverance, for you to continue, no matter how impossible things might look. Those words, when played out in prayer with faith that God will intervene, call God into action and bring His plan to override all others.

This story is about a woman who would not give up. Would you give up hope if your child had been kidnapped? Would you not eat? Would you not sleep? Would you stop seeking your child, and stop crying out for help from those who would join you in doing whatever it took to bring him or her home?

A woman lay crossways on her king size round bed, with her face buried in the pink, furry bedspread and cried out in prayer for her oldest son, Mike. Mike had not been physically kidnapped, but his soul had been. The life that God had planned for Mike had been stolen by anger, hatred, bitterness, and brokenness. The devil, himself, was after his destiny. Mike had become involved with an outlaw motorcycle club and was living the lifestyle.

Another son, Teddy, Mike's little brother, didn't quite know what to make of their momma's tears or the atmosphere of crises. Hour after hour Mike's little brother heard his mom and wondered what was wrong with his big brother that would cause this relentless prayer and prevailing intercession.

Teddy was only five years old, and though he felt afraid, he was drawn to the Lord's presence in the room. Teddy wanted to be next to mommy, so he climbed up onto her big pink bed. It would be the first of many times that he would join her there. For many days, and often for hours within those days, the travail in prayer went on. Here he would listen and learn to pray, too.

Her prayers ultimately brought change to Mike, above and beyond what she could have imagined. But, God was not going to waste those prayer-filled hours spent beside Mike's little brother, whose conception, by the way, was a miracle. You see, his dad had been told he could never have children. God had a big plan for little Teddy, as well. There, as they lay side by side in prayer for Mike, unknown to this mother, she was being used by God to model a life of prayer to her younger son. God was training him to sow in tears for those who do not know Jesus' great love.

Her young son would one day grow up to be my brother-in-law, Dr. Ted Rose, II, one of the great prayer mobilizers of our nation, author of the book, *Pastors Need Prayer*, and founder and chairman of the *United States National Prayer Council*. (www.usnationalprayercouncil.com)

His older brother, Michael Eugene Sumstine (Mike), born March 9, 1950, would one day become my handsome husband, and I would become the love of his life.

How would an outlaw biker, riding a chopped-out Harley and living at the tip of Florida in a tent, end up marrying a Christian girl who, at that very same time he was in Florida, was attending *Western Pentecostal Bible College* in Vancouver, British Columbia believing she would become a missionary to Africa?

This story and the next few stories in this book will share all that. I will start here by going back and sharing Mike's story from the very beginning.

Mike's mom, Rosemary Heckerman, was born and raised in Ohio. She met and married Ralph Sumstine when she was 15 years old. By the time she was 19, they had three children. Mike was the 2nd child with an older sister, Sharon, and a younger sister, Judy. I was told Mike was an ugly baby, and his mom would be embarrassed when people would be awkwardly silent, withholding the normal verbiage. However, by the time he was 18 months old, Mike had developed into the cutest toddler you had ever seen, with his big brown eyes and dark wavy hair, he never quite outgrew being a "cute boy." I am a witness to that!

Mike had a wonderful sense of humor! After looking at himself in the mirror, one of Mike's favorite sayings was, "I can't wait for tomorrow!" Of course, you would ask, "Why?" And he would respond with a gleam in his eye, "Because I get better looking every day!" His statement would always end with his contagious laugh! He said it often enough, that when He did, I would roll my eyes and let out a huge sigh while simultaneously shaking my head back and forth. But, I must say, I did agree!

As a young woman, Mike's mom felt overwhelmed. She and Ralph moved from Ohio to Tucson, AZ, where she found her childhood dream of being a movie star could be fulfilled. She had married for the wrong reasons, and now, though she loved her three young children, her dream became her escape. She and Ralph soon separated and eventually divorced. Ralph eventually married again, and he and Pat had three sons, giving Mike three brothers, Mark, Matt, and Chris along with Pat's son, Rick.

While still in her twenties, Rosemary worked as an actress in some of the old westerns movies, including, "3:10 to Yuma." She became friends with Glenn Ford and Audie Murphy out at Old Tucson. She was named a top model in Tucson and did many live commercials. During this time, she had another son, Mike's brother Dewey, and she married again; but that ended in divorce, as well.

In those first 11 years of Mike's life, his mom, who had become an alcoholic, was rarely home. He remembered as early as the second grade he would wake up in the morning, after there had been a party in their home the night before, and walk through the living room picking up the half-smoked cigarettes and leftover glasses of wine. With the adults in the house still asleep, he would head out into the Arizona desert, smoke those cigarettes and become drunk, finishing off the alcoholic beverages.

Mike's mom, having lost all hope for happiness, and with her life spiraling downward, attempted suicide once, then twice, and then a third time. The third time she came

5

dramatically close to succeeding. She was only 28 years old when she purposefully drove her convertible into a telephone pole. The transformer attached to the top landed "live" in the front seat right next to her. That experience shook her up enough that she responded to her mom's pleading to come home to Ohio and spend some time there with her.

Rosemary knew her mom was praying for her. When invited to church, she agreed to go. She heard the gospel message of Jesus leaving heaven to be crucified on a cross to pay for her sins. She knew her sins were many. She had heard it before, but this time she was listening. With the truth penetrating her heart, she believed in Jesus' resurrection knowing *she* needed that same power. It was as if the minister spoke directly to her, offering her hope for her shattered life. That night, as she encountered God's love, and gave her whole heart to Jesus Christ, she was radically changed. To represent her new life, she chose a new name for herself. She became "Angel."

Angel soon met and married Ted Rose, Sr. When Angel came back to Arizona from Ohio with a husband, it was a difficult adjustment for Mike. He went from a home life of parties, alcohol and no boundaries to being told they would be Christians, attend church, and that they were all moving to California. Mike did not want anything to do with this new life.

It was anything but an easy transition, and the soon discovered personality clash between Mike and his new stepdad did not make for a peaceful home. Ted made it clear that he was in charge. Mike did not want to obey. Confrontations became physical. Mike said that many mornings he would wake up "seeing stars," as Ted's authority and his rebellion each rallied to have control.

Ted and Angel had invested in a restaurant business in Southern California, but the endeavor soon failed. A move to Christmas Valley, Oregon to build a church not only would provide income for the family, but brought what Mike remembered as the happiest times the family had together.

Even with this, sadly and simultaneously, there was another building project in process. It was in Mike's heart as he, stone upon stone, built personal walls of anger as protection from hurt and the brokenness in the family's dynamics.

With the church construction completed, relocation took the family to Lodi, California. There they looked for and became involved in another church. Mike was forced to attend, but no one could force his heart to respond. He had a few encounters that planted seeds of God's love in his heart. His disappointing personal experiences with Christians formed his negative perceptions, which became a fortified barrier to the gospel's real message.

By age 12, Mike walked the streets of Lodi carrying a gun. He wasn't in a gang, but he, and the others with whom he hung out, were often in trouble, and he became their leader. When Mike was about to enter high school, he heard that a boy named John Addington was the leader of a group of guys at another junior high school in Lodi. When Mike and

John realized that they would soon be attending the same school, they planned to fight one another and agreed that whoever won would become the new leader of their high school group. The day they were to fight they took one look at each other, something clicked, and they said, "Hey, let's join up!'" And so, they became instant friends.

Mike, known then as "Mike Rose," from being enrolled using his stepdad's last name, John, and his friend, George Johnson, were placed in a special class for high schoolers who were troublemakers. I'm not saying this is how it was, but Mike's perception was that they were shoved into a room and a teacher was paid to babysit. He was labeled his entire years in school as "unwilling to learn." It wasn't until he was in his thirties that he took a class offered at a local junior college and discovered that there were phonetic sounds to letters. As he learned these sounds, he began to read words! Even with this, he felt he had a reading disability, likely a form of dyslexia that was never diagnosed.

Mike would never complete high school, but he, John and George remained lifelong best friends. John and George are both godly men today, but back then they were running from troubled home lives just like Mike.

One time, Mike decided to run away and steal a car, driving it all the way to Los Angeles. As usual, he involved two of his best buddies. When Mike and his friends were caught and taken into police custody, Ted and Angel would not only bail Mike out but his friends, as well. This became routine. The cycle was ongoing: anger, rebellion, abuse, run away.

It came to the point where Mike ran away and would not return. He had stolen a couple of motorcycles for some friends, and this began his involvement with a biker club. At 18 years of age, Mike was managing an adult-themed bar and running with the biker crowd. He moved back to Tucson where his dad still lived and owned an automotive garage. He joined a 1% Outlaw Club named the Hessians and was often called "Top Hat," because of the hat he chose to wear when riding his bike, or "Crout," because of his German last name.

Just as in high school, Mike was often considered trouble within the ranks of his biker club. To keep his rage outside of his club their officers would assign him out of state club business. He would be sent east all the way to Florida, and then back west, as far as Los Angeles. He would then travel up the California Highway through Oregon and into the state of Washington. He took this route several times, buying and selling drugs and guns along the way. He stole motorcycles for parts and resold them for club money.

During this time, Mike also owned and traded women. In biker clubs, the girlfriends are the property of the men with whom they ride. Mike once traded a woman to another man for a burnt book of matches. He so wanted to degrade her that he told the other man if he would give him a burnt book of matches, he would trade her for them. What a cold and hate-filled heart he had.

Later in life, when we would officiate at biker weddings, we always did the ceremony together. Mike wanted to show the bride and groom his love and respect for me, and that women are not meant to be property, but rather to be loved and honored. Multiple times a day, throughout our 33 years of marriage, he told me he loved me; and he always introduced me as *his bride.* Yes, God was going to warm his heart and fill it was His love!

Mike took all sorts of drugs: reds, whites, morphine, cocaine and heroin. He always smoked marijuana, but his true addiction was alcohol. He drank two to three cases a day. And, he was not a happy drunk.

There was a time when someone stole his motorcycle and began to date the woman he had been seeing. Mike was not upset about the woman, but he was quite upset about the bike. He went on a rage-filled search for the man who stole it. When he found him in a hotel room asleep, after he kicked the door in, he opened fire into the bed. How the bullets missed the couple was another miracle of Mike's momma's prayers. To Mike's knowledge, in his lifetime, he never killed anyone. He was always thankful for that prayer covering that he believed acted as a shield to protect others from his actions.

One night Mike and some of his club brothers were riding on a dark desert road when one of their members went down on his bike. This accident practically tore off this member's face, and he begged Mike to shoot him. Mike refused to do it. He called an ambulance for him and made everyone lift the damaged bike onto the top of the sweeper van that always followed the pack of riders. When the ambulance driver arrived at the scene, he informed them that he could not transport the injured man to the hospital if he had no insurance or payment for services.

Mike always shared, "Bikers didn't have insurance, but we had 9mm handguns. So, I took mine out and stuck it in his face, and we owned an ambulance. When we got to the hospital, before the police could be called, I disappeared into the crowd." The man lived, and when he recovered, he felt he owed Mike for his life.

There were bike wars going on. Clubs were killing other club's members, and Mike knew he was a target. After about a year of this, out of fear, Mike decided he wanted out of his club. Back in those days, once you joined and became a patch holder you were considered "a lifer." There was no getting out. When Mike announced that he wanted out, he said, "They sent Tiny, their fresh-out-of-prison, 250 pound, six-foot Sergeant of Arms, to come knocking on my door. And the door came off its hinges."

Mike was put in handcuffs and taken to the club meeting where, as a control factor, he was forced to sit through all the club business before they discussed his request. It was only because the man whose life Mike had saved on that dark Arizona desert road had become their local club's president, that they didn't bury him in that same dark desert.

Instead, the man whose life Mike saved, was going to save his. Still handcuffed he put Mike in a headlock, and said, "Bear with me, Crout," and then beat him half to death.

After the beating, the president said to the others, "You don't know this man. If you see him on the street, don't speak to him."

Turning to Mike, he said, "We keep your patch, your van, and your bike. Now get out of here."

Owning nothing except the clothes on his back Mike left with his life but felt an overwhelmingly deep void in his soul. He would share, "I walked the streets free from the club, yet I was lonelier than I had ever been. I felt totally lost."

As he was partying one night, Mike saw a woman using Tarot Cards and reading palms. He went up to her and asked for his turn. She looked at him, let out a gasp and told him to get out of there, and that she wanted nothing to do with him or the spirits around him!

Mike always believed that what she saw were the angels of protection his mom was praying over him. He believes the fortune-teller saw God's call and the kingdom assignment on his life.

About a year after he left the biker club Mike was still so lonely and felt such a loss of identity; he decided to go back and ask to be patched with them again. He knew the dangers involved, but he wanted to return to what was familiar. He was desperate for acceptance, and putting on his three-piece patch, or biker "colors," would give him that, along with the status of having full club privileges.

He was in a bar negotiating with a couple of former club brothers about what they could do for one another if he re-joined the club when another couple of bikers came in and stripped an AMA rider of his colors. With that, an all-out biker gun fight ensued.

Obviously, the bike wars were not over. Mike remembered stepping over bodies trying to get out, and just as the cops showed up, he managed to slip away, and once again to avoid arrest. At that moment, a woman miles and miles away lay on her pink bedspread on her son's behalf fighting that war and its outcome in the spirit world. He never did re-sign with the club!

Mike made his way back to Lodi and asked his mom and stepdad if he could stay with them just for a few days. The answer to years of prayer was in full motion. Although, no one knew it. God's blue intervention was already penning Mike's story.

Mike and I were about to meet for the first time, and both our lives would take a major turn. That will be another story. But, I saved this next story to end this first story. It serves to share the value of perseverance in prayer.

A couple of years earlier, Mike had made another stop in Lodi on one of his trips up through California making his way to Washington state. A few of his biker club brothers were with him. His short visit was over, and Ted and Angel had said goodbye, both having done their best to show their love and kindness.

Back inside the house and looking through Venetian blinds in her kitchen window Angel watched her son get on his Harley as a member of the 1% outlaw club he had been a part of for the past five years. Her heart was breaking in grief. With tears streaming down her cheeks, she asked God, "However can You get glory out of this?" She was referring to one of God's promises to her about Mike. God had told her that the lifestyle Mike was caught up in would one day bring Him glory. But, at this moment, that reality seemed impossible.

Angel would walk away from those Venetian blinds and into her bedroom. She would lie across her bed and begin, again, to pray. She would never regret one hour or one day spent. Her perseverance in prayer would see the promise fulfilled. Her son would come home, but for now, she prayed in faith.

Make your commitment to persevere in prayer. There is every reason to hope when God is involved. The same deliverance that would happen for Mike *can* happen for your loved one. Never, never, never give up!

Story 2:
A Day Like No Other

A day like no other: it was a Sunday that would start out like any other, but would hold within its minutes and hours a miracle. It was going to be my spiritual birthday! I was 11 years old, and that day, I was going to be born again.

My first birth was on September 15, 1951. My parents were Ira and Dorothy Smith. Dad was a brave World War II veteran who had spent the war in an artillery unit, riding in the back of a half-track personnel carrier on top of crates full of 105mm Howitzer shells. My mom was a warrior of a different sort. She was an intercessor, a prayer warrior, who, on her knees in prayer fought spiritual powers of darkness for the souls of men to be set free so they could live in the kingdom of God.

My parents had married in 1949 and my sister, Carole, was born the following year. I was their second daughter, born 16 months later. Within seven years, two brothers, David and Stan, would be born to our family. But as far back as I can remember, our family was also part of a greater one—our close-knit church family. *Calvary Tabernacle* in Stockton, California, was where we met to worship. My entire growing up years, our lives revolved around the services and social events held there.

We certainly were not a perfect family, but I always knew I was loved, and my parents provided me with an invaluable Christian heritage. As adults, our relationship was strong and our family close. I always wished there had been a more one-on-one interaction with them when I was a child. I wished they would have known how to sit on my bed and talk heart-to-heart. I have that same desire now as I look back on interactions I missed in the lives of my children.

My dad worked hard for the family, often at two jobs. I remember him being gone a lot. He was either at work, church events, or out visiting the elderly or the sick, which he loved to do. My heart was tender, and a stern word from him was always enough to bring me to tears, so discipline rarely went past that. Financial stress probably caused the greatest tension in our home, and any disagreements between my parents were usually over money.

Mom's love was gentle, and her voice in prayer was a strong support to me. My youngest remembrances of my mom, at age two or three, are hearing her voice in her bedroom and peeking through the door to see her on her knees in prayer. That was consistent throughout my entire growing up years. She had wanted to be a missionary but was responsible for the care of her mother and younger siblings. In what seemed to be a conflict of a call to world missions, versus the priority of family here at home, God made way for her to fulfill her lifelong passion. God told her she would go to the mission field, but she would go "on her knees" in prayer.

I have wonderful memories of yearly vacations with my family. We would drive up to Oregon to visit my Uncle Marvin and Aunt Rose and their two sons, Kerry and Bryan. Or they would drive to California to spend their vacation with us. I don't know how we all fit in each other's houses, but we crammed in and knew our time together was special.

There was a season where my family vacationed every year in Yosemite National Park. We'd camp out for a week and watch the fire fall from Glacier Point each night. We visited the beautiful waterfalls, and look forward to swimming in the river that ran through our campground.

I remember my childhood as being happy. I was extremely shy growing up, yet I found myself as teacher's pet in school and being brought into leadership positions in my youth. I had my siblings and neighborhood friends, friends at school and our close youth group at church. But I remember a prevailing loneliness clinging to my soul.

As I grew older, I cried myself to sleep most every night. I didn't know how to overcome it, and so it became part of who I was. I lived with this loneliness tucked away in my heart, and the only time I could acknowledge it was in the dark of night. Though I shared a bedroom with my sister, she never knew. I cried in silence.

Between church and parents, I received the foundation of the gospel of Christ in truth and power. I was taught God's Word and high standards. Those years were laced with law and legalism; or in other words, a lot of "we are permitted to do this and not to do that." I gleaned from those rules that some behaviors should be avoided just because they stir the flesh. When our human sin nature is given too much permission to thrive, it can lead us down a path that we never meant to walk. I think that's what my church and parents were trying to warn us about all along.

My earliest memories of Sunday go back to when I was just a toddler of probably two years old. Mom had left me alone, perhaps for the first time, in my Beginners Sunday School Class. I didn't want to be there and did not want anyone to talk to me. I took control in the only way I knew how. I closed my eyes. My little child's mind believed that if I couldn't see them, certainly they could not see me!

One Sunday, nine years later I was in the sixth grade. Although my Sunday school teacher was very kind and I liked her, I felt uncomfortable as she asked me to remain behind after the class was dismissed, as she had done all my other classmates, one by one, each Sunday. She looked directly at me and said, "I wanted to ask you if you have personally accepted Jesus into *your* heart? That is the most important thing you can ever choose to do in your life."

I wanted to give her the answer that would make my exit the quickest possible, so after nodding my head up and down, I forced out a barely audible, "Yes." It wasn't a lie because I automatically associated my reply with the fact that I had been going to church with my family my whole life.

Though I didn't realize it then, my response was the same as when I was two years old on my first day in my Beginners Sunday School Class. On that day, I did not want to be there either, so to escape an uncomfortable situation, I took control, and I closed my spiritual eyes, disassociating myself from understanding and answering truthfully. But, God was not about to let me believe, at 11 years old, that because I closed my eyes that He did not still see me *or* hear my response!

I left the classroom relieved that our interaction was over and began to walk up the stairs. There, midway up, I heard for the first time, the voice of the One that I would follow for a lifetime. This clear voice of God's Holy Spirit challenged my answer and forced open the eyes of my heart when He said, *"No, you haven't."* His voice of truth cut straight through my exit strategy and my incorrect assumption that church attendance and family status meant I was heaven bound.

I don't remember what the pastor talked about that morning. I just knew what I was going to do when he finished.

I was going to the altar. It was as if a veil was lifted from my eyes and my mind and heart understood what my ears had been hearing all my young years. I needed to have my personal encounter with Jesus.

At that altar, it was as if I came to His cross where He died for me. There, I asked Him to forgive me for *my* sins and to come into my heart. I knew He gave His life to pay for my sins and now I would give Him my life in return.

At 11 years old, it was just like what Jesus had talked to Nicodemus about in the Bible story of the third chapter of the Gospel of John, that my Sunday School teacher had just taught me. Now I could answer, "Yes!" to her question and it was the truth. I was born again, born of the Spirit. I understood what it meant, and my young heart felt clean.

It was the first day of what would become a lifetime journey. I would learn much in the years ahead of how to walk the Calvary Road and to choose to live in the Kingdom of God.

That Sunday, God and I entered a covenant relationship. The moment I received Christ the Bible tells us that angels celebrated because *now* I was going to heaven! That very hour *my name* was written in the Lamb's book of Life! That evening of the same day, I would seek for and receive power to be His witness and share His love through the infilling of the Holy Spirit.

My eternal destination changed that morning. There could never be a day that marked my life more than that one did. Though I would struggle with loneliness for many years, and then compromise my morals and beliefs later in life; because of this day, I would have truth to be light in my darkness and hope to always guide me back to the cross.

Has anyone ever asked you the question my teacher asked me? You, too, can have a day like no other!

Story 3:
Whitewashed Wedding Vows

It was my wedding day, November 16, 1974. It was very different than I had imagined it from the time I was a little girl. There had not been one bridal shower. There had been no wedding rehearsal the night before. No waking up to a glorious morning of anticipation of the day's events. There would be no joyful drive to have my hair and makeup done, no gathering of family and friends at the church, no bridesmaids and no walk down the aisle on the arm of my dad. We were eloping. Just a handful of people knew where I was.

What had transpired in my life to make way for my eyes to open on the morning of my wedding in a motel in Reno, Nevada, where my family had no idea what was happening on this day? Denial of the truth, lies I told myself and others, compromising choices, and whitewashing Mike's lifestyle had led my way there.

I had pushed past warnings from God, family, and friends. I mishandled heartbreak and took things into my own hands when my dream fell apart, and it took me down a path that would change my life story.

I'm not saying Mike was not a good person. I saw much good in him. But, life had put a painful mark on his heart, and it was going to take time and perseverance for us both to make our way through the journey that was about to begin. I certainly had my baggage as well, but, in the end, love, God's love and ours for each other would prevail!

I had met Michael Eugene Sumstine at a church in early March 1974. Mike had returned to Lodi and asked his mom and step-dad if he could stay with them a few days.

Angel had invited her son to come to a church where they were holding services. This church was my home church that I had grown up in. She had told him she had met a cute strawberry-blonde there and she thought he would like to meet her.

As Angel pointed him out to me through a glass partition that separated the main sanctuary from the foyer, she didn't tell me, "That's my son the alcoholic, the drug addict, the outlaw biker." She also didn't tell me that God had spoken to her heart and told her, referring to me, "That's Mike's wife." Her momma's heart, which had poured out a river of tears for years in prayer on Mike's behalf, only allowed her to simply say, "That's my son."

Along with my first grade Sunday School class, I was part of the illustrated sermon that they and their ministry team shared as they visited my church that night for the first of special weekend services. I knew Mike had seen me as we played our parts, so after the service, I planted myself by the aisle door, so this very cute boy I had been shown would have to walk right by me. That is exactly what he did without saying a word.

However, when the service started the next night, we were all instructed to turn and greet those around us. I was startled, and my heart skipped a beat to realize Mike and his brother, Dewey, were sitting directly behind me. He *had* seen me!

Six months before Mike and I met, the young man I had dated for over a year, who was still attending *Western Pentecostal Bible College* in Vancouver, B.C. Canada, had called off our relationship. I had worked to pay my tuition, dorm room and board costs for both years that I attended there and had graduated their two-year program. For those two years, I knew I was exactly where I was supposed to be. When this relationship ended, I was not only broken hearted, but confused. My hopes and dreams fell apart leaving me extremely vulnerable.

I'd loved this person and had imagined us married and being missionaries… maybe in Africa. I had not been able to move on with my life. I had not yet been able to let go of love in the hope that we might be reconciled.

Now, as I sat there in church, I realized that the man behind me *was* interested in me. I knew nothing about him and, because my heart was still attached elsewhere, I had no interest in a serious relationship.

But, I believe it was there that I brushed my first stroke of "whitewash" as I assured myself that I could remain in control. It would be fun to go out just once and "just for fun" as the attraction between us made a light-hearted promise to ease my sorrow. I remember my loneliness feeling flattered as I wondered, "What does this 'worldly' man see in me, a church girl?" I would hide our first date from my parents and meet him at a friend's house. They'd never need to know.

As we continued to see each other, I continued to "whitewash" by telling myself that moving out from my parent's home and getting an apartment with a childhood girlfriend had nothing to do with wanting no accountability. I whitewashed my friends' concerns as I told them that he drank a little, but it wasn't a problem. In fact, it *was* a problem. He drank heavily every day. I kept attempting to reassure myself, "Its ok, we're just going on a few dates. I'm not going to marry him."

I had never been to and had no interest in frequenting bars. But, at Mike's continued invitation, I began to go and sit there to be with him, ordering 7-Up or a cola. I felt personal guilt in being there, mixed with compassion for every broken life that was represented on each bar stool. I found myself over and over brushing up against the world I knew nothing about: alcohol, marijuana, and people whose daily lives were void of God's presence.

Little by little sin invaded my territory. And what is a sin? Sin is choices we make that separate us from a relationship with God. I soon surrendered to Mike's persistent offers and tried alcohol for the first time. It was not a fun experience for me. I could not understand why people paid good money to feel like they had the flu! Everything felt off balance; my footing, my thoughts and my spirit.

I felt lonely, separated from the reality of relationship with Jesus. I knew this could not take the place of the peace I had always known with Him. But Mike did not yet know this peace and could not understand why anyone would want to face life sober.

One baby step at a time, I walked deeper into a relationship with Mike. There was a connection between us, a true romance growing. Life was becoming complicated. He said he loved me. Weren't those the words I so longed to hear? I was still torn in my feelings for this other person. Why hadn't he spoken those words to me? Where was he?

There were times I made attempts to walk away from Mike, or he made attempts to walk away from me, but he would always come back. I would catch glimpses of a wonderful man, the man God wanted him to be. In so many ways Mike was a good, gentle and caring man. I could hear him crying on the inside for answers and true love. He saw in me a stability for which he had longed. I was different. I cried out for God to help him, to help me, and to help us.

I knew and began to share it openly with Mike that there cannot be true inner happiness and fulfillment in life without a relationship with Jesus. It wasn't about going to church. It was about the healing that comes to us when we know our God. I stopped going to the bars. I was not going to live my life there.

Mike attended church with me one Sunday evening and went forward for prayer. He asked God for help and asked Jesus to forgive his sins and wrong choices. I immediately saw the changes that followed and these changes gave me much hope. At this stage of our relationship, however, I had no understanding of the stronghold of alcoholism that prevailed in Mike's life.

I did not know there was a spirit already attached and in control... one who did not plan to be tamed for long or to give up without a fight. It is true that we become slaves to sin. Sin takes charge and makes demands on our will. For now, this stronghold was content to remain undisclosed and unnamed where it could be easily whitewashed by my naivety and denial.

I carried an increasing weight of guilt and then shame as our relationship progressed. Seeds of my sin were being planted. Boundaries were being crossed. Morals were being compromised.

These sin seeds would sprout and spread quickly, almost as a ground cover on the other side of our marriage. My young heart didn't understand that insecurities and fears, because of these failures, would remain as an infestation of weeds even after our marriage vows were given.

With a dread in my heart, knowing things would not go well with the purpose of our visit; we went to my parents and told them we planned to marry. I saw manifested on their faces a deep concern for my future and a loss of their hopes and dreams for me. They tried their best to respond calmly to our words that had just turned their world upside down. They could only ask if we were sure this was what we wanted to do. We didn't stay long. It was too awkward and the atmosphere extremely tense.

Dad called me later that night and asked me to meet him at the church so we could talk. I couldn't tell him no. He wept like a baby and sobbed trying to find words as he begged me not to marry. I wept too, but could not articulate to him that I was no longer the daughter he could be proud of, and because of my compromises, I felt I was without options. I would not hurt him further by speaking the details.

I held back a deluge of tears until I could release them in my car on my way home. I believed my relationship with Mike had gone too far and our emotions were too fully involved. No matter who I was hurting, it was too late to turn back. The only way I knew to manage all this was to once again pick up the whitewash. We needed to make legal the relationship we were having, and everything would be alright.

I avoided my family and close friends. I hardened my heart and hid my fear. We began to follow through with plans to marry. I moved out of the apartment I was sharing with my childhood girlfriend without giving her any real notice, which put her in a difficult financial situation. What should have been a fun experience for us of being out on our own for the first time, I ruined. I couldn't face her words of true concern for me, so my choice to leave abruptly deeply hurt our relationship. I moved into a small single wide mobile home with Mike, and we prepared to elope.

After driving to Reno where Mike received his divorce papers dissolving a two-week long prior marriage, we purchased our marriage certificate and then drove on to nearby Virginia City. The next morning, we went to a little wedding chapel on the side of the Silver Dollar Saloon. My mom and dad never did know that's where our ceremony took place. I just couldn't bring myself to pierce their heart with another hurtful detail of their losses on that day.

I wore a long dress, but it was not bride white. There was nothing borrowed and nothing blue. No one sang.

I had no doubt that Mike was giving me his love that day. I spoke the words to give him mine. I was fully aware of the commitment I was making. I felt the ring slipped on my finger. We looked into each other's eyes and repeated our vows to be kept "until death do you part."

I felt the emotions of excitement, but there was also a gnawing fear of what would become of our life together. Would the whitewash act as glue? How long could it cover the sin that had forged our path to this far-from-home altar?

When we follow the passions of our hearts rather than the path of God's heart, those choices lead us to isolated places. I thank God for Jesus, the Good Shepherd who will leave the ninety-nine sheep in the fold to go after the one that has wandered away and is lost. I would, in time, see Him come for Mike and for me. But on this day, I was not only far away from my family, I felt far away from my faith. God says marriage is called holy matrimony. My heart desperately searched for the "holy." Where was the holy?

31

Two things were now true. It was done, and we were one. But, before I could try to feel like a bride, I had to find the courage to make the dreaded phone call to tell my parents that it was my wedding day.

Story 4:
Reception Shadow

A shadow cast over the beauty of love withholds it from blooming. It was Saturday, January 4, 1975, and on this day a shadow would be cast over my heart and my marriage that would remain for the next seven years. I was blinded to God's truth that there was a holy remedy available, healing for my smothered soul.

After our elopement, my parents called and asked to come by for a visit. They greeted us with a smile and Mike with a hug of "welcome to the family." I know now this demonstration came after unconditional love sent them to their knees in search of how to respond to and accept our marriage. God had come through with His perfect answer: to love unconditionally and to pray unceasingly.

They shared about their plans to provide and pay for us to have a wedding reception. We would invite family and friends including those from our church, many of whom had watched me grow up. I would wear my wedding dress, and Mike would wear his Western wedding suit.

My parents and sister, Carole, were taking care of all the preparations and decorating. All we were to do was come and enjoy the celebration. This would be the opportunity I longed for. My hopes were high. I wanted everyone's approval and for them to see that I had not made the mistake of my life.

The day of our reception arrived. It was time to start getting ready, but Mike had not returned from working at what he said would be a short day. I waited, hoping and pleading in my heart for him to pull into his parking space. It had become my experience that when Mike was gone too long, I would know he had likely stopped at one of his bar hangouts. It would be the case this day, as well.

I finally got ready and thought of going without him. I could give the excuse that he got sick and just couldn't come. But, the sober Mike was not the same Mike that drank. With alcohol in his system, I didn't know what he might say or do. I feared he would show up and cause a scene. So, I went looking for him.

I found him at my second stop. He had been drinking Tequila all afternoon and had lost track of time. He saw my great disappointment and immediately agreed to come home and get dressed. I managed to hide my panic and anger.

By the time we arrived at our reception all of our guests had been there for what had become an uncomfortably long wait. All eyes were on us as we walked in, but in the awkwardness of the moment, there was no rejoicing and clapping. There was, also, no hiding the fact that who was present now with me was a very drunk groom. And I was a humiliated bride. I felt their pity and the conclusions they'd drawn. I wanted to disappear as I realized that the meal had already been served to shift the focus off the absence of the guests of honor.

We all put on smiles in what became an endeavor to proceed as if things were normal. My sister, Carole, beautifully sang the *Hawaiian Wedding Song*. We cut and served the cake. The gifts were opened. But, all of this was done in an unmistakably uneasy atmosphere.

I knew there were whispers in the crowd, eyes rolling and heads shaking at this first and, what I knew would be, lasting impression. Every bit of whitewashing I had managed to deceive even myself with was stripped bare that night.

I was deeply embarrassed for my mom, dad, and my family. I was embarrassed for Mike's mom and step-dad. I knew how uncomfortable they must have felt in front of all their friends, but I didn't realize in my distress the great sadness they all felt for me because of Mike's actions that day.

My dad was extremely angry with Mike and sought me out privately to make a declaration that our marriage would not last six months. I understood his justified outrage and wondered if it might be true.

Mike was deeply remorseful that next morning. Again, and again, he asked me to forgive him. I acknowledged that I knew he was sorry, but, was unable to adequately share what I felt his drunkenness on such an incredibly special day had caused. How could I share the active bleeding going on in my heart? I felt a tear in the very fabric of our relationship. The wound was deeper than I knew how to bandage. We were married, and the Bible says that the two become one flesh, but beginning that day I struggled not to feel we were two.

35

Not knowing what was transpiring, my hurt became a hidden seed of unforgiveness buried in my soul. I did not realize this seed would take roots by my revisiting it repeatedly. From those roots, a tree would grow for the next seven years. A tree of death would block the light of love, and on every intimate moment cast a shadow.

Story 5:
Tired

A dozen red roses were in the hands of the deliveryman who stood at the entry way to where I worked. My eyes sparkled with delight when he called my name as the recipient of this surprise gift. I enjoyed the jealous teasing from co-workers and proudly put my bouquet on display to validate that I, a newlywed of three months, had a loving and thoughtful husband. It was February 7, 1975, a full week before Valentine's Day, so I wondered out loud if he had misread the calendar.

Because Mike and I had eloped to escape the unfavorable response of family and friends, I was very aware that we lacked the blessing that can easily be taken for granted by those who experience a traditional wedding.

Our new relationship as a married couple was weak and insecure, and I was struggling to give it strength and stability. This was Mike's thoughtful, tangible effort to show his love and I immediately looked romantically ahead to the evening and weekend that would begin in just a few hours.

My built-up fantasy instantly faded at Mike's appearance in our doorway later that evening. The thief of alcoholism, that had hidden its true agenda from me as we dated and had turned my parents attempt for a wedding reception into a bad dream for us all, was in control of him again.

Just after Mike announced his plans to leave me and the marriage that night and head to Florida with a bar buddy as if on cue, his mom and step-dad drove up blocking his exit.

Angel had insisted they come. Ted would have rather not, because he was exhausted after a hard week's work at the church he was building in the small town of Escalon, 20 miles east of Stockton. But, Angel had heard God's voice, and Ted knew to pay attention. They were there by divine appointment, and they brought with them the right words at the right time.

Angel, hearing Mike repeat his intentions to leave me, was led by her love and the power of God's, to simply ask him, "Son, aren't you tired of sin?"

When we are tired of living under pride, rebellion, immorality, hate and numerous other sins that forge our separation from God, all we need to do to be free from the cumbersome ball and chain that attaches itself to our heart is to ask Jesus to forgive us.

The power of God's love was about to triumph as God answered the prayers of many on Mike's behalf. God would burst through the spiritual darkness and break off the chains that were binding Mike's heart to the slavery of his terrible addiction. Ask anyone who has been imprisoned for any length of time how it feels to be free. Living free from the slavery to sin is what being a Christian is about.

Mike's answer to his mom's question would forever emboss February 7th as our special day; a day when hearts were exchanged, as Mike gave his heart 100% to God's Son, the Lord Jesus Christ. That night the miracle of God's grace turned the course of our lives as Mike's manipulative alcohol addiction lost its grip!

Before Mike's mom led him in a simple sinner's prayer of asking for forgiveness, he paused to say one on his own. He said, "God, You know who I am, and You know what I've done. If You're real, I want You. If You're not, then I just want these people (referring to his mom and stepdad) out of my face!"

I watched Mike become instantly sober with my own eyes! Joy filled him, and he began to laugh. Then, Mike reached over and took one of the roses that I had brought home with me and handed it to his mom. It was something he had done for her since he was a little boy. He would proudly bring her a dandelion or a stolen flower from the neighbor's garden. Tonight, that rose said, "Here I am. I'm back. Thank you, and I love you, mom!"

Mike didn't go to Florida but stayed to also give his heart to his precious son who was conceived on that special night. I loved the association of God's gift of new life to Mike and then His perfect gift to us in creating a new life in my womb.

Mike would stay to give his heart, as well, to a beautiful baby daughter who would be born to be a forever blessing to us, to bikers as a motorcycle missionary and to me in our 33-year heart and soul love affair.

Roses have become my favorite flower. The roses sent that day were no calendar mistake. They are known to be the flower of love, and God knew from the moment they were sent that they were going to be a part of the story of His divine intervention planned for that evening. They were arriving early to be a symbol and a proclamation of His redeeming love.

Yes, Mike may have ordered them, but it was God who sent a dozen red roses.

Story 6:
The Long Night

"What is God saying to you these days, Sherri?" Jeff's question vibrated through me, penetrating my total being, shaking me awake spiritually as someone would do to one who was in a deep sleep. I was caught off guard and was totally unprepared to answer. I instinctively searched for my spiritual bearings and was forced to realize it had been a long time since I had heard God's voice. It had been years since I was in a spiritual place to have that kind of relationship with God. It had been *seven* years.

The first seven years of our marriage were held together by God's strong cords of grace. I wanted to believe that Mike did love me because he told me multiple times a day and did his best to show me often, but my heart edges were frayed, and my emotions were in distress. I felt I was going through the motions of marriage in which the atmosphere was always thick with an unnamed feeling of separation.

Mike's actions in those first few months of our marriage had impaled my heart, and I couldn't seem to recover. An undercurrent eroded our already weakened marriage foundation, like waves against a house built on sand. That undercurrent was fear stemming from that night he came home to leave me, coupled with our reception chaos and his occasional one-night drinking binges that I feared would evolve back into a full relapse of alcoholism.

I tried to will away the hole in my soul and accept life as it was, but out of that empty place, a voice constantly harassed me with a despairing accusation that we could never be whole and we would never be one, as the Bible said we should be.

Two separate statements Mike had made early in our marriage fed my fears. They constantly played over and over in my mind. These statements perhaps seem trivial now, but for an already wounded heart to hear that if you were to die today your husband would only wait two weeks to begin to date again, might undermine a newlywed's belief in his true love for her. And, following the birth of your baby, if your husband said that he wasn't attracted to heavier women and that you needed to lose the baby weight, it would be very easy for insecurity to set in.

Both statements brought deep insecurity and robbed me of my self-worth and confidence that my marriage was based on his love for me, not only on my looks. After our son was born, I hardly ate until I had lost the 20 pounds gained and was back to weighing 118 pounds.

As you read the several mini-stories within this story, you will see how the voices would become my perceived truth and the belief of them the source of my struggles. It's a classic example of how our actions can speak louder than words, but, also, the fact that words do hurt.

Our First Home, Our Son and Then a Daughter

During the early summer of 1975, we bought our first house, in Stockton, California. It was very tiny and brought me to tears the first time Mike took me to see it. I had just found out I was pregnant and wondered how I could bring my baby home to live in it. I wondered how I could keep my friends and family away so they would not see it at all! The ceiling was lying on the floor in parts of the house! I had no understanding then of Mike's gift to build and that He was very capable of giving it a major makeover. He kept his promise, and I watched an amazing transformation happen over a period of just a couple of months, including a custom-made space for a baby crib! What a visual illustration this little house would become of our own broken-down hearts and what God would do to restore them!

Mike loved people, and people loved him. He was very social and the type of a person who never met a stranger. He was fun and would, without thought, say things that would bring spontaneous laughter. Most mornings his first words would be something quick witted. I loved that about him and, though I held secrets in my heart, I enjoyed his outgoing personality that was so different from mine.

We began to attend a different church than the one that I had grown up in. It was smaller and across town. I couldn't quite bring myself to worship with the same faces that were present on the night of our ruined wedding reception. I was hopeful this would provide a place for Mike and me to both grow spiritually. They reached out to us inviting us to dinner in their homes and some of the women blessed me with a baby shower, generously allowing me to invite my friends and family.

We moved out of the mobile home and into our little place a couple of months before the birth of our first baby. It had been exciting to watch the house develop and to watch my belly grow at the same time. Those months went fast as Mike remodeled the house and I looked forward to motherhood.

Michael Todd, born three weeks early, came into our lives in October of 1975. I thought I wanted a girl as a first baby, but when I saw my son, I wondered out loud, "What was I thinking! I want *this* baby boy!" As we held him in our arms for the very first time, we felt a new kind of love wash over us.

Mike's soul and spirit were experiencing the bond of true love in a three-dimensional form: love for God, love for me and, now, love for a son. His escape in the past had always been to run away. He would share with me years later that with his new responsibility of being both a husband and now a father, he would be forced to face his fear of commitment and would find that God's power was greater for him to stay than the pull of the world to run away.

When we realized that we were going to have our second baby, we sold our little 800 square foot house, paid off debt, and moved to a triplex in nearby Lodi, CA. Mike agreed that I could quit my job at Western Lumber Sales, where I had worked off and on since the first summer in between my two years of Bible College. I was so excited to be able to be a stay-at-home mom. Our daughter, Stephanie Marie, arrived on her due date in January 1977, but not without a wild ride to the hospital in the middle of the night.

We made the foggy 40-minute race to Stockton where I was taken straight to the delivery room, ten short minutes before she was born! Mike was one panicky dad believing he just might have to be the one to deliver her in the car. I found out what it was like to give birth without an epidural!

Your whole heart is in love when God gives you your first child. But, then, when the second one arrives you realize that you love this one just as much, with your whole heart! I was overwhelmed as my heart validated this truth and gave full room for this tiny new life. Though born at 2:41 AM, there would be no sleeping that night. All I could say over and over was, "I have a daughter!"

Western Lumber Sales called and asked if I would like to come back to work and my mom agreed to watch our baby and toddler. We moved back to Stockton where Mike and his step dad were working as partners in a construction business they named "Half and Half Builders."

Their new company's name and slogan came out of an inquiry about their work and building technique. Mike's quick-witted response was "we build half of it sturdy, and we build the other half 'purdy!'" (His slang pronunciation of the word "pretty.")

I came to realize over the years that Mike was naturally gifted as a carpenter and flourished in the construction trade. Though he had learned much from years of working with his stepdad, he also possessed an inborn gift from God, and he loved his work.

Marriage Strain and "Nice Day for a Beer."

Just as I felt our marriage would begin to stabilize, without warning Mike would make a stop at a bar. Because of Mike's past alcoholism, and the pain it caused, I could not help but have a no tolerance attitude for alcohol at any level.

I'm not saying that having a drink is a sin to everyone, but it was to Mike. Alcohol put Mike in a destructive zone that was precarious for him, and put those around him in damage control. Social drinking was not an option for him. Alcoholism begins with that one social drink.

Alcohol was Mike's "besetting sin." A besetting sin is one we continue to give in to because, usually in some form, we enjoy it and its enticing call to our sin nature wears us down. Once we surrender to the momentary pleasure, we can be bombarded with regret that piles on guilt and shame.

Mike's relinquishing of his control to alcohol every so often left me feeling like his progress was one step forward and two steps back. I was grateful that he never did fully return to everyday drinking, but I was depressed by the dread of it. Fear forces you to live as if it is happening.

Mike would share with many in his later years how the enemy would work in his mind:

"When I would begin to face a spiritual attack, I would resist, sometimes for several days. I knew drinking held serious addiction issues for me.

I would be doing just fine, no problems and nothing bothering me. I would be driving home, and I would hear this whisper in my mind that would say, "Nice day for a beer." I would ignore it.

A few days later I would be driving along, and there would be that voice again, "Nice day for a beer." I would ignore it again.

After a few more days the voice would add to its seduction and say, "One won't hurt you."

So, I would have one beer. And do you know what, that voice was right! It didn't hurt me. But then the next day I had two, then three...

That voice once led me straight to a DUI arrest and jail. When I look back now, it makes me angry how the enemy played me."

Mike saw how the enemy tempted him with a weakness and then taunted him at his failure. He always felt conviction after these downfalls. The enemy is the one who puts guilt and shame on us. The Holy Spirit does not condemn us. The Holy Spirit convicts us so we will not only regret what we have done but repent of it so we can live in relationship with Him.

Every time this happened Mike was quick to repent and would ask God to forgive him. He would always say to me, "I'm sorry, I did a stupid thing!"

God forgave Mike 100% every time. I would say I forgave him, but I was angry, hurt and fearful. Those emotions played into more lies that consistently harassed me: "I wasn't ever going to be happy, I wasn't ever going to experience true love, and I made a mistake and married the wrong person."

These voices of hopelessness kept reinforcing discontentment in my marriage. My viewpoint was justified in my eyes, and it left me without the understanding of the work of grace that God was doing in Mike's life and wanted to do in mine.

Grace is not permission to sin. Grace forgives, but, more so, contains within it the strength for us to do the right thing, and to live in right standing with God. All along, God was walking with Mike and teaching him. All along, God heard Mike's repentance and saw in him a man He could use.

A Perfect Dream House, Imperfect Parents

Mike came home one day full of excitement and dreams. An opportunity presented itself for us to buy property up in the foothills about 30 miles east of Stockton, in an area known as Valley Springs. His mom and step dad also bought property, and the plan was that we would help each other build.

Mike worked hard to build a beautiful home for us, and our first months there were exciting. It was up on a hill, and that first year we decorated it in detail with Christmas lights. You could see it for miles down the highway! We raised some chickens and even a few pigs. The kids had a tree swing out front and a huge inside playroom big enough for them to ride their little trike bikes around in circles, yet safe from being outside with snakes or traffic on hilly streets.

Mike had built us a beautiful waterbed bedroom set with night stands and hanging lamps. It was stunning with its cut-out stain glass design on the headboard and lamps. Cissy, our nickname for our little daughter, had a white canopy bed with a dresser that was perfect for a princess! Our son, Mikie, as we loved to call him, had bunk beds and he thought it was the coolest thing ever. Mike also built the kids a child-size picnic table with attached benches. They played for hours sitting at that little table, and I would often serve them their lunch there as if they were at a park picnic.

I became a stay at home mom again, during this time, and Mike worked separately from his dad in his own construction business. It seemed we were living the dream, but our life issues, our real struggles, were still there. They were just kept out of public sight.

Dysfunction is often passed down from generation to generation. The enemy loves to harass one generation after the other with the same set of problems played out from family to family, father to son, or mother to daughter. It is in this way that the sins of a parent can be visited upon the lives of their children.

All children need correction, but as purposed discipline, given in love. The Bible says that we know we are true sons/daughters if our Father disciplines us.

I knew without a doubt that Mike loved his children, but when it came to discipline, the anger that had been visited upon him sought to be visited on our children. Anger itself is not a sin. It is a proper response to wrong. But, if anger becomes a reaction out of our dysfunction instead of an action out of our love, it can have lifelong negative effects.

Mike didn't yet know the spiritual power tools to use to be free from this unwanted legacy. That day would come when his bottled-up hate would be totally defeated, but now he only knew to respond as had been modeled for him.

No parent is perfect. Most of us wish we could undo or redo some of our actions or decisions as parents. But, we usually do the best we know how at the time. Hindsight shows us our failures from a different perspective. I would one day deeply repent for my fear that Mike might leave us if I spoke openly to him of his sporadic episodes of anger towards the children.

My failure to communicate my anger at his angry displays only drove the separation I felt between us deeper into my heart, and my children had to experience discipline in ways that caused them to be afraid of their dad's outbursts instead of feeling the love he had for them.

Mike and his step-dad struggled for years with anger toward each another. Years later, towards the end of his life, Mike's stepdad would share, "When you look at my life take the good and let that be useful to you; and take the bad and let that be useful to you. Don't do it." He was a man who let God heal and renew his heart on his life journey, and God used his voice and testimony in gospel music for many years. I know Mike's heart would echo that same quote, as would mine.

We don't get "do-overs" but, oh how grateful I am for a Savior that can help us revisit the past for healing, as He visits us daily to take us forward. Our God is devoted to us from day to day that leads from generation to generation.

One of the comforts spoken to me by God years later was, "As I have been faithful to you I will be faithful to your children!" I knew that my Heavenly Father was saying that as He healed me from my sorrows, strongholds and broken places, so He would be faithful to heal my children of theirs.

A New Identity

The enemy of our soul wants to kidnap us and force us into a wrong identity. He tried it with Mike and almost succeeded.

When we feel unsafe, it is our instinct to protect ourselves. A wall can be quietly built up in the heart of a person, even a child, and Satan will have willingly issued the building permit!

Satan will hand us a stone for every word that hurts us. He will hand us a brick for every action that bruised our heart at two years of age or age 20. Stone upon stone is placed on the rising wall of preservation, promising us a place to hide where no one can hurt us. The problem is that Satan makes sure his stronghold also isolates us from hearing God.

So, when Satan begins to call us by his different names for us, we listen. Our false identity is crafted out of the injuries to our soul whether they were caused intentionally or unintentionally and the wall of lies protects it.

I am thankful that our Heavenly Father has all power. The ongoing work of God's grace breaks down our long-standing walls. Sometimes we need to be forgiven; sometimes we need to forgive. If we ask for His viewpoint, he will show us how to align our thought process with life from His Word. With the power of the Holy Spirit living in us, we can make changes in our lives and live differently.

Nothing is too hard for the LORD. No stronghold is too strong! No weight is too heavy. No lie is too deceiving, and no identity is too hard set! God writes a new life story for us that enables us to claim our true identity in Christ.

A Blue Warning

By the time we had lived in our mountaintop home for about two years, unfortunately, a recession had hit the nation.

As the recession was dawning, we experienced the intervention of God's protection in a powerful way!

We were struggling financially when Mike became involved with another contractor who seemed to show up out of nowhere. This man approached him on becoming partners together in the building of several houses in the Valley Springs area.

We felt it was an answer to prayer and like our ship had come in! This man would front all the money, and Mike would build the houses. We began to intermingle and socialize with him and his wife, and they seemed like a very nice couple.

We shared this possible business merger with Mike's mom and step-dad. Angel called us the next day with a strong warning she felt in her spirit. She said she could not shake it and to please do some inquiring about this man before we signed any papers.

Mike remembered this man had talked about living in the Tucson area, so Mike called his uncle who had been a contractor in Arizona for years. Mike's uncle immediately recognized the name. He was tied to the mafia and was looking to launder money through our business!

We immediately cut ties, and this man just disappeared from the scene. We could have blindly been pulled into a very dark world! How thankful we were that God sent us His warning and that we listened!

Lots Of Loss, But An Invaluable Gain

As the recession fully hit, we watched all our investments, and all of Mike's hard work to provide a beautiful home for us, disappear. We were forced to sell the house of our dreams on the mountain top, at basically no profit.

We moved to a rental not far away, able to pay the rent upfront for six months, using most of the meager proceeds we received from our house.

It was there in that rental house that Jeff McEachron, the friend who would ask me (about a year later) that spiritual awakening question at the very beginning of this story, came to visit us on church business. Distance had kept us from attending regularly, but we still considered *Evangel Assembly* our home church. I was thankful to see him.

Mike had been feeling down, with work slow and finances low, and I feared another bar episode. Jeff sensed Mike's struggle and invited him to talk privately out in his truck where Mike received the infilling of the Holy Spirit that day.

I was thrilled and understood the power that came to dwell in him. We may have felt beaten down with the loss of our house, but Mike's body, his spiritual temple, had just gained immense strength for his spiritual journey!

The recession hit the construction trade hard. Mike was looking for avenues of work. He was encouraged when he and a local realtor decided to partner to build a couple of small homes. Mike already had an account at the local lumber yard that he used when he built our house, and to run his business. So, it was logical that the building materials for this new project would be largely charged to that account, to be paid off when the house was sold.

After the first house had been built, our new partner swindled the profit that was made and moved out of the area, leaving Mike owing a $25,000 lumber bill. Eventually, over a few years, after we paid some of it off, the lumber yard "forgave" the balance. We were very thankful, yet this whole experience also had taken a toll on Mike, and he was struggling with feeling defeated in life. But, let me tell you how God would use this experience.

A few more years down the road God would use this debt to test Mike's, heart. God tests us to reveal our personal spiritual progress and what we have learned. God had been healing and restoring, teaching and training. Now it was time to test.

Mike happened to run into the person who had left him holding that large note at the lumber yard. Mike looked him straight in the eye and spoke curtly to him saying, "You had better be glad that I'm a Christian now!" The look in his eye told this man, who knew of Mike's biker past, that he could expect to be seriously hurt if Mike were not a Christian now.

After several days of that statement hanging in Mike's heart and leaving a bitter taste in his spirit, he purposefully drove back to Valley Springs to find this man. In obedience to

God's dealing with him, Mike wanted to ask this man to forgive him for the resentful words he had spoken to him!

Mike loved to share in his testimony, "This man took me for thousands of dollars, and *I'm* asking *him* to forgive *me!*" God had forgiven Mike of a great debt of sin, a debt he could never repay. Now it was Mike's turn to forgive. The man was shocked, and the Holy Spirit's purpose was accomplished in both men's hearts to show them that God loves forgiveness!

After all these losses, Mike and I had to turn our vehicles over to the banks that held their titles. We purchased a couple of cheap used vehicles but were thankful for transportation.

We felt it was time for us to move out of Valley Springs. Our son would be starting kindergarten in the fall, and we needed to be located where Mike could find work. His dad in Tucson, Arizona made us an offer to move onto their property, and he would help us get a new start.

To Mike, it sounded like a good opportunity. We began to sell off large pieces of furniture and other items in anticipation of this big move, but all the while, I had no peace about it. It was more than, as some suggested, my not wanting to make a move to be with his family because it meant being away from mine.

I couldn't put my finger on why, but it may have been because Mike's dad was currently using alcohol. (Though that would change later in his life as he, too, was born again and gave up all his destructive alcohol abuse.) Living so close to someone you love would have been easy for Mike to fall back into his old choices. I silently asked God to block the move if it was not His life plan for us.

Instead, we chose to move back to Lodi until we could raise the money to go to Arizona. But, we never moved to Tucson.

With a very limited income, we moved into a one-bedroom apartment where Mike and I slept on a hide-a-bed couch in the living room, and started attending a church that was right across the street, *Century Assembly*.

We enjoyed a renewed friendship with a couple who had been Mike's friends since high school. (Remember John Addington?) John and his wife Bobbe had recently been born again as well! Our families enjoyed being together and our fellowship extended outside of church on a regular basis. We shared dinners and spent weekend evenings together, the kids swimming, and us playing card games or dominoes.

Mike and I enjoyed the services at church; yet, Mike would later say that we went from the back row in one church to the balcony in this one. In other words, he was saying that we were staying detached. We never searched out a small group Bible Study which would have given us needed life tools. We were still functioning on our own, each dealing with personal struggles without the help of others.

Within just a few months, we found a two-bedroom duplex in Stockton. I could return to work at Western Lumber Sales, and Mike began doing side jobs and selling at a local flea market. It was during this period, at the duplex, that Mike had his final bout with alcohol. But, then it was done. Mike would defeat that besetting sin, and it would never win again!

Black and White to Living in Color

I was now 29 years old and my life, unknown to anyone, was reaching a crisis point. Feeling out of control with my fears, I bought a pack of cigarettes and began to smoke, as if that was going to help in some way. I would smoke in the morning before Mike or the kids got up, and then behind a locked bathroom door. I smoked on my way to and from work. Why was I choosing such an unhealthy behavior that I disliked, and wanted my husband to stop? I was trying to fill that hole in my soul with something that would only damage my lungs!

I began to entertain thoughts of escaping from my unhappy life. And my options became the two things that I had feared the most that Mike would do. I was tempted to stop off at a bar on my way home and have a drink, and a voice was telling me to put my two kids in the back seat of my car and drive far, far away never to return.

Except for the fact that I deeply believed in the wedding vows I'd spoken "for better or worse, in sickness and health, till death do us part," I don't know what I might have done.

Thankfully, there was Another who believed in His vows to us. At salvation, God had entered a covenant relationship with Mike and me. He promised never to leave us or forsake us, and He was not about to break His vow. He was going to do His part in an amazing intervention to transplant us into a safe and thriving environment where we both would come into relationship with Him in a fresh and life changing way.

How thankful I am that I did not choose to do those wrong things. I believe Satan thought, since he hadn't succeeded in Mike destroying our marriage, he would get me to do so. He had set his trap well.

I know the Lord had people on their knees on my behalf. Those escape mechanisms would have destroyed my life and my marriage. My life story would be totally different. But, life was about to change from black and white to living color!

It was at this crisis point, and on a very unsuspecting, ordinary Saturday morning that Jeff knocked on our front door. Mike had run into him earlier in the week. Jeff wanted to ask Mike to do some carpenter work at a new church outreach facility that his in-laws were heading up right there in Stockton.

This new church, named *The Youth Connection*, had just moved their location to Pacific Avenue, which was the main drag for the youth in Stockton. Its mission was to reach out to the youth in a coffee house setting and produce Christian concerts on the weekends.

I remember that morning perfectly. I was standing in my kitchen, and Jeff was standing behind the counter that doubled as a breakfast bar. I believe, to him, what he was about to ask me was just a casual question. He looked at me and asked, "What's the Lord saying to you these days, Sherri?" I must have mumbled back some unimpressive response, but this was no chance question. His question hit me like a ton of bricks, and the weight of it stayed with me for days. I would hear it as an echo again and again.

What was God saying to me? I realized I had no *real* answer. My life for the past several years flashed before me throwing back at me a barrage of more questions. Where was God in my life now? How far off track was I and how could I ever get back? Did He even have anything to say to me?

Jeff's question rang as a wake-up call to my spirit. It would become a major marker on my spiritual journey and the catalyst of turning my seven-year walk in the wilderness into a season of freedom and reestablished faith.

Mike and I took our children to visit this new church fellowship, and it was the first day of a near 30-year attendance. This time, we would be fully involved, heart and soul together with God. I believe God hand-picked this fellowship because it was the perfect fit for us and where we could join in with those who would become like family.

I had lived behind a weak wall for seven years. It had not sheltered me. I was in pieces. I felt like Humpty Dumpty who had fallen off, and as the nursery rhyme says, "all the king's horses and all the king's men could not put Humpty Dumpty back together again."

But, there at *The Youth Connection*, under the spiritual authority of Pastors Dick and Edie Patterson, the true King of

Kings was completely and thoroughly able to put me back together again. My wall was torn down, and in its place, a strong foundation on Christ would be built. Upon that foundation of Christ Mike and I, together with Him, would build a new marriage relationship. It would be a whole new journey!

There, from a shattered egg, I would grow up from being a broken baby bird into an eagle, able to mount up with wings and soar high above the circumstances of this world. There I would discover heart connection with other Christians and heart healing from my disobedience to God. Following His commandment of love would mean more and more freedom from sin, and an abundance of peace that conquered all my fears.

Mike would grow astronomically there, as well. Pastor's Dick and Edie Patterson would become our spiritual parents and our mutual love for one another, to this very day, is one of God's best gifts to my family and me. I still say to them, "As you follow Christ, so I follow Christ."

So, where are you in your life? I will now ask you the question that turned my world right side up! Can you give an answer? "What is God saying to *you* these days?"

Story 7:
A Supernatural Memory

Dreams are supposed to come true on your wedding day. Mine was a dream lost, and I didn't even allow myself to think of it. As I shared in a previous story, though it was certainly a special day, it was missing so many key elements that I could not begin to call that day a fulfillment of what many of us wait our whole lives to experience.

It was a day without family and friends; it was miles from my home, in a small, side chapel of the Silver Dollar Saloon in Virginia City, Nevada, it was performed by a Justice of the Peace and, most lacking was a parental blessing. My memory of that day was so difficult that I had taken all the pictures of the wedding and our reception and put them in a brown paper bag. Then I set the bag back behind other items on a shelf in the garage.

My run-away marriage memory was where the Lord began my journey of inner healing and chose to personally engage with me in a remarkable way. This was the first of several interventions God would make in my new season of restoration.

We had been attending *The Youth Connection* for a while. I remember my first Sunday there, walking in and feeling like I was "home," but more than that, like I had just discovered buried treasure!

The power of God's presence was palpable. I could hardly wait between services. I didn't yet grasp how I could walk in His presence all week long. Pastor Dick taught under a gifted teacher's anointing, and the Holy Spirit moved through Pastor Edie in her strong gift of prophetic words and prayer.

They nourished, encouraged and challenged us to go deeper in our relationship with God. There was something about them that drew you to listen and hang on to every word God spoke through them. I would come to know that this "something' was the Spirit of God upon them, and at work in them, as they walked their daily life on "Calvary's Road."

"Calvary's Road" is a term used for a fully dedicated heart walk with God. It's a walk with the Spirit of God as He gives us an understanding of the price Jesus paid for our sin. With that understanding, we must choose to no longer participate in issues of pride, arrogance, greed and lies, to name a few.

The sin nature that we are born with must be "put to death" so that our life is pleasing to the Lord always. We walk The Calvary Road every day that we choose to closely follow the teachings of Jesus. It's not always easy, but the reward of living in close relationship with Him is worth giving our all to experience.

The Word of God tasted like eating fresh bread. As I read it as if for the first time, the words brought strength to my spiritual walk and peace into my everyday life. The stories stirred my spiritual hunger to read more.

The Word of God became as if I were looking in a mirror. As I looked at my "reflection" or my actions and my thought patterns through the Word of God, I wanted to change how I must look to God. I didn't want dirt on my face or my hair disheveled from rushing through my morning without spending time with Him!

The Word of God was as living water for which I thirsted. The Bible is about Jesus from beginning to end! I wanted to drink it and receive eternal life!

Mike and I were both ready for this new beginning, this spiritual awakening, and journey. We both said yes to this sacred stirring in our spirit, and I was ready and willing to let God do what only He could do to put my pieces back together again—His way.

It was here at the Youth Connection where Mike and I began our deep friendship with Jeff and Cheryl McEachron. Each would play a vital role in our lives. To this day, they are among my closest friends.

God showed me one morning on my drive to work that no matter how far away we stray from God it is always only *one step* back. That step is repentance. The second step is obedience. Then obedience is the third step, and the fourth, and the fifth. Obedience is what keeps us on track.

I could follow obedience, and God gave me the strength in grace to quit smoking. I began to hear the call to walk on Calvary's Road. As I took a few baby steps toward Him, He responded in a huge one towards me.

One evening I received a phone call. A couple of new friends from the church had me on their heart and wanted to know if they could come by to pray for me. My heart leaped, and I responded, "Yes!" They came and began to pray a sincere prayer, but honestly, I could not tell you what they said. As they prayed, God gave me a vision.

Almost immediately I "saw" myself in a church setting and it was obvious that there was about to be a wedding held there. As I looked, I was surprised to see that I was the bride. The pews were full of people, and the organist began playing the traditional wedding march. I saw myself being walked down the aisle on the arm of who I believed to be my dad.

We arrived at the front altar, and the minister said, "Who gives this woman to be married to this man?" I turned to look into the eyes of my dad, but instantly, in the spirit, I knew He was my *Heavenly* Father! He said, "I do" and took my right hand and placed it lovingly and firmly into Mike's.

God knew for my healing to begin I must see that He is a Father of love and forgiveness. He was addressing one of the enemy's haunting accusations that said I had married the wrong person.

God, my *Heavenly* Father, gave me a white wedding and in it, with me on His arm, He gave me away to Mike! He was showing me that He saw us as one flesh. God knew that His blessing on our marriage meant everything to me. I'm not implying He approved of how we had done things, but that He forgives and restores. God was doing an inner healing in me. He was removing shame and pain so my heart could truly embrace my husband in the miracle of marital love.

God embedded the wedding vision into my memory as a living experience. From that time on, when others would talk about their wedding day, my mind immediately went to this memory where God made our marriage as it was intended to be—holy.

A wedding is a once in a lifetime event, and the God of the universe created, especially for me, a supernatural memory! His blessing came to fill every empty hole with hope as He transferred my disappointment in the past into a divine appointment in the present. He rescued what was lost and, as others prayed over me, God turned back the clock and returned the day to me in beauty, holding within it a redeemed white wedding dream.

Story 8:
Forgive Me

A lesson in forgiveness freed my heart to love and showed me a man of God.

Though I grew up in church and had attended Bible College for two years, never had my spiritual life been this alive. I am not saying I had not known God. I truly did. And because I knew Him and His Word I had a very hard time accepting the compromises I had chosen. I was very hard on myself. I had not just hurt myself. I had hurt my family and friends, and, also, my Lord. I guess in some ways I was punishing myself over and over.

On my way to work, I often found myself singing a song that is taken from Psalm 51. *"Create in me a clean heart, oh God, and renew a right spirit within me...."* I loved this pursuit of my heart for God. And I meant it. I wanted a right spirit within me.

The Youth Connection, our new-found fellowship, was nontraditional in its coffee house style setting but was rich in the deep truth of God's Holy Word. Mike and I were both beginning to thrive there.

I decided I would attend the women's Bible Study held in one of our member's homes. This was a big step for me. I was painfully shy! I had learned to depend on Mike to make our new introductions. It came so easy for him. I would have social anxiety. What would I say? Would I make a fool of myself? I usually kept quiet and waited to be approached. So, my decision to go was proof of my fresh hunger for God's Word. I was willing to face my fear in a room full of women who were strangers.

I remember walking into that living room that first evening. I nervously searched for a place to sit where I hoped I could melt into the chair and be inconspicuous. The Word was shared with anointing and power. I felt awkward and left as soon as the prayer ended, but not without looking at each face and wondering if I would ever know the lives behind them.

I continued going to the Bible Studies and soon was visiting and getting acquainted. I not only came to know them all, but some of these women have become lifetime friends. Fellowshipping was so enjoyable that we began to open our home on Sunday evening to get to know people on a more personal level.

In this season of time, I had felt impressed to do some spiritual fasting. This was one of the earmarks for me that I was back on track with God. I began to hear His voice again. I would wake up in the morning and hear the Holy Spirit say, "No breakfast this morning," or "no lunch today; instead, leave work, park somewhere and pray." I had been doing this for a few weeks.

The Holy Spirit had led me to talk to each of my parents separately and ask them to forgive me for the pain and sorrow I had caused them in my early relationship with

Mike. I knew I deeply hurt them in our elopement and leaving them out of our wedding day. I knew we hurt them, again, at our wedding reception that they had paid for, as Mike arrived drunk and ruined the event.

They did forgive me and were thankful for my heartfelt apology. The wall I felt between us came down. I knew in their heart they had forgiven me, but it meant a lot to them to hear me say it. I knew they had been praying for Mike and me for years, and they were thrilled at the new spiritual life they saw growing in us.

I continued to go to the women's studies, and it was at one of these meetings that I had another major spiritual breakthrough. I don't remember the Bible passage Pastor Edie was teaching from, but it was on forgiveness. As she spoke, I remember sitting there, and in my mind, I was rehearsing, again, the list I kept in my heart of the places Mike had hurt me in our first seven years of marriage, especially the very early years. The biggest hurt was our reception night where I felt humiliated and shamed before so many who had not only watched me grow up but saw me as a young woman called to ministry.

Pastor Edie continued sharing as I went over these places one more time. I said to myself, "Mike hurt me. Yes, he needs to ask me to forgive him!" As I was accusing Mike in my mind, the Holy Spirit shocked me with the words I heard Him say, "Mike does not need to ask you to forgive him for anything. He already has. *You* need to ask him to forgive you! *You* are the one who has held bitterness in your heart!"

71

You could have pushed me over with a feather. I was stunned by this revelation of truth. Truth, when spoken in love, comes with the power and purpose of setting you free.

How could I have missed this? *This* was the thick separation that was still lingering between us. Even though God had given me the memory of a white wedding, *this* was what was keeping my joy from being full. The thick separation I felt for years had been exposed and identified. Over time my lack of forgiveness had grown into full blown bitterness that blocked and locked out love. Bitterness rots the roots of our life tree.

I could not see how ugly my heart looked housing this sin against Mike, until then. My unresolved anger was hurting me so much more than Mike's original offense. Forgiveness would remove my anger, which then would immediately cause my bitterness to lose its support.

Along with the separation I had been feeling from Mike, this inability to forgive had also caused a breach to be revealed between my Heavenly Father and me. I knew Jesus was my only way to healing. I had asked for forgiveness for many wrongs in the past weeks. And now, as I asked forgiveness for this unwanted bitterness, I felt grace wash over me. I felt the anger and the bitterness leave.

It was not enough for me to only ask God to forgive me. I knew for my forgiveness to be truly effective there was more to do. I had not forgiven as His Word tells us to in the Lord's Prayer. The Word says that I am to ask God to forgive me, *as I forgive others*. I knew this was a part of walking the Calvary Road. I wanted to do the right thing.

I was nervous about how I was going to go home and tell my husband that I had held this offense against him all this time. How could I tell Mike that I had harbored anger and bitterness against him because of my inability to forgive? He knew nothing of it, and he had no idea how this thief had stolen happiness from my life with him. He had asked for forgiveness a long time ago. He was always quick to repent. Would he be able to forgive me for not forgiving him?

I didn't want to wait one more day, so that very night I went to him and told him my sin. I confessed it to him and asked him to forgive me. I looked into his eyes to try to read his response and what I saw was Jesus. Mike said, "Of course I forgive you, honey." And that was that. No grilling, no questions; just immediate forgiveness. I felt like I was floating. That huge weight tied to me like a ball and chain had been unlocked and removed from my heart, my soul, and my mind. Forgiveness is so freeing

That amazing night God came and showed me a hidden sin, not to condemn me, but to bring reconciliation in so many ways. I thanked my Heavenly Father over and over that I had received mercy twice that night, first through His Son, Jesus, and then through my husband, as they both covered my sin with love and a lesson in forgiveness.

Story 9:
A Life Prayer

Prayer is our privilege to communicate with God. Knowing our prayers are heard and answered brings a dimension into our life as we would experience with a heart-friend! We can talk to Jesus quicker than we can text or call someone to share our everyday concerns or the crises that have come up in our lives. A "life prayer" is born out of one of those in-depth conversations with Jesus, your best heart-friend, and is shared within the context of that deeply committed relationship. A life prayer begins as that one communication, but over time, you find you want to repeat it to keep it active.

My lifetime prayer began in 1986 when I was 35 years old. We had been doing a Bible Study from the book, *Release of the Spirit* by Watchman Nee. His writing was not light reading, but it drew me in with its deep and powerful contents in a challenging way. It compelled me, called to me and led me to pray for the release of God's Spirit to work in me in this mysterious life-changing and life-lasting way.

This was one of those events that causes you to remember forever exactly where you were when it happened. We were living in the house on Apple Blossom, in Stockton, California and I went into our bedroom and sat on the edge of the bed. I'm not sure of the exact day, and maybe not the exact words, but I can remember as if it were yesterday, the very heart and spirit of my prayer.

I had made my decision to step onto Calvary's Road with Jesus. I was ready to commit my life to Him in a deeper way than I had ever done before! With my heart pounding, I purposefully began my prayer:

Dear Jesus, You know how much I love You. You have done so much in my heart and Mike's heart these last few years. You have placed us in a wonderful church, and our pastors are teaching us Your ways and Your Truths. They are teaching us to walk on Calvary's Road, that spiritual road where our flesh is put to death so that Your Spirit can rule and reign in our hearts.

I know the seriousness of what I am about to pray. I choose to set my life apart for You. I know what happened to You on Calvary's Road. You were persecuted, beaten and crucified. You did it all for me, for all mankind, to pay for our sin and to make way for us to have reconciliation back to Your Father. I am choosing to be a close follower of Yours.

I want all that You have planned for me in my life. I give You permission to do whatever it takes to bring me to the exact place You want me to be. Whatever circumstances You might choose to use, I give You permission for them all.

I know that there will be some amazing places that You will take me, but there will also be some hard and difficult places. These "places" will be my circumstances and experiences You, Holy Spirit, will choose for my good.

I don't want ever to cut short the work that You will be doing in my heart during these circumstances and experiences. So, when I am in a very hard place, and I ask You to stop, saying that this is too much, saying that it's too difficult and that I call off our deal, don't listen to me. Don't stop. Keep going!

Encourage me, yes. Help me, yes. Teach me, yes. Empower me, yes. Draw close in a relationship like I've never known, yes. But, don't stop. Please, don't stop, because I want deep fellowship with You. I want all of You and I want Your perfect plan in my life.

I want to walk the next 10, 20, and 30 years on Calvary's Road. And when all these years have passed, I want to be thankful that I choose Your Road and Your Way.

My Life Prayer may have started as that heartfelt one-time prayer, but, as time went by, I returned to the essence of that prayer and prayed it again and again. I would pray my Life Prayer, again, at the age of 45. I remember feeling how much had been accomplished through some very difficult circumstances since I had first prayed the prayer.

We had been forced to sell our house (again), there was more loss of property, and our call and transition into full-time ministry all brought, at times, extreme financial challenges. But I was ready to pray it again, "Lord, whatever it takes to bring us into that place of fruitfulness, of reaping a harvest of souls for your Kingdom, I give You permission to do in our lives." How could I have known we were going to face years of such hard health issues with Mike….and such divine God-thing intimacy and intervention?

When I turned 50 years old, I chose another specific time to pray my Life Prayer over the next decade of my life. I had walked with Him on Calvary's Road for 15 years, and He had taught me how to live in dependence on Him and His Holy Spirit! He met every need, every time, in His time. My trust had grown and was still growing! My faith had enlarged, and I wanted more! My hope was secure! My marriage was the best! And, I had a relationship with my God that was real and interactive! I knew this was pleasing to my God. And it so pleased me to please Him!

When I prayed my Life Prayer at age 50, I added a new dimension. Instead of just stating as before, "Whatever you, O God, need to do, I give you permission…" Now I felt that it was not only what I gave God ongoing permission to do, but it was, also, what I needed to do. I felt I needed to abide and live in a new level of resting in Him. What I meant by resting was that I wanted to live in constant confidence and trust. I wanted to be paired with Him in His yoke. Whatever place He led me to live, to whatever He spoke that He wanted me to do, if He would give me His Presence in every hard circumstance, I would choose to find my place of rest and peace in it all.

Now, here I am exactly at the 30-year mark of praying my Life Prayer! I am so thankful that I prayed this prayer and that I prayed it again and again. What a history with God I can now look back on! The fruit of this prayer has seen me through my darkest of days, through grief and loss of family members and of my beloved husband. It pulled me forward many times when I felt I could not take one more step. It caused me to strategically seek to heal in my sorrows and grief so I could continue to stand where He wanted me to stand and to be who He wanted me to be now.

If I knew back then what I know today, I would say the prayer all over again. God is the One in control, and I want Him to oversee every aspect of my life. All things He has worked together for good. And if not yet, He will!

This prayer has kept me on track with God. It has kept me in His story written for me so I could experience His glory for myself and to see it displayed in the life of others. My great reward has been Jesus and to experience the heights and depths of *knowing Him* and His personal love!

My Life Prayer has now become an almost daily prayer, but, one thing remains, and that is we still must choose to walk Calvary's Road day by day. The world is right there to pull us away, and we must guard our time and our choices. At the end of our life, we will not regret the fight to stay in step with Jesus.

There are all kinds of prayers in the Bible: prayers of faith, prayers of supplication, prayers of intercession and prayers of seeking direction. In fact, we can take most of the Scripture and make it into a prayer for our family, friends, pastors and ministry partners. Praying Scripture is a powerful and extremely productive way to pray.

The most beneficial part of our day is when we carve out our special time to pray and spend time alone with Jesus and in His Word. There have been countless times that I have left my "prayer closet" and thought of how sad it would have been to have missed this awesome encounter. And, I would have never *known* what I could have had!

Prayer gives us the opportunity to hear what's on God's mind and to feel the joy of Him sharing His heart with us. Everyday prayer is of utmost importance. I encourage you to make it a priority. Your Life Prayer gives God the green light to "write in blue" His plan for *you*! There is nothing that will make a difference more than prayer!

Story 10:
No Ordinary Garden

Ordinary living is life without Christ's power at work in it. Extraordinary living is experiencing our day with the supernatural being added in. Our garden, our life, is not meant to have ordinary plants in it. God does not plant ordinary flowers in our garden called life, nor does He want to let the weeds of the world grow wild there.

Mike and I were happy in our new garden in life. We were still living in the duplex on Hammer Lane, the place where God came and rescued us from our brokenness by planting us into rich fellowship. The Holy Spirit was continually at work, growing us and changing our hearts. We loved our *Youth Connection Church* and were thriving there.

A vital part of plants thriving includes addressing the weeds in the garden. As God was walking with Mike in his life garden, God saw an ugly weed that had turned into a thorny choking vine. It was very much alive, and He began tilling the soil around the vine with the plan to personally remove it. In other words, God wanted to address and deal with a long-standing stronghold in Mike's life that, if not removed, would likely choke the spiritual life out of him. This stronghold was hurt, turned to anger that had turned to hate and was affecting Mike's Christian walk.

Mike had been hurt as a child. That hurt had planted a seed that grew a weed and now, over time, remaining unchecked was affecting the fresh fruit of God's Spirit (love, joy, and peace to name only a few) that was wanting to grow in Mike' life.

This stronghold was against his step-dad. From the time Mike was a youth, when his step-dad first came into his life, up to that moment, Mike's joy and peace were being strangled by this thorny vine wrapped around his heart.

There had never been a resolution between them and, even as adults, there was a control that came into play. Mike had rebelled against it as a youth, but it was still a part of every job they worked on together. Mike was growing fearful that he would become enraged and do something he would regret. He could feel the rage building up inside him.

One night Mike came home from a particularly hard day and made an extraordinary life changing decision. He called his friend, Jeff, and Jeff called Pastor Dick. The three of them met at the church and Mike shared about the anger and hatred that he feared he could no longer hide. They prayed. Mike repented of his participation and renounced the hold those emotions had on him. Pastor Dick and Jeff spoke to that spirit of anger, hate and rage in the authority of the Name of Jesus and commanded it to leave Mike's heart and loosen its grip on his mind. And it did!

Mike came back a different person! The forgiveness was complete. The peace was visible all over him, and it never left. Mike saw Ted in a totally different light from that moment on. Mike even asked Ted to forgive him for his rebellion and for anything that was his part in their long hard relationship.

Though they often saw things differently, Mike continually weeded his garden pulling out any growth that did not look like love or peace. In both Mike and Ted's gardens, love took root, and fresh fruit grew. Their lives would eventually take different paths, and they would no longer work together, but Mike genuinely loved Ted, and they would always help each other out physically or financially whenever they could.

I love how God is the Great Gardener. He wants others to look at our lives and see the beauty of a well-tended garden. He does not want our gardens to be ordinary. If we ask God to weed through the ground of our hearts, He will do it. He will help us pull the weeds of sin out by the root! Then He will cultivate the perfect vegetation that will shade us and grow the best vegetables that will help to open the eyes of our hearts. He will grow glory grapes and peaches of peace.

Our spiritual gardens have a purpose. They are meant to satisfy us and to feed those around us. How awesome to give a golden apple to a friend who needs a word of wisdom!

Our lives have been bought by our Lord and paid for by the sacrifice of His life. We are an extraordinary planting of the Lord. We can grow into oaks of righteousness that can withstand life's storms and can offer shade and safety to others. We are called to a greater purpose than just ordinary living.

Story 11:
Lean Into the Curve

"Lean into the curve" was an instruction I received from Mike when I was a "newbie" motorcycle rider. Your natural tendency is to pull yourself up to sit straight as the bike leans into making a curve, whether it is just turning a corner or making a wide sweeping bend out on a country road. To lean into the curve seems opposite of what your senses tell you is safe. Leaning requires that you position yourself in trust of both the natural movement of the bike and the skill of the rider.

What Mike and I could not see then was that God had put us on one of those wide sweeping bends. His long-range plan for us required spiritual growth and a walk of faith that would develop a deep trust in Him. We would grow spiritually on this long slow curve, and our confidence and trust in our Heavenly Father would be challenged and tested through difficult circumstances. God's goal was for us to learn to lean into Him!

We moved from our duplex on Hammer Lane in Stockton to a house on Apple Blossom Way. We switched places with Mike's sister, Sharon. She took our Hammer Lane duplex, and we moved into the house that she had been renting. It was an easy move as 15 trucks showed up that morning to help us! Our new church friends were awesome.

It was there that Mike bought our first motorcycle. Mike had not owned a bike since his "old days" with his outlaw club and had not talked to me in detail at all about that time in his life. Later Mike would share humorously that after his years as an outlaw biker, God had to teach him to be a human being before allowing him back on a bike.

Up to this point, I could only remember one statement when Mike had even mentioned riding again, and I remember how off guard that comment had caught me. We were at a restaurant, and it was raining. A few bikers left and, as they took off in the rain, Mike said, "Someday that will be us." At that moment, I had *nothing* to associate our present life with the words he said and had no clue how truly prophetic it was.

But one life-changing day, Mike came home more excited than I had seen him in a long time. He started sharing with me about a motorcycle he had seen parked out at the end of a driveway with a "For Sale" sign on it. Unknown to us then, God was writing the first words in what would become His destiny for us and His calling on our life—motorcycle ministry.

This motorcycle was an older bike *with a side car*! Given Mike's history of only riding a Harley, he didn't seem to mind at all that this was a Honda. We did not have the money to buy it, and I felt a bit of relief. However, because God had a plan to use this as the beginning mark of our "slow curve," when Mike prayed, God provided "blue money" to buy that motorcycle through an unexpected bonus check that was the exact amount we needed.

This first, fun bike would soon be replaced with a newer Honda and then the inevitable Harley. That was also when we joined the *Christian Motorcyclists Association* (CMA). It would be a while before we got involved, but God was at work in connecting us with new relationships there, and they were going to play a major part in our lives very soon.

Mike was feeling the dream and the urge again to build another house. God was going to use this dream for early-stage training in our lives. God's long-term goal would be to transfer our priorities from a search for this world's opportunities to asking for His Kingdom to come and His will to be done on earth. God's will is that all should come to know Jesus Christ, His Son, as their Savior.

With my blessings, Mike went into a construction partnership with a friend, Joe Reiff, who we had met at our church. Joe owned a motorcycle as well, and he and his wife sometimes rode with us to CMA events. Joe would provide the financing and Mike would be the contractor. The lot they purchased was on Majestic Lane in Stockton. They both had high expectations of each of them making a very good profit from the sale of this house.

We always called it the "Blue House." Yes, they painted it blue! Looking back now, God's fingerprints were all over it: built on Majestic Lane and painted "Blue!" But, it wasn't selling, and no one understood why.

The house was sitting empty, and Mike's business was struggling. It had become difficult for us to meet our financial responsibilities, plus they felt uncomfortable having it sit there vacant. Both agreed that we would move into the blue house where we could use our future profit like a cash advance to cover our "rent." Joe would continue to make the loan payment to the bank until the house sold. We would not pay actual money, but we would keep a running total for each month we were there that would then be deducted from our part of the profit when the house sold. They still believed it should sell any time giving us both a good overall profit. Surely God would *bless* the dream.

I had already left my job at Western Lumber Sales to follow a coworker to a new place of business, Robertson Homes, where she had greater potential for advancement. It had always been my desire to work part time, and this company gave me that option. I was also taking my second class to learn American Sign Language. I went first to *Delta*

College, and then I commuted 40 miles to *Ohlone College* in Fremont. This had real potential for me as a career change from office work to becoming a certified interpreter for the hearing impaired, but my true goal was to use signing as a ministry in my church.

After staying at the Blue House for about a year and it still not being sold, we moved out and into a duplex not too far away. It was a stark environmental difference, but we had used up all of what could have been our part of the profit from the sale of the house. We signed off all rights, and Joe took it from there. We knew God was with us, but we did not understand why He did not bless Mike's dream so we could relax, enjoy life and perhaps buy our own home.

A few months later, the dream still burning in his soul, Mike sat at dinner one night and shared another opportunity for us to own our home. But, this opportunity would require us to go back to Valley Springs. In many ways, we had a pretty bad experience there the first time. I was surprised he would even consider going back, but the land was still much more reasonable there, and building was in his blood!

He promised with all his heart that *this* house was "where we would live for the rest of our lives." There were persuasive statements made to us about the simpler life of country living and of him, with my son, building a dog kennel for breeding dogs. There was a promise of a swimming pool for us all and no working outside the home for me! We discussed how we would continue to commute to our church which had recently relocated to Lodi, CA. No way did any of us want to leave our church family! And so, with a fresh feeling of adventure we all agreed, "Let's do it!"

We felt this was God's direction for our family but did not recognize it as the hand of God that led us deeper into "the blue curve." The building process was fun and exciting. We saw the stick structure and the trusses raised in one day, as our friends all came to a house-raising party. We had taken out a construction loan and finances were tight, but we managed. We all enjoyed living temporarily in a travel trailer. It was close quarters, but it brought us closer as a family as we looked forward to our future on Berkesey Lane.

We moved into our new home the night before Thanksgiving. What a perfect morning it was to wake up in our new home! We were beyond thankful with such hopes and dreams. But, very quickly our hopes began to be dashed and *our* dream, again, began to crumble.

Mike had jobs he had bid on and was completing, but *every* penny was budgeted. There was no time for side work, and so the money from the contracts he had signed would be our total income. Our budget showed that it would be a stretch to adequately cover our expenses, but we hoped for the best and were perhaps in a bit of denial.

Then we made a couple of large purchases based on emotion. I learned a lesson that new furniture looked nice walking into our home, but in the dead of night, it was not worth it. This purchase would keep me awake as I tried to figure out how I would pay for what I bought on credit. Mike purchased, on sale, a large doughboy swimming pool, to keep his promise to the kids, but once it was filled-to-the-brim, the pool collapsed, dumping all the water and sweeping away the promise. We could not replace it, and there never was extra money enough for the kennel Mike wanted to build.

We celebrated Mike's 40th birthday shortly after moving in. I was so thankful that I could pull off surprising him with a huge party in our church basement. The look on his face was priceless! Also, our daughter celebrated her 13th birthday, which was exciting for her to have a slumber party with several of her friends. Both were bright lights in hard times, and both still bring joy as we reminisce about each one.

Overall, we were not making it financially, and I began to see the handwriting on the wall. The refinance of the construction loan gave us high house payments. Mike had work, but after he paid his help, there just wasn't enough for us to live on. I considered going back to work, and even applied for a job at the lumber yard in San Andreas, a little town about 20 miles away, but the door to employment did not open to me.

Not even a year after moving in, we began to face the fact that we were going to have to sell. It was extremely hard to tell our children. They were both attending Toyon Middle School and would have to process the loss of changing schools as they were just feeling settled with new friends.

I was thankful for the consistency that attending our same church brought to each of us. I was also thankful for the positive Christian growth we were experiencing in our increasing ties with the *Christian Motorcyclists Association* chapter. Both connections kept us focused on what was important and were a strong source of strength to us personally and spiritually.

However, Mike and I felt the anxiety and stress of facing another loss. It was as if we were on a huge merry-go-round and *this time* we thought we had managed to grasp the gold ring, only to watch it dissipate into thin air, right before our eyes. We could not understand why this kept happening over and over.

We moved out of our "forever home" with great sadness and after a quick stay in a home that we knew was for sale when we moved in, we ended up in a rental across the valley, but basically in the same general area. The kids could remain in their school for now. Mike would commute to work in the Stockton-Lodi-Sacramento area and, from early dawn to late at night; he would give his all to support his family. He loved driving, and that was never an issue, but he could not be content with renting and was not ready to let go of the pursuit of his dream to build.

I was weary, but Mike was not going to let even this loss stop him. God would use Mike's tenacity for His glory in the years ahead, but now, one more time, God watched Mike launch another dream. He found property in the little community of Burson, CA, a small town about 10 miles south of Valley Springs on Highway 12 East. The property had no water on it, but Mike was blindly confident that the perc test would pass, so we purchased the land. A percolation test has to do with the absorption rate of the soil if you are planning to put in a septic system.

I still could not see how God could use loss to help us let go of the things of this world. We were in the full throws of our curve as God was using Mike's very gift to build to break our flesh and build in a different realm, the realm of our spirits. As I look back now, I can plainly see that God was turning our life path, be it ever so painful. This season of dead ends and failed dreams that had been our training ground was almost over. There would be just this last big bump in our road.

My parents were willing to lend us money to get things started, believing once Mike had the septic system in and the water hooked up he could get another construction loan. After investing many hours of manual labor, we were informed that the land would not pass the percolation test. Without this, it was determined unsuitable for a house. Without this, we could not get water, without water, we could not get a loan to build on the land. The work Mike had done so far, he had to turn and walk away from.

Moving our family in with my parents, into their tiny three bedrooms, one bathroom, 900 square foot house in Stockton felt like a failure. It was the summer of 1992. Six of us had lived there as I grew up, but somehow it seemed bigger then. My parents were sacrificing their privacy and lovingly offering us all they had. We were very appreciative, but it was an extremely difficult move. After 15 years of marriage, after so many attempts to build, we were all going to live with my parents?

This seemed like too much. It was one of the few times I saw Mike loose it emotionally, not out of anger, but deep frustration and loss. He had tried so hard. We couldn't see that God had us "leaning hard" into the wide sweeping curve and, though it felt like we would skid off this road, God had His hand firmly holding on to us, keeping us steady and safe.

Mike was finding some sporadic work, and I applied for an employment opportunity in the Lodi Unified School District to be an aide to the teacher of a new class for the hearing impaired. Some sign language skill was required. I was excited about this possibility! Lodi was only about 20 miles north of Stockton, and I could easily make the commute from my parent's house. I applied immediately upon hearing of the opening but found out I was one day past the application process deadline. As it turned out, I was the only one who applied at all, so I received a phone call almost as soon as I got home that I had the job if I wanted it.

This job was such a blessing to me. Mike and I both struggled, but here was this amazing place, right in the middle of our stress, emotional pain, and chaos, that had been carved out for me! My pastor, Dick Patterson, had preached a couple of sermons out of Joshua Chapter 1 about being strong and courageous. I listened to those sermons over and over during my commute to Lodi and back. God talked to me through them, and every time it was like a personal word from the Lord as God would encourage me in the spirit of adventure that we needed to be strong and courageous. We were going to be overcomers!

Though I'd often cry to work and back, I loved every minute of my day and knew God had a bigger plan going on outside of the realm of sight! I was gaining so much experience in my signing skill and was able now to sign and speak at the same time very efficiently. I felt happy and needed. This joy also provided the money to enroll our teenagers in Brookside Christian High School in North Stockton. I thought this might be the time for me to consider more schooling to become a certified interpreter. Having that certificate would bring in more money and give me that opportunity to use my signing as a ministry in the church. Those were the dreams dancing in my head!

After a few months of us living with my parents in my childhood neighborhood, sometime in the fall of 1992, Mike came home one day and shared that a friend of ours, a member of our church, Dave Sproul, wanted to help us relocate. He owned an almost new, 1989 34-foot Cimarron travel trailer that was parked out on his warehouse property outside of Lodi. He said we would have first option to purchase it. For now, we could live in it and have our son and daughter stay in a part of an older vacant house that was on the same property.

Mike and I decided to test it out, and the first few nights we spent there felt like we were in a small, but a very nice hotel room, if we didn't look out our window. If we did, we saw the warehouse grounds piled with all sorts of junk, equipment, and parts. We didn't care. It offered us our space! The kids were as ready as we were to be out of the cramped living quarters at my parents' house, and we unanimously decided to move.

We had renewed hope and believed things could only get better. And they would, but there was still this last stretch of the way. God's writings in "blue" would still be obscure. We would live here in this warehouse setting for the next three years continuing to lean into the wind and choosing to believe that God arranged it. In the least expected place, with the least amount of money, God would call us into full-time ministry. How would we respond? It would challenge us and set our course in faith and endurance.

Here we would lose all, but not in the ways of the past. It would be here in this warehouse as our home that we would "lose our lives" and surrender to God's call. We had gone through much of what looked like a failure. But, here we would release to God our past dreams and finally understand that there was a difference between losing and letting go.

95

We were about to transition out of the long bend in our road and find out that, all this time, we had been on the narrow highway named "Calvary's Road." This road would still require a few more miles of perseverance as God continued to develop His character in us. But, we were becoming experienced riders, and we had learned that all we needed to do was to keep our eyes out ahead, put our trust in Him, relax and lean into the curve.

Story 12:
The Song

"Mike's Song" was sung over a 20-year period of our life together. The song is one I still love to hear because I connect it to Mike's adventurous heart and soul. A song is composed of your heart-thoughts, and this one revealed Mike's. I can still hear Mike's voice singing it.

The Song was *What A Day for A Daydream*, originally sung by Bobby Darin. "What a day for a daydream... What a day for a day-dreamin' boy!"

At first, I believed this song was one of those catchy tunes that get embedded in your mind, and you find yourself humming its tune, or singing the words whether you want to or not. In all the times I heard Mike burst out with this song, he almost always sang just those first two lines.

But, not too far into our marriage, this song became my cue that Mike's dreamin'-heart was about to take flight, and his imagination was creating a plan to make it happen. It would be my "heads up" that he was "cooking up" some deal. It was usually a plan to "make us rich." The ideas rolling around in his head of a new project he was focusing on had a voice through this song,

I came to know the pattern.

Step One: The Song. It would begin. We could be walking from our car into a store or Mike could be coming out for a morning cup of coffee. It could be anywhere, anytime or any place, but if the words to that song rolled out his mouth I knew what was coming!

Step Two: The Sway. His dreams were big, and he was going to persuade me to agree to give my blessing. I would wait for the sales pitch and the sweet talk that would make me want to shake my head and even sometimes to roll my eyes.

I was not a dreamer back then. I think that was something that I "caught" from him as the years spent with him meshed our hearts together. At least I like to believe it to be so. In those first moments, his ideas most always seemed impossible to me. But, somehow, someway he would convince me he could make them work.

He was a leader, a dream caster, and he always found those who believed and wanted to dream with him. I became one. What an adventurous life I had because of them!

Step Three: The Soar. Once I agreed to enter his dream world, his idea would set flight like a kite! He was on a high! A dreamer is never happier than when his dream is alive and in action.

I believe I heard The Song for the first time in the single-wide trailer where we lived when we first married. Mike took me to see that first little house he wanted to remodel. The Song was sung in the years that followed before he began every building project that ended in disaster. The Song continued to be sung when we moved out of my parents' house and into the 34-foot Cimarron travel trailer at the warehouse. Full circle, trailer to trailer, and many dreams later, God was about to let me witness Him change not only The Song but also to give me a very special peek into Mike's heart.

It was 1993, and we were in the early beginnings of entering full-time ministry. I will share more of this in the next story, but we were having a pretty hard time financially. There was barely enough money and never extra. At the time, we were both sick with bad colds; Mike more than me. I remember feeling so helpless that we didn't have the money to buy him cough syrup to allow him to sleep.

We had gone to bed, and I laid there listening to him cough. I knew this was a testing time for him. The decision to enter full-time ministry was his, yet we were already struggling to pay our bills.

We had been lying there for a while, and I know he thought I was asleep. Then it happened. A hush filled our little bedroom as he began to worship and sing the song, "Oh, How I Love Jesus" by Frederick Whitfield.

"Oh, How I love Jesus,

Oh, how I love Jesus,

Oh, how I love Jesus because He first loved me."

He sang almost in a whisper, but I knew I was experiencing a holy moment between Mike and his Lord as He put His whole trust in God for himself, his family, and the ministry he was being called to.

From that night forward, The Song in Mike's heart changed. Not that I never heard him sing, "What a Day for a Daydream" again; but never like I had all the times before. Now, just as he had with the old song, he would spontaneously burst out singing this new song at any given moment or random place! I had been allowed to witness the great exchange of the dream. Mike's dream had been remarkably replaced with a vision, a vision for all people to love Jesus as He did.

Now, Mike was not scheming on his next dream job. God's purpose through all the testing had been accomplished. Mike was ready for full-time ministry and to dream God's dreams. The old dream song faded fast as this new bright, and joyful love song endearingly became "Mike's Song."

Story 13:
Fight It All You Can

"Fight it all you can," was Pastor Dick's advice to Mike when Mike began to share what he was feeling in his heart about going into full-time ministry. This wasn't the response Mike expected. He was feeling the call to take a step of faith and expected his pastor to encourage him.

Pastor Dick explained why he gave that advice. It was because too many people don't realize how challenging ministry is. He said, 'Mike, sheep bite!" And they both laughed. Mike understood what he was telling him. Pastor Dick shared that often people jump in, thinking full-time ministry is glamorous, but they haven't counted the cost. When the going gets hard, they aren't prepared to stay the course. Pastor Dick wanted to spare Mike from that. He wanted Mike's faith to arise and for him to know that he knew he was called to do this and that it wasn't just a passion. Pastor Dick was not saying to fight God, but to hold steady and see if this was Mike's desire or God's. If this were God, Mike's faith would increase as would the calling.

We had been involved with the *Christian Motorcyclists Association* (CMA) as "weekend warriors" since 1985. Once the reality that they were much more than a Christian ride group was realized, Mike was all in. We loved CMA and the people that were a part of its many chapters. CMA had become, in part, an amazing answer to a specific prayer for

Christian friends. We were now making friends all over the state, the nation and that would eventually include the world.

We had become officers in our Chapter, the Delta Ambassadors Chapter #30, out of Lodi/Stockton area. Mike had been elected as the chapter's President, and after first holding the office of Secretary, I become the chapter's Chaplain.

It was at one of our first campouts with CMA that Mike shared with me that he was walking through the camp late at night and he had a flashback memory. He "saw" himself back in his outlaw biker days and had this wave of God's presence roll through him. He wondered in his heart if God was calling him back to them, to share the love of Jesus Christ with them and to show them that there was a different way to life.

Of course, Mike loved to ride! Soon more and more of Mike's weekends would be to go out on rides and poker runs wearing his CMA colors, including Sundays. I understood why he went, yet I felt he should be in church. I had a mindset that to be a good Christian you were to be in church every Sunday. And though true in the sense that we do grow spiritually when we are an active part of a church fellowship, Mike was not sleeping in or playing hooky on Sundays. He was riding to look for ministry opportunities.

My little jabs spoken to make Mike feel guilty didn't work. My resentment of having to go alone mixed in with some judgment was obvious to him. One day at lunch Mike addressed the issue by saying, "So, in church, this last Sunday, how many people gave their heart to Jesus?" I said,

"None this Sunday." Mike then asked, "So, should Pastor Dick stop preaching?"

I looked at him not quite getting his point. It was then he poured out his heart of compassion for the bikers. He said he felt compelled to be with them. He loved them and knew in his heart that God was calling him to go to where they were. He said, "No, I don't get to lead someone to Jesus every time I go, but if I don't go, how will they know that it is Jesus that is missing in their life?"

I gave my full permission and more that day. I gave my blessing and felt so proud of him in my heart. I was seeing a man with the heart of God for the salvation of bikers. From that point on I was 100% behind him!

What I still didn't see coming was that God was pulling what I now call a "slow, fast one" on me. Slowly He had been turning our path, giving us a new identity as "bikers." But, in my mind, I saw it as God giving *Mike*'s old identity a spiritual makeover. He had been an outlaw biker, and now he would be a Christian biker.

I did love CMA and began investing much more time in it. I had progressed from being the occasional rider to feeling led by God to give up my Sunday School Class in the fall of 1992 so that I could attend more of the biker events with Mike. Now, I was also the one missing church to reach the lost on the highways of life.

By the fall of 1992, we were already functioning as Motorcycle Missionaries, yet Mike still had his construction business, CBC Construction (Complete Building Concepts).

We ministered within the *Christian Motorcyclists Association* and our local CMA chapter, but we were not supported, sponsored or singly sent out by them. We were sent out under a home missions status and the covering of our church body, *Zion Christian Fellowship, Outreach Ministries International* and, also, by those whom God had asked to be a part of our ministry through their financial and prayer support.

Mike's heart was moving along toward being in full-time ministry. He arranged for us to each have our testimonies recorded and put on cassette. Our intended purpose for this was that they could be used to either help us raise support or as a tool of extended personal ministry. I think in their entire existence we only sold very few. God instead chose to use them as that extended voice to those we would share with one on one.

I fully believed in the mission of the *Christian Motorcyclists Association* to win the lost one heart at a time, and I fully enjoyed the people in CMA. I did not particularly love camping, the look of "helmet hair" and that gritty feeling your face has after being in the wind on a long ride. I was willing to go and to be involved, but, if I was honest, in my heart it was still Mike's thing. I went to support my husband and to be with our friends, but the people were still "Mike's people." I was seriously considering acting on my dream to go back to school for my sign language certification.

It was now the summer of 1993, and it had been over a year since Mike first talked with Pastor Dick about entering ministry full-time. Mike had taken his advice and waited and held back all he could. He was bursting at the seams and finally, one day he said to me, "I know financially it is almost the worst of times. But *I must go full time.* It's time. Let's go talk to Pastor Dick and Edie."

I tried to conceal from Mike the little panic attack my heart was having, and I comforted myself with the thought they surely would say to him he should wait a while longer.

Before, Mike had talked with Pastor Dick alone, but this time he wanted me there, and we made an appointment for a visit. Pastors Dick and Edie both gave their blessing! They said they saw that God had made way for this ministry and felt positive that Mike was called to it. Our long-time friends, Jeff and Cheryl, also felt it was God's time and confirmed Mike's call in agreement with our pastors. The four of them encouraged us to move forward.

Mike was beyond excited, but there still was this hesitancy in me. I was just not sure about how this was going to work. All my insecurities kicked in. How would we live? What about money? How would Mike "make a living"? Mike felt that he had fought it, and could fight it no more. He was ready to step out and trust God.

I was not so ready for him to do that. Was it *God's* plan? Though I would keep my job and still work, it was not only Mike going into ministry; it would be me with him to a large degree.

If we wait for all our "ducks to be in a row" it isn't faith, is it? I was still struggling with "our ducks." They were not lining up! Not only would our ducks not line up, I felt a few were missing! I knew I had to hear from God myself. He knew He still had to speak to me personally. It was not enough for me to have another person tell me it was time. The practical side of me was not hearing the voice of faith in which Pastor Dick had spoken, but was hearing the voice of fear, my old enemy, and he was saying in a whole different tone, "Fight it!"

Story 14:
A World in My Heart

Asking God to add to our heart something that we know we lack will get a response from Him. This is especially true, when that something relates to the leading role we will play in the story He has written. For me to ask God to put a biker world in my heart was, to Him, already answered.

My world had always been my husband, my family, and my church. The deaf community had made its way in, and I believed my heart would make full room for them, but now it was being stretched in a whole different direction through our involvement in the Christian Motorcyclists Association and Mike's call to full-time motorcycle ministry.

We were like two little kids on a Christmas morning the day of August 4th, 1993. We were waiting and watching out the window of the Cimarron Travel Trailer that was home, for the first glimpse of our beautiful "new" Harley all freshly painted pearl white with blue trim. We commented, "It just doesn't get any better than this!" We were leaving for Sturgis, South Dakota for our very first of what would become ten straight years of travel and ministry there.

I had not originally planned to go to the Sturgis, South Dakota Black Hills Motorcycle Rally. Mike had been before, 20 years previously, back in his outlaw biker days. Mike had been asked by his friend, Roger of *Christ's Christian Riders* in

Sacramento, to help distribute 25,000 Commemorative Edition Sturgis Bibles! I still saw the biker ministry as Mike's, and I was happy to let him go. I would be his prayer support.

The Word of God says that things are confirmed by two or three witnesses. God was going to say something through others, three distinct times before I would grasp that He was sending me to Sturgis too. First, one friend, then a few days later another made direct statements that they thought I should be going to Sturgis with Mike. I brushed the first one off, but the second one lingered in my thoughts.

I wasn't sure Mike thought I should go with him, but when I mentioned it to him that I was thinking about it, He got excited. He thought I didn't want to go and wasn't going to pressure me. We had purchased a small motorcycle tent trailer that was pulled behind the bike, and Mike began talking about how great it would be to travel together. Riding the bike using our new "off the ground" tent at campgrounds would be "comfort" we were not used to. It would be traveling first class!

We discussed the financial issue and determined we would need another $200 for me to go. We had no resource for this extra money to come, except "out of the blue." To my surprise, when I went to pick up my check from work it was for exactly $200 more than usual! I was on summer break from my job at the school district, and so there were no medical insurance deductions. Had God just provided?

Still unsure, I went to the church to talk to my heart-friend, Cheryl. We loved to share about what we were discovering in God's Word or what new precept He was establishing in our hearts. I just knew my friend would tell me that I should not be going to such a secular biker rally, especially since it was so far away. I was wrong. Immediately out of her mouth came the words, "I always thought you should be going with Mike!"

God knew I was having some issues feeling connected with the bikers and He was going to use this trip to answer a prayer of mine. I had seen on the wall of the church office a picture of hundreds of people all inside an outline of a heart. I told the Lord I did not have Mike's bikers in *my* heart. If He was going to call us into that full-time ministry, He was going to have to somehow put all of them in there like I saw in that picture.

I knew that if I went to biker events to appease God and Mike, but my heart was detached and me not wanting to be there, that the bikers themselves would pick up on it and sense that my heart wasn't with them. It would do more harm than good. If God was going to call me to them, He would need to put them in my heart, which He did on our first trip to Sturgis together.

I wrote an article for our *Christian Motorcyclists Association*, Delta Ambassadors Chapter Newsletter and this, in part, is what I wrote:

A View from Mt. Sinai/Looking at Sturgis

As viewed by Sherri Sumstine

As we traveled our last day back home after being in Sturgis, I still felt the high of being in an extraordinary experience. I likened this trip, the sovereign events leading to it, the days there and even the ride home as a mountain top experience. I thought, "It's like being on Mt. Everest, the highest mountain in the world!" But, then my thoughts changed to, "No, not Mt. Everest, but Mt. Sinai — the Mountain of God!"

Why? How could a 3,000-mile ride on the back of a motorcycle, camping in someone's backyard for seven nights or being one of among approximately 200,000 bikers (which included the full spectrum of the casual rider to the hardcore patch holder) be a Mt. Sinai experience? It was because in this experience *God stamped a people upon my heart* and then filled it with *His love* for them. He showed me I could have divine intervention, direction and provision and that if I called upon Him, He would answer me and show me great and mighty things. We will say to the captives, "Come out," and to those in darkness, "Be free!"

We were a part of putting a Bible in the hands of 25,000 bikers, of handing the plan of salvation via CMA water cups to thousands and

111

of participating in a divine appointment with two biker couples whom God saw had open and searching hearts.

My view of Sturgis? It was AWESOME! *My first bike ride down Main Street* I will never forget. But, I will also never forget the last one of the week as I asked Mike, "Please, can we take one last ride?" The emotions were overwhelming, as I thanked God again and again for His unconditional love and for putting "the world in my heart."

God was making way for my call. He was going to use me in this mission field too. It wasn't Africa with people living in huts where my heart had felt drawn so many years ago, but it *was* a very special people group all its own, camping in tents and needing to know the love of Jesus. There weren't snakes on the ground but tattooed on their arms. There weren't native tribes, but there were biker clubs. Caring about their world was laid before me and going to them with love was now my opportunity—all for the asking!

Story 15:
I Have a Word for You

God's interaction with us proves our faith is more than religion. There are many religions in our world, but none have what Christianity offers in mutual love between God and us. As we worship Him and pray, we can hear the inner voice of God speaking to us in response to our shared relationship.

God uses the Bible, as a light to our path and as His living Word to our souls. He speaks to us regularly by specifically matching our situation, our current storyline, *with* a story or verse recorded in His Word. When this happens, divine communication occurs Spirit to spirit and brings comfort, peace, hope, and often a promise in perfect alignment to our need.

One of the first times God matched Mike's and my situation with a particular verse was in late 1993. We had traveled to Sturgis, South Dakota for the big motorcycle rally in August of that year for the first time. A few months later, in November, we felt that to be faithful to the call of God and to follow His leading, we were to close Mike's current business, CBC Construction, to make way for him to enter full time into the work of the ministry. This was not a decision we took lightly.

Mike was more than ready to shut the business down. He had been waiting on God's timing. I had been doing some spiritual fasting. My fast confirmed to us God's green light for the ministry. We decided that I would continue to work at the Lodi Unified School District with the hearing-impaired class. I loved my job following the students to their classes and interpreting PE, Art, Math, and Biology.

When I started working at the school district, my check covered our children, Mike and Stephanie's, tuition at the Christian High School in North Stockton, bought groceries, provided our health insurance and allowed a bit to cover expenses while we stayed at my parent's home. When we moved to Lodi into the travel trailer and the kids into the little apartment house we took them out of private school and put them in public school. That freed up some finances, but, money was still very tight.

We had made our decision for full-time ministry, and so Mike was not taking on new jobs. In the past, when things got hard Mike would always find a side job and was able to pull in the needed resources. But now, as his act of faith to bring in some finances for our expenses, as well as his needed ministry expenses, Mike began to *sell* some of his construction equipment and tools. His trust in God, and the decision we had made said that we didn't need them anymore.

Watching his cargo trailer roll out of the driveway hooked to the back of someone else's truck wasn't easy. Knowing each time, he handed me money it had come from the sale of his tools that he had used to *make* our living, took us deeper into our commitment. I remember taking deep breaths after those sales and praying, "Ok, God, we're trusting You."

God was going to give me His Word in response to my honest concern for our provision. We made plans to attend a *Christian Motorcyclists Association* (CMA) Christmas banquet in Santa Nella, CA. We had attended this event in previous years, and it was always fun to see everyone all dressed up instead of in their leather jackets and chaps.

This year was special because we were going to make our big announcement that we had crossed over into full-time ministry. It was an honor to have our CMA Regional Evangelist, Wayne Henderson, share our decision with everyone. His words validated to others our call and he encouraged everyone to pray for us.

After the banquet, so many friends came and congratulated us with many asking excitedly, "How is it going?" I responded, "God's good! Faith is very exciting!" This was true, and I meant it, but I was thankful that they could not see the shaking in my heart that our steps of faith were causing.

Once we arrived home that night, Mike said he was going on one of his "prayer drives." He loved to drive, and it would help him clear his head. If he couldn't sleep, he would often get up and take a drive. If he needed to pray, that's what he'd do.

After Mike had left, I began to pray myself. I sincerely asked God, "What am I to say to all those people who ask how were we doing? How am I to respond to everyone when they ask?" I did not feel free to share with them how hard it was, or that I wasn't at all sure how we were going to do this because I did not want them to think my hand was out asking *them* for money. We needed financial supporters, but I did not want to appear begging for their money! I genuinely poured out my fear and frustration to the Lord.

As I cried out to God as to what to say to people, I heard Him in my spirit say, "Go get my Word. I have a Word for you." My heart leaped. I went into my room and picked up my Bible, opened it, and my eyes fell on this passage.

It was as if Jesus, Himself, in great love, cupped my face and held it in His big strong hands. With the most tender loving voice you have ever heard, I knew He was looking me straight in the eyes as He spoke this promise to me:

> *"Then Jesus said to his disciples: "Therefore I tell you, do not worry about your life, what you eat; or about your body, what you will wear. For life is more than food; and the body more than clothes. Consider the ravens: They do not sow or reap, they have no storeroom or barn, yet God feeds them. And how much more valuable you are than birds! Who of you by worrying can add a single hour to his life? Since you cannot do this very little thing, why do you worry about the rest?*
>
> *Consider how the lilies grow. They do not labor or spin. I tell you, not even Solomon in all his splendor was dressed like one of these. If that is how*

God clothes the grass of the field, which is here today and tomorrow is thrown into the fire, how much more will he clothe you, you of little faith! And do not set your heart on what you will eat or drink; do not worry about it. For the pagan world runs after all such things, and your Father knows that you need them. But seek his kingdom, and these things will be given to you as well.

Do not be afraid, little flock, for your Father has been pleased to give you the kingdom. Sell your possessions and give to the poor. Provide purses for yourselves that will not wear out, a treasure in heaven that will never fail, where no thief comes near and no moth destroys. For where your treasure is, there your heart will be also" (Luke 12: 22-34, NIV).

I had received a Word from the Lord before, but never quite like this. I knew that I had experienced an encounter with God and *He was* going to take care of us. A solid faith settled in my heart. I felt my faith had substance. God said not to worry! He would provide for us!

To this very day, I look for and ask God for a word from His Word. I must know what story from the Bible I am in or what verses match my story today. It gives me peace, brings direction and sheds insight into how I live in my current circumstances.

I encourage you to find your life story in the Word of God.

Story 16:
Highway Prayers

Highway prayers are what I call those prayers that I pray when I am out driving. If I am alone in my car, it is natural for me to engage in worship or conversations with God. Within my highway prayers, I regularly pray "one-line prayers."

One-line prayers are all about *God's heart*. His heart calls to my heart to notice a person and to pray for them, whether they are beside the road as I'm driving by, at a specific event I am attending, or even those standing ahead of me in line at the grocery store. My spirit responds to Christ's love rising for that person. I ask Him to meet their need for salvation or assist them with a struggle they might be facing. As my faith connects with God's desire to bless them, a holy moment is observed in Heaven.

Life can be changed on earth as I talk to God on the highway, and in my one-line prayers. Sometimes the life that's changed is a stranger's. Sometimes it's mine.

It was March 1994. Mike and I were not only active as chapter officers of our Christian Motorcyclists Association Chapter but also as motorcycle missionaries. We had been busy doing "Ministry Presentation" services using a slide projector to bring awareness to our ministry and to look for financial support. We also began meeting every morning at

6:00 AM with a few others from our church to pray. Each of us was praying for God's purposes to be done in our lives, and in our church.

One morning after prayer at the church, I came back home, as usual, to get ready for work. Later, I drove my normal route to work, which would take me on Highway 12 East/Victor Road to make my entrance onto Highway 99. That morning, at that entrance, there stood a hitchhiker with his thumb out. Obviously, I was not going to stop to give him a ride, but I did "shoot up" to heaven a quick one-line prayer. I said, "Lord, please send someone to share Jesus with this man today." And that was that. I drove on to work.

Later that morning I needed to call Mike to ask him something. He picked up the phone, but as soon as he heard my voice he said, "Honey, can you call me back later? Ron Poletti (our friend) was at UJs having breakfast. When he walked out, he saw a hitchhiker there at the Hwy 99 entrance. He picked him up and brought him over here. We're sharing Jesus with him."

My eyes popped wide open, and my mouth dropped to the floor! Could it be? Was it the same man I prayed for? Yes, it was. That same hitchhiker was at that very moment in my living room being prayed for by my husband! I know that God allowed me to see the answer to this one-line prayer to show us He sees the individual, and as we ask Him for a need on their behalf, He is listening to every word we say.

This season of seeking God continued. We wanted to hear His voice of direction and were asking for His anointing

121

as we moved forward in ministry to the bikers. We were always at bike events on the weekends. I had been on school break loving the Track A schedule of having January/February, and July/August off. Going back to work after this two-month break seemed hard. My days had been full, and now I would have to fit back into a work schedule. Mike began to feel I needed to join in the ministry full time.

I felt torn. I loved my job, but God had been leading me in this new direction for a while now. Was He going to ask me to lay down what He had specifically given me permission to pursue? I felt I knew the answer was going to be a "Yes," but I was not going to jump into a decision. I began to process the change and pray for God's timing.

We continued to meet for prayer each morning. It had been a couple of months, and I had been struggling in my spirit about laying down "my dream" to join Mike in biker ministry. God had specifically given me clear permission to take my sign language classes. He had given me this job that had increased my skill and my love for the hearing-impaired. Was He asking me now to lay it all down? If I were going to quit and not come back after the upcoming break, then I would need to give the teacher I worked with and the school the proper notice. I was feeling the pressure.

While at early prayer at the church one morning, I was doing my best to convince God of two major benefits that my job provided and why I should not quit. I told Him that my job provided our family with groceries and health insurance and if I quit what we would do for both? *Just* as I finished that question, I heard a noise immediately to my right that sounded like paper rustling. My eyes opened to the empty chair next to where I was kneeling and there laid a $100 bill. As soon as I saw the money, I heard God say, "I will take care of you!" One of the men had laid it there as a blessing to Mike and me. I was stunned. That money could not have been any "bluer!" God's answer could not have been any clearer.

As I drove back from the prayer time to get ready for work I was still in shock. I knew that what had just happened was not a coincidence. As I offered one of my Highway Prayers on my ride home, God had, even more, to say to me. I was on Highway 12 East/Victor Road again, and the radio was tuned to a local Christian station. Suddenly I caught a devotion that was being shared. The words being spoken were as if they were being directed specifically to me.

There had obviously been some Scripture reading and perhaps even some dialogue and discussion. But, where I picked up on the devotion segment was when the speaker said, "God is your provision. God is asking someone to take a step of faith. He is saying as a Father would to His little child, 'Jump! I will catch you!'" I knew this was for me.

God continued to speak to my spirit. He said, "But, you do not have to do this. You *can* keep your job if you want to, but then, *that* will be your provision. You will never know all the ways I would have provided for you. It's your choice."

My heart was pounding as I realized the personal interaction God was having with me. There was no way I was going to miss this adventure with Him! I was ready to lay down my dreams for God's dreams, and the call He was now asking of me. I would join my husband in full-time biker ministry. I could hardly wait to tell Mike, and I wrote out my resignation and turned it in within the next few days.

God loves talking directly with us! He has unlimited resources for us to hear His voice. For me, He used a $100 bill and a radio program!

Another amazing part of this story is that on *the last day of my job,* Mike was invited to meet with Ken Vandergrift, one of the founders of the *Good Samaritan Training Center* in Stockton, CA. Ken had felt led to talk with Mike and hear his story. Ken gave Mike a tour of their facility including the offices and the big food room where they handed out boxes of food to those who needed help.

After their time of sharing, Ken handed Mike a full set of keys to their facility! He offered us free office space, and he sent Mike home with boxes of groceries that overfilled our cupboards. Ken had given us full access to use the food room personally, as well as to freely hand out groceries to any of our bikers in need!

It was no coincidence that this happened on my last day of employment. God immediately began to fulfill His promise to take care of my family's needs! In the future, I would see God provide the best healthcare for Mike in the same way.

Prayer sees a need and believes it will be met. Prayer is all about faith. Perhaps God has been talking to you. Is there something He has asked you to do or to believe for? Does it involve risk and the unknown? Take "a chance" with God. Close your eyes and tell Him, "Here I come," and take that leap! If you don't, you will never know what the outcome would have been if you had trusted in the One who challenged you to "Jump!"

I believe when you open your eyes you will find that you are on an extraordinary journey with God. His ultimate destination for you is spiritual maturity found in a devoted relationship with Him. He travels exclusively on the road of faith, and you will come to know it as the High Way!

Story 17:
Burning Our Plow

Confirmation that we are doing the right thing or going the right way reassures us that we are on track with God's plan. Confirmation brings peace to our minds and validates that our struggles are worth fighting through for the greater purpose of our mission.

Sometimes God will use a situation as a test of our commitment to our mission. It's easy to make a statement of faith, but eventually, our statements will require acts of faith.

It was spring of 1995, and we were still living in the warehouse setting. It had been 18 months since Mike had closed his construction business to go into full-time ministry; and almost a year since I had quit my job at the school to join him. Our good friends, Rich and Jennie Hardesty, were our constant companions in ministry. They blessed us in so many ways, more times than I can record. Their family became our family, and we had many personal and ministry times together.

God was keeping His promises to be our resource for all our needs. We never missed a biker event because of lack of funds. Our personal bills were sometimes delayed in being paid, but the money always came.

Our church secretary, my friend Cheryl, and I called our ministry finances "manna;" a direct reference to God's sovereign provision for the Old Testament Israelites. He fed them from heaven every morning when they were in the wilderness. He wanted them to learn that He was their Provider.

Manna was also a foreshadowed revelation of Jesus, the Bread of Life, who is our Manna from Heaven. His mercies come to us new and fresh every morning. Just as the Israelites would gather manna, so we go to Jesus at the beginning of each new day to receive our spiritual nourishment. My personal morning times with Him fed my soul as the Word brought nutrients vital for my spiritual growth.

As the children of Israel gathered only enough manna for that day, so it seemed that God was providing financially for us the same way. It became my procedure to call Cheryl and ask her, "Is there manna today?" God's supply for us miraculously appeared as donations from others in amounts of $25, $50, or whatever God put on their hearts to give. It was always just enough.

One day we received mail from the State Contractor's Board. Mike's construction contractor's license annual renewal fee was coming due. The law had changed regarding how a contractor could share his license, so if we let this renewal lapse, Mike's stepdad would not be able to add Mike back on his license as he was then.

127

I don't remember the exact amount they required, but to us, it was a lot of money, and I knew if we used our "manna" to cover this expense it would overstretch our very slim budget. However, I still thought that for our long-term security, we should pay it.

When I brought it up to Mike, he looked straight at me and questioned, "Why?" I reasoned back, "Just in case." Without thinking twice Mike's faith responded with, "Just in case what? Just in case God fails us?" I let out a big sigh and knew he was right.

Shortly after we made that decision, I was reading the story of what Elisha did when he was called into full-time ministry with Elijah. It's found in 1 Kings 19:19-21. First, Elisha slaughtered his yoke of oxen. Second, he burned the plowing equipment to cook the meat and then he gave it to the people to eat. With no expectations of God failing him, he set out to follow Elijah and became his attendant.

Elisha made sure he had nothing to fall back on; he had no oxen and no plowing equipment to make a living. Elisha was 100% sure he was called, and he would abandon his very livelihood as proof to confirm his faith and answer that call.

This was another place in God's Word where we found our current life story, as we fully identified with Elisha. I saw that we, too, had "slaughtered our oxen and burned our plows" when we sold all but a few basic tools and pieces of equipment.

What had been our statement of faith, now required an *act* of faith; and we did not renew Mike's contractor's license.

We burned our plow. Our commitment was to trust in God alone. What peace filled our hearts knowing we were in 100% reliance upon God. I believe He was pleased, too, because at our point of faith He told us the story of Elisha as a perfect confirmation!

Story 18:
"Highway Travelog"
Experiences and Encounters

Adventures on our motorcycle came often, and we loved the fun and fellowship! We learned to watch and wait in these adventures for our God-assignment to kick in and transition the moment into a live opportunity to be a part of the great commission.

The following paragraphs are excerpts from our *Travelog Newsletter* during our first couple of years as motorcycle missionaries. They will give you a glimpse of our encounters.

June 1994 Travelog. There was a woman at the Bike Fest who God told me about early in the morning as I prayed before we got there. I had a sense she had gone to church as a child, but had become involved with a boyfriend and had compromised her lifestyle that went against all she knew to be right.

I prayed for her all day. About 10 PM we were at the CMA First Aid Station, and a young woman came up shaking and crying. When it was realized she was not physically sick but had been battered by her boyfriend, I was asked to talk with her. The Lord immediately spoke to my heart and said, "This is her."

I shared with her that I understood how she felt she was a long way down a wrong path and very far from God, but that it was only two steps back! She looked at me with tears in her eyes and said, "I can take two steps." I explained, as God had shown it to me, that the steps were first repentance and then obedience.

She said she was going home, moving out and back in with her mom. God promises to leave the 99 and go to look for the one that wandered off. The Good Shepherd looked for her. He'll look for you. He'll look for your loved one.

September 1994 Travelog of our trip to Sturgis. We traveled round trip 3,000 miles. We towed the bike with the van and, other than losing our trailer hitch, water pump, belt, fan, clutch and tires on the trailer, we had no mechanical problems. We had numerous opportunities to share one on one including with: a satanic priest, an agnostic, and a young man who said I was saying to him exactly what his praying mom would say!

January 1995 Travelog. (Followup about five months later) Mike received a phone call from the former Satanic priest he had shared with at Sturgis. This man told Mike that back when he was at Sturgis his wife had left him and their two-year-old son had been taken away by authorities. He said that though he was doing drugs the night Mike spent talking to him, the Holy Spirit continued to deal with him. This man would not let Mike pray with him then, but he had agreed Mike could pray *for* him. Mike told him he would pray for "divine discomfort" in his life. And he did.

This man called now to let Mike know that a short time after leaving Sturgis he and his wife went to a Teen Challenge Ministry and both received Jesus as their Savior! They are attending a local church and were able to have their son with them during the holidays; and he will, in time, be returned to them.

This man also called to tell Mike about his nephew who was being dishonorably discharged from the service and in deep spiritual need. He wanted Mike to pray for "divine discomfort" for his nephew!

February 1995 Travelog. We received a phone call asking if we would do a graveside funeral for an 88-year-old man who was at death's door. We agreed but then inquired about his spiritual condition. He had known the Lord when he was young but had not lived with him for many years. On the way to the rest home, we prayed and asked God for His mercy and for this semi-conscious man to be alert and responsive.

He was no longer talking. We began to pray for him and softly share with him that Jesus died for his sins so that he could have eternal life in heaven. He began to respond and was able to say, "Yes," as we prayed the sinner's prayer. He kept reaching for our hand to hold and stroke.

There was an awesome presence of God there that night. I told Mike I felt as if we had walked out to the very edge of eternity, where God met this man lingering between life and death. This man was allowed the last opportunity to ask Jesus to forgive him of his sins, and he took it. One never knows when they've been given their last opportunity.

September 1995 Travelog. The Friday after our long trip to Sturgis there was a campout that we knew several of our bikers were at. We were very tired from our trip and only planned to

133

stay the day on Saturday. Shortly after arriving we were approached by a club staff member and asked if we were doing church the next morning. Of course, our plans changed immediately as we said, "*Yes!*" The band announced the service Saturday night, and on Sunday morning one of the biker vendors walked through the whole camp yelling on his megaphone, "There's church in the bar at 9 o'clock!" We had eight people, including our announcer, come to biker church that morning.

Mike used a T-shirt with a picture of the Grim Reaper on the front to give an illustrated sermon on how even the dark side knows their time is almost up and they cannot stop the move of the Spirit of God or the fulfillment of the end time events God has said will happen.

Mike's message will now be triggered in their heart every time they see a Grim Reaper shirt.

May 1996 Travelog. When our loved ones aren't living spiritually, as we know they should, we can allow worry or even depression into our heart and tend to want to shut down until all is okay. It can be a struggle to feel like going out and being about God's business.

One day when I was struggling, God said, "If you will go and be the answer to another mother's/father's prayer for their son or daughter (by reaching out and touching a life with the truth of the gospel), then I will be faithful to send someone to be the answer to yours."

The painting on the back "boot" of our bike is finished! The artist that painted it spent hours and hours—often stopping to weep as the reality of what his hand was expressing came back full force upon him. That reality being the mass of lost humanity blindly walking on the Broad Way Road which leads to a burning hell and eternity without God when all the while the cross was there to be the bridge—the only way to escape and walk into heaven's gate and eternal life with Jesus. This mural was a labor of *love* not only for this ministry but for the work of the Kingdom of God. A picture says a thousand words!

July 1996 Travelog. Mike has been recently appointed as a Christian Motorcyclists Association Lay Evangelist by CMA West Coast Evangelist, Wayne Henderson. This is not a paid staff position, but Mike accepts this privilege as an honor to work in a greater capacity within this great outreach association.

August 1996 Travelog. A Poem; by Sherri Sumstine.

Will you listen to the taunts of the enemy

that results in depression and a lack of Godly self-esteem?

Or will you listen to the voice of the Lord that says,

"Is there anything too hard for me?"

You lack motivation because you allow your flesh to rule.

I will give you direction and purpose and then the anointing to carry it through.

Lay down your life—give it all to me.

I will take you one step, then two, then three.

It will be a process, but you'll never regret,

because I know the beginning and the end— they're already set.

So, call upon me with all your heart

for in my Kingdom you do have a part.

September 1996 Travelog. We were just home from Sturgis one day and then off to another campout that was a Statewide Run for the Modified Motorcycle Association, the biker association we target. We were tired and, out of that physical state, I was telling the Lord that I didn't want to hear the language I was hearing or see the things my eyes were seeing, that I was just tired and asked did we need to be here today?

He answered using the scripture from Ezekiel 2:4-5, "They will know that a prophet has been among them." *Then,* Mike came in from having a conversation with one of the men in the MMA leadership. This man had shared with him that he had been going through crises in his life in a court situation.

He shared that as he laid awake unable to sleep that all he could see was Mike and Sherri walking around the campground and he wondered if our God would hear his prayer. He said, "So, I prayed to the God of Mike and Sherri, and He answered my prayer!"

At that, I grabbed Mike's hand and said: "Let's go walk around the campground!" This man was in our Biker Worship Service that Sunday. We had a total of 22! After hearing our message on Nicodemus and Jesus' statement that "You must be born again!" he came up and asked for one of our CMA New Testaments. This indicated to us that he had repeated the sinner's prayer! Please pray for him that he will take a full stand.

Our lives became as an open book for men to read as we loved the people and let His light shine in the darkness. Our heavenly assignment was always the purpose of the day and became the passion of our heart. We thought it awesome to discover that besides redeeming broken lives, God was using our riding bikes to write action adventures!

Story 19: GodThings!

"GodThing" began to be used in my daily conversations and exclamations about God. This word was birthed out of a conversation I had with my friend, Patricia Reilly. In our discussion, it was said, "Men do men things, and women do women things. And God does "GodThings!" GodThings are things that no human can do or make happen.

I began to use this word often and to include it in my newsletters that went out to various parts of the country. An out of the country choir came to sing at my church, and I spoke it to them to each take back to their nations.

Mike and I spoke at a church in Arizona and used the word "GodThing" in our services there. The word was "catchy" and captured an expression in the unique terminology of what God does! I began to use it everywhere we traveled.

Am I taking credit for the word "GodThing," now common most everywhere in Christian and even in some non-Christian circles? Well, just let me say that I had never heard it used anywhere before. I still delight when I hear it spoken on a television program, by a celebrity, or even by new and old friends. I guess I do not have proof that it is "my word," but there is *very* good reason to believe that it is. And I use it a lot.

It was April 1995, and we had been living on the warehouse grounds in the Cimarron Travel Trailer for almost three years. A lot had happened in our story in those few years. God was leading and providing, but living in the trailer with our teenagers in the old two-bedroom apartment type dwelling had been challenging, to say the least. Most of our household furniture was in storage on the same warehouse grounds.

Don't get me wrong. We were more than grateful for the free storage space. We would have lost everything without it. But, as a woman, I could feel time ticking away, deteriorating our belongings. It was too overwhelming for me even to go look at all of it covered with tarps, the dust thick on top, and, yes, mouse droppings.

Our friend who owned the property and the trailer approached Mike and said he and his wife wanted to sell the trailer and they were giving us first option to buy it. He was also going to begin work on the warehouse site, and that it would be best if we could find a place to move to.

Though our church offered to finance the Cimarron for us, we both felt that this was not God's plan. We said thank you, but no to our friend, knowing we would need to move out of the trailer immediately, and off the grounds as soon as possible. Where were we going? We did not have money for a deposit. We did not have a consistent enough income to prove to a property management service our means to pay rent.

Another friend of ours, who rented shop space that included an office on the warehouse site where we were staying, offered to let us move temporarily into his office and use it as our bedroom. That would give us time to search for another place to live.

It was an answer to our need to vacate the Cimarron, but to live and sleep in a shop office? We were moving from a small hard place to an even smaller harder place. There was no privacy. The bathroom was just outside the shop office door, and one that was used all day by the public. It looked very much like a warehouse bathroom. I cleaned it the best I could, but there was no shower. We would need to walk across the grounds to where the kids' little apartment-house was. We were thankful for a roof over our head, but life was beyond difficult. It felt tailor-made to work humility in us.

The Holy Spirit used those circumstances to make a truth real in my heart. I discovered it does not matter where I live physically because *where* I truly live is to Him, in Jesus. I agreed with God that as I lived spiritually in Christ, I was well cared for, and deeply loved by Him. Every cell of my body would testify to that.

Within these truths, God revealed Himself to me as the Great I AM, the Eternal One. This office was not my eternal home. My furniture was not stacked in a dusty warehouse. Heaven was my home. His Word said that He was preparing a place for me! My furniture was being built by The Great Carpenter. Where I physically lived now was not a concern. I did not *need* beautiful décor. All that I needed, God said, "I

AM." He also whispered in my heart that the house He would provide for us *here* would be above and beyond what I would ask for!

In a precious and rare way, it was here, also, that Mike and I grew together as we never had before. Our hearts had been healed for a long time, and our love for each other had only continued to deepen and grow, but it was there, in that little office shop, that God made Mike the love of *my* life. In that least romantic place, God breathed on us a taste of heaven.

That summer Mike worked hard on remaking an old small camping trailer into a bike trailer. It turned out beautiful! We had purchased a van and painted it Harley orange; and a friend, Don Vigil, had gifted the van with awesome flames down both sides! Then, friends and supporters, Curt and Amy Sandberg, gave it an amazing inside makeover with oak cabinets. The carpet was donated as were the oak skins to redo the paneling. We painted the bike trailer black and Harley orange to match the van. Together, they were something to behold!

Mike had made the decision that it was time to sell our bike and get an upgrade. He began to make it known at the Sturgis Rally we attended that August. We no sooner got home, than we got a call from a buyer in Utah. We towed the bike back to Utah and sold it, then began our prayer search for a new one.

Now we were "on the hunt" for a house *and* a bike which were two big orders. We had the money from the bike sale but were at least $3,500 short of the cost of the bike Mike had looked at and dreamed of owning. He had sat on "this dream" and said, "OK, Lord. This is it!"

He had originally looked at a smaller bike because of cost, one with not much of a back seat and without an arm rest or backrest. But, the Lord spoke clearly to him and said, "No, because Sherri needs to be comfortable." Yay, God! I was so thankful. Mike agreed to trust God for the extra funds to buy a bigger bike for our ministry and travel needs.

Then GodThings began to come back to back! About the first part of September my friend and church secretary, Cheryl called and said a very large "manna" drop had been made. It was a check for $3,000 specified for our housing. We were blown away and very excited! We found and answered an advertisement for a house to rent about three miles out of Lodi, in a country setting. The people viewing the house after us were driving a Mercedes. Insecurity tried to knock on my heart, but this house would be above, and beyond what I would ask for, just like God had spoken to my heart it would be! We prayed and asked God if this was it.

The landlord inquired about the stability of our income and Cheryl told him that all she could say was that she had witnessed first-hand God be our Provider. To our benefit, Geoff Grinols was also a Harley Rider and was intrigued with our ministry and service to God. We knew it was God's favor on us that Geoff decided to take a step of faith with us.

We paid him the first and last month's rent, plus three more months in advance. After that, to come up with $600 a month would require God's participation again. We took the huge step of faith and were told we could move on October 1, 1995! God encouraged me in His Word that when He gives us a blessing, He doesn't take it back. And God was faithful to us for the next ten years that we lived there. It would be the longest we had stayed in one place during our entire marriage. It would be a "GodThing!"

About a week after getting our "GodThing" approval to move into the house, Cheryl called again and asked me if I was sitting down. Another check had come in. This one was for $3,500 and specified for our motorcycle. Another GodThing! The same weekend we moved into our new house, we brought home our 1992 FLHS Electra Glide Harley Davidson with 21,000 original miles. We had just enough for the basic cost of the bike but were short the tax and license fees. The same couple who had sent the $3,500 inquired about those issues and immediately sent another check to cover them!

We called that October our move to the Promised Land. We had been living in the "wilderness," though definitely under God's provision. I had surrendered to "the office shop bedroom." Now we would be living in a 1,300-square foot, two baths, three-bedroom home with beautiful wood throughout, including a large oak dome kitchen ceiling. Sun shined through a kitchen window, and every morning rainbow prisms appeared on the walls and dome ceiling from the crystals hanging there.

The home was surrounded by beautiful trees, a huge back deck with a live Koi pond where Mike and I often read our Bible and prayed together on our porch swing each morning. Isn't God amazing?

What if Mike had not closed his business two years earlier? What if I had decided to stay at my job and to let it be our provision? What if we had complained and sulked in our "office shop bedroom?" What if rather than listening to the Lord, Mike had bought the smaller bike? What if we had let fear cause us to purchase the Cimarron trailer? For sure our life would be void of these stories, and we just might be without the use of that great word that expresses God's miracles as a "GodThing!"

Story 20:
Crises

Life is a gift. God gave us a love of life because He loves life! When a health crisis hits, we are forced out of our fantasy thinking that we will live forever, and are thrust into a hyperawareness that we have no guarantee of tomorrow. We come face to face with our mortality as we measure the time we've had, and the threats to our dreams for the future.

In our appeal to God for His intervention, we recognize and acknowledge His Sovereignty as we cry out to Him, "Not yet, not now!" We realize we have no real control over what happens. It is He who numbers our days on earth, and it is His will that He mysteriously hands back to us His gift of time. God's omnipotent sovereignty and His ways are higher than ours. They are constant reminders that *we* are the created.

We had been in our new house on Locust Tree Road almost a year to the day. Our Sturgis trip had been the highlight of our year, as usual. Before we left, another GodThing provision added to our stack of stories of His faithfulness to meet our needs when we were out of options.

We had been behind in our rent and some personal bills. We, also, had no funds available for our trip to South Dakota. We were standing in faith, just not sure how God was going to do it this time.

Mike had an appointment with the pastor of the First Baptist Church of Elk Grove. They had supported us monthly almost from the beginning. He went for this already scheduled visit and came home with a miracle. The check in his hand covered our back rent and bills, allowed for a few items to purchase to get ready to leave for our trip and covered the entire cost of the trip itself! And, as a cherry on top, this pastor informed Mike that their church's monthly support for us was going to increase substantially. We couldn't have been more thankful. This was, again, divine favor.

It was remarkable to experience these "blue money drops" from heaven. After so many years of learning to trust through lack, now we were living as if eating the fruit of the seeds we planted. God's Word says He will meet our needs. It was still God's call of how He would do things, so we did not presume as we waited in hope, but we did trust knowing that we were in His plan for our lives. It was awesome to see our faith produce substance.

It had been a wonderful whirlwind summer. We would just get home from one rally or campout, and we were off on another. We loved it and would have had it no other way. I was truly enjoying what God had called us to, and I was not faking one bit my love for the people He had called us to share His love with.

How could we know we were taking our last steps of what had become our normal? We were about to step into another new season filled with GodThings, but it would be characterized by challenges we had never yet known. It would validate that an all-out commitment to God does not mean life itself is "safe." And we would come to understand there can be a mysterious and profoundly different meaning to living happily ever after.

On September 29, 1996, our path took an unexpected and very sharp turn.

Mike came home from a men's barbecue held at our church. He wasn't feeling good and felt worse as the night went on. We thought he might have food poisoning or, more likely, sick with the flu.

I'll spare you the details and just say that the vomiting had subsided during the night, but by morning he was throwing up blood. I realize now that I was in total denial that Mike's life was in crisis. He had lain on the bathroom floor for quite some time too weak to get up. My daughter and I managed to get him in the back of her SUV, and because we didn't have health insurance, I drove him the extra miles to the county hospital.

By the time we got there, he was immediately put in ICU. The nurses were calling it an upper GI bleed, and I remember the stark panic I felt as I watched him continue to lose blood. A specialist was called in to do a procedure that they hoped would stop the bleeding. The doctors told me they did not know if he would make it through the night or the next couple of days.

I remember walking the hospital halls in a state of shock. How could this be? Was Mike going to die? Had God brought us through all the hurt, forgiveness, healing and spiritual growth to get us into full-time ministry, with all the provisions of the house and the bike, just to let Mike die now in this hospital? I could not make sense of it all.

In my heart, I frantically looked for faith, but I was afraid that if I asked God what was going to happen, He was going to say, "I will be with you through the valley of the shadow of death." I knew He would be, but I didn't want to hear Him confirm my fear. So, I didn't ask. I prayed. I prayed for mercy, and I asked God to please spare Mike's life.

Our good friends, Rich and Jennie Hardesty, were immediately at the hospital and hardly left our side. The prayer call went out. We asked everyone we knew to pray.

Dale, one of the bikers with whom Mike had been sharing Jesus, called and asked if there was anything he could do. I told him we were asking everyone to please pray, would he please do that. Dale replied, "Sherri, you know I don't pray." I responded back, "I know, but that's what we're asking people to do."

The next day Dale called back to tell me, "I wanted you to know I prayed! Yesterday, after we talked, I went into my room and talked to God for the first time in a long, long time. I asked Him to spare Mike's life!" He was so proud of the fact that he had prayed for his friend. God used Dale's love for Mike to open their communication.

To fast forward a few years, we received another call from this man while we were at a campout. He wanted to tell Mike that he had prayed that prayer that Mike had asked him

151

to pray called "the sinner's prayer." He had asked Jesus to forgive him of his sins, and that he believed Jesus was God.

Dale too had a lot of health issues. Several years before he had been the victim of a bar shooting, even though the bullet was not intended for him. He had lost his leg because of it and had suffered greatly. But now, his heart was filled with hope and peace.

Finally, after Mike had been hospitalized for three days, I realized that I needed to talk to God. I was ready to hear whatever He said to me. So, in a very deliberate conversation, I went to my Heavenly Father and asked, "Where are we going in this crisis?" I knew then I would trust whatever He said. As I braced myself to hear the worst, the image of Moses standing at the Red Sea flashed through my mind. I heard the Lord say to me, "You are not the Children of Israel standing there with Moses, asking if they were brought there to die. You are *Moses*! So, raise your rod over the sea and see the deliverance of the Lord your God."

Oh, my gracious! I was Moses! I could have received this word three days ago! God says in Exodus 14:13-14, *"Do not be afraid. Stand firm and you will see the deliverance the LORD will bring you today. The Egyptians you see today you will never see again. The LORD will fight for you; you need only to be still."*

So, that is exactly what I did. Mike was already calm. So, I now joined him in peace.

In this story, in the context of what God was saying, we never would see "those Egyptians" again. We had a long, even difficult, road ahead of us, but Mike would not die at "this Red Sea." God was going to extend his life for another 11 years. God had much more for him to do.

We all watched the waters begin to part. Mike spent seven days in ICU, four days in progressive care and two days in what he called "who cares," as he was moved into a normal hospital room. We all laughed at that one! But, after much testing was done the double diagnosis came in.

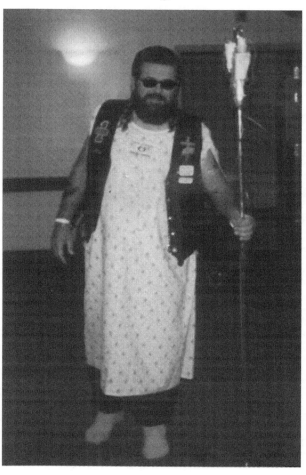

The first diagnosis was that Mike had Cirrhosis of the liver. It would be determined Mike's upper GI bleed was caused by a weakened esophagus. The weakened esophagus was because his liver was not allowing the blood and fluids to process through it at a normal pace. These fluids were "backing up" and putting extreme pressure on other veins and arteries in his system, of which the veins most affected were those leading to the esophagus. The pressure would create swollen veins in the esophagus; and as these veins grew they would eventually break open and bleed.

There was a procedure called Endoscopic Band Ligation, or "Banding," where they would put a scope with "fingers" attached to it down the esophagus and wrap a band around the bulge, kind of like tying off a balloon. Once those bulges were tied off, they would not break open and bleed. Mike had this procedure done several times over the next four years. We were told Mike's liver had less than 50% function and that would decrease as time went forward.

The second diagnosis came a couple of days later, and it would be more dire than the first. The cirrhosis was caused by a very aggressive blood born Hepatitis that mainly targets the liver. Mike had Hepatitis C, and he had the highest of all levels.

We had no reason to suspect Mike was sick. I had noticed fatigue, but not in our wildest dreams would we have thought it could be something life-threatening. I had never heard of Hepatitis C, and my understanding of Cirrhosis of the liver was that it's what happened to alcoholics.

154

Mike had not had a drink in many years. However, the damage he did do back then, along with the Hep C virus that had likely been contracted through some drug use before we married had either laid dormant, or had progressed slowly over the years. Never the less, it had finally taken its course.

His body had filled up with over 50 pounds of fluid, but with medication and rest, within a few weeks, he returned to his normal weight. His liquid intake was limited to 6 cups in a 24-hour period. For a coffee "addict" this was tough.

Before we left the hospital, God sent us another personal word through Acts 27:13 – 28:16, which tells of Paul's storm and the trip to Rome where they were shipwrecked. It says, *"...not one of you will be lost,"* and further down in that passage we read of how Paul's ship would again be *"in the wind."* I read those passages as God's insight to us that though Mike was in a storm, he would live. And that phrase of Paul's ship being in the wind I heard it as if it was a biker term... that our faces would again be "in the wind."

As the Red Sea remained parted for Moses and the Israelites until they reached the other side, it was as if the waters were held back for us to walk through our crisis, as well. Mike would recover to resume a sense of normalcy, with a few changes made due to his health limitations.

The ministry was put in my name as Mike's doctors put him on full disability. Social Security Disability accepted his case without question the first time. That alone was a miracle. Mike's acceptance onto MediCal was quickly approved. This insurance covered the astronomical cost of his hospital stay with just residue copay amounts.

When the day came that we got back on the bike, we remembered the word God gave us in that hospital room. It felt good as we rode and felt the wind in our face.

At Mike's first post-hospital follow-up, he saw Dr. Robert Gish, a world-renowned liver specialist who practiced out of *California Pacific Medical Center* (CPMC) in San Francisco. Dr. Gish held a clinic at San Joaquin General Hospital where we had taken Mike that first day, so Mike was automatically referred to him. He informed us that Mike only had a 50% chance of living past two years without a liver transplant. I remember after hearing the words liver transplant for the first time, I immediately went into full denial. It all felt surreal.

This doctor agreed to take Mike as a patient and sent him to San Francisco in January of 1997 to undergo tests to see if he was a good transplant candidate. Mike would be accepted into the liver transplant program and begin phase two of this life changing journey. This phase was all about waiting.

We had taken for granted that health would always be there. We would now come to understand the daily struggles and hindrances brought when it was lacking. I never knew when Mike's health would plummet and so I always had our suitcases packed and ready to head to the hospital in San Francisco on a moment's notice. First and foremost, we put our trust in God, yet we were extremely grateful for the team

156

of doctors, whom we believe God put on assignment for Mike's care.

God had encouraged us not to worry about our life in Luke 12:25, where we read, *"Who of you by worrying can add a single hour to his life? Since you cannot do this very little thing, why do you worry about the rest?"* To God, *adding one hour* to our life is a *"very little thing."* When we are facing a serious illness, to us, it is not a very little thing to realize there is the possibility we might not be breathing in an hour. We knew Mike was "on the clock," as far as his doctors were concerned. Time was ticking away.

At that moment, we stepped into a blue timeline that would stretch to just over four years. There are 8,765 hours in a year. We were in the first hours of what would be 35,063 "very little" miracles that God would perform in one-hour increments on behalf of Mike's life!

Story 21:
Beyond Our Own Perspective

Perspective can change everything. We can have a perspective based on fear, or one based on faith. Fear gives us negative viewpoints that smother our capability to see the value of adversity. A perspective of faith gives us viewpoints of hope that cover adversity with open-ended possibilities.

If our viewpoint is changed to that of our unlimited God, then what we see in front of us is the same as what He sees. "There could be dozens of people along the way the Lord has planned for us to minister to." That was Mike's perspective about his diagnosis of Cirrhosis of the Liver and Hepatitis C. If what the doctors were saying was the road he would walk, there would be many hospital and doctor visits that would become a part of life for us. Hospitals are full of people, whether they are doctors, nurses, support staff, patients or visitors, and people need the Lord. Our perspective would be: How can we share hope here? How can we share Jesus? Our attitude would be that God is good and His plan is greater than we know now.

God did have a purpose in play. First, He was going to encourage us in perseverance to go forward in the difficult months ahead. Then, He was going to display what a relationship with God looks like, and open ours up for others to see.

Those first few months after Mike's diagnosis were filled with thankfulness:

- We embraced the prayers at meal time with new understanding. "Bless this food to the nourishment of our body, and our bodies to your service" had never meant so much! I remembered having to spoon feed Mike just weeks before and asking God, with every bite, to strengthen his body.

- The *Good Samaritan Training Center* staff and volunteers recommitted their open door to us. We had already distributed over 6,500 meals to our bikers, and others we saw in need of food.

- *Feeding God's Children* ministry started bringing the men from their men's home to do our yard work, which depending on the season, could be an all-day job.

- Our church, *Zion Christian Fellowship*, supported us in love, prayers, and finances.

- One of the local biker clubs, the *Devil's Horsemen* out of Sacramento, made it a mandatory run for their club to ride out in honor of Mike and to visit for the evening.

- We attended one of the biker swap meets we normally attended. The man was there who, a couple of months before while in a crisis, had prayed to "the God of Mike & Sherri," and God had answered him! Pointing his finger at Mike, he said to a group of friends, "He's alive because I prayed for him!" Our hearts smiled as we realized how God had put a love for Mike in their hearts and, through Mike, God was showing them that He was someone they could talk to!

Mike's body may have been declared sick, but his spirit was alive and healthy! In January of 1997, while filling out an annual Support Update/Questionnaire sent us by the *First Baptist Church of Elk Grove*, God began to move in Mike's heart. One of the questions asked about our long-term goals and our vision for the future.

Mike knew his life had no guarantee, but in this time of great uncertainty, God was about to initiate his biggest dream ever! God lit in Mike's heart the beginning embers that would one day be an all-consuming fire. As a promise to live for, God gave him the dream *to establish a place, a facility, for "our bikers."*

Mike did not know how "long term" the goal was. God doesn't always share timeframes. Although Mike never knew that this dream went beyond his perspective of its purpose,

God, in His foreknowledge of His people's needs, planted this vision in Mike's heart so deep that he would receive it as a mandate from God, and see it through to the end, at all cost. God determined this dream would live because He heard in Mike's spirit a cry to build, not for his reasons to build as he had in his past, but for God's Kingdom purposes.

Mike began to pray for a place where bikers could come during the week after we had spent time with them at weekend events. He dreamed of a place where we could build friendships with them, and they would experience Christian love in action. Perhaps it could be a place for them to spend the night if traveling through. People could donate new or used motorcycle parts, and bikers could come in to do repairs. Most of all, Mike felt God's heart was for it to be a place where they could change the life road they were on by accepting Jesus into their hearts. Mike was all in. His dream began to make its way into almost every conversation Mike had with anyone.

Mike had been officially added to the Liver Transplant List in February 1997. The next three and one-half years would be quite an emotional roller coaster ride, and we would always be amazed and grateful to discover that Jesus was right there riding that roller coaster with us!

At the beginning of this period, Mike diligently began to pursue the dream God had placed in his heart. There were two pieces of property that we seriously looked at, and one even that accepted our offer, but as the bank financing fell through the door shut tight. By the end of 1998, we knew that

God was saying we should lay the vision down, for now. Mike would have to get well first.

Though we struggled, we were determined to stay in peace. Mike wanted to do so much, but physically could not. The doctors told us that Mike had technically "put in his time" on the transplant waiting list, but there was an extremely high number of patients on the list, and those who were critically ill kept being added in front of him. Obviously, this prolonged our wait. Mike was told that before a new liver would be made available to him, the current protocol required him to be in the hospital in a crisis state. We felt our emotions plummet, but we refused to trust in our perspective, but chose to trust God's timing.

During what would become *two more years of waiting*, 1999 through 2000, I was constantly doing a quick mental and physical "scan" of Mike's overall heath as I looked for signs to detect impending crises. High ammonia levels would send him into a condition called encephalopathy, which meant the liver was not doing it's hundreds of functions, and was unable to purify his blood. When the dirty blood passed through his brain this would cause a stupor like condition, sometimes getting so bad I called them "open-eyed comas."

Several times, when encephalopathy would descend like a dense fog, I would somehow manage to get Mike into my car and then drive him from our home in Lodi to San Francisco. Our local hospitals did not have the liver specialists nor did they know his history. Much time was saved, and precise care could be given much quicker if I could get Mike to San Francisco as soon as possible. I was thankful that I did not have rigid job hours, and I was free to be by his side throughout his hospital stays. Often the hospital would give me a hotel voucher, or someone would cover the cost. When that didn't happen, I slept in a chair next to his bed.

In those days, Mike still never wanted to miss a biker event. He wanted to be there when I wanted to protect him from people seeing him so very sick. But, he would not stay home even when he might be experiencing a mild form of the encephalopathy. At our events, I would see him staring off into space with this far off look on his face from the toxin buildup. Everyone else saw it, too. But, in the proper context, no one cared. Underneath it all, Mike was aware he was there. More importantly to him, his bikers knew he was there for them. They saw love come at great cost.

I would easily say that from the time of Mike's diagnosis at the end of 1996 through the end of 2000 we attended 200+ events, many not-so-near to us, including traveling to South Dakota for the Sturgis Rally every year. In the early months, Mike still rode the bike when he could. Later, I did the driving, and we traveled in the van. Eventually, we traveled in the small motorhome we purchased, towing the bike.

Mike's personality and trademark humor came through no matter how he was feeling. They so often made way for the gospel to be shared. One night, at Sturgis a man walked up to Mike fully dressed in black as the Grim Reaper. His face was veiled, and he had a sickle in his hand. He paced his deliberate walk up to Mike and in a deep slow voice announced, "Your time is up! I've come to take you with me!"

As only Mike's wit could readily respond, he answered, "My doctor also says my time is up. However, I'm expecting someone ELSE to pick me up!" We all laughed as the Grim Reaper's neck snapped back as his service was clearly refused, and he walked away with his head shaking back and forth! Oh, but realize he understood who the "someone else" was! A seed was planted.

At every doctor's visit, every hospital stay, every biker event and to anyone who would listen, Mike shared the love of Christ through his laugh, his stories, and his life. Mike knew how to make conversation relevant. He always found a way to make the turn in a conversation that would captivate his listeners. His most effective was when he shared the story of his former lifestyle as a 1% biker who became tired of sin.

We were determined we would throw caution, not to just any wind, but to the wind of the Spirit. We would go to an event if Mike possibly could. We would see our adversity develop Godly character in us and a deeper dependency on God. We would continue to live out our purpose from God's faith perspective.

Story 22:
A Perfect Day

A perfect day shares a similar quality as a perfect diamond. It's priceless. A perfect diamond may require it to be flawless, but that is not necessary for a perfect day. It just requires someone to wrap the imperfection in grace and set it outside of that day's story. The power of love will overrule the evidence as if it wasn't there at all. Then the day will always unfold in your memory as one without blemish.

That is what I did on the day Mike and me, and over 250 guests celebrated our 25th Wedding Anniversary. To have this main event missing in our life story would be like not experiencing the "Amen" at the end of a prayer.

Our original wedding day, as I shared earlier, was 1974. Mike was 24, I was 23, and we had eloped. We began our life together alone. So, to have a "white wedding" celebration with family and many guests present would magnificently display God's goodness and great faithfulness to us. It would certainly be a highlight in our lives, seen as written with His signature blue pen.

What a year 1999 was for my family! We celebrated my parent's 50th wedding anniversary in June, as their guests witnessed the renewing of their vows. In September my sister, Carole, having never been married before, had a beautiful white wedding as she married George Good, the love of her life. She was truly a Cinderella bride!

While shopping with my sister for her wedding dress a couple of months earlier, we were at one of the outlets in San Francisco. I saw a beautiful long dress. I couldn't have loved a dress more if I had been out searching to find the perfect one. It was a steal being on super clearance for only $19.95! I tried it on, and it fit perfectly, so I said yes to the dress! I had thought, "If we should end up having a big celebration I have my dress. If not, no big deal. It was only $20!

After my sister's wedding, everyone's thoughts turned to Mike and me renewing our vows for our 25th anniversary. I felt all of our family's energy had already been spent on two grand events, so, when the talk began, I downplayed the idea. But, everyone kept encouraging us to do it. It was our turn they said!

When my good friend, Jennie Hardesty, offered to be my wedding coordinator the plan was on! Though our anniversary date was November 16th, the best day for our celebration was Nov 6th. We had barely six weeks to get everything in place.

We sent an open invitation to family, friends and of course, our bikers! There was lots of preparation to do, including planning the music, ordering the flowers, deciding on the cake, choosing our toasting glasses, shopping for bridesmaid dresses and a dress for our flower girl, tuxedo fittings for the guys and ring bearers and a detailed list of the food needed for the reception. Somehow, we did it all and the excitement was high. Many of our friends donated a huge amount to cover the cost of these items, making our "wedding" as special as it could be.

Wayne Henderson, our CMA regional evangelist, was to be our emcee. However, he had to decline due to his health issues. Another friend, Kent Textor, was happy to be our next first choice.

The day of the wedding itself, I arrived at the church and looking at my sister, Carole, my daughter, Stephanie and my friend, Jennie, I said with excitement and tears, "I told the Lord I didn't need this day… that He didn't have to do this for me. I told Him I was perfectly fulfilled by the vision He had given me as He walked me down the aisle and gave me away by putting my hand in Mike's."

But, my sister responded, "Well, He wanted to give it to you anyway!"

I wanted to take most of our pictures before the ceremony. It was planned that I would make a special entrance to Shania Twain's song, "You're Still the One." I would be in my dress and veil, holding my flowers as I walked down the aisle to meet Mike, who would be standing in front at the end of the aisle.

I can still hear that song playing, and I can still see the look of love's awe in his eyes as he saw me walking toward him. Our eyes never dropped until we closed them in a beautiful kiss. It was one of the most special moments of the day.

Since our trip to Sturgis that August, Mike's health had continued to downgrade, and I could see that he was struggling, but I was thankful his heart was present. I mentally and emotionally took Mike's liver disease symptoms and the toll the illness in his body had taken and wrapped them in delicate tissues of grace. In my heart, I set them outside of our story for the day. Today he would be just my beloved Mike, the man I planned to marry all over again.

As we were finishing up with pictures, to our surprise, Mike's dad, Ralph, and his stepmom, Virla, came walking in! They had told us that they would not be able to make the trip from Arizona because of Ralph's poor health, but there they were. We felt so blessed to have all three sets of parents with us on that special day.

It was time for the ceremony to begin, our guests were all seated, and the special music began. I stood there soaking in all I had missed out on 25 years ago. I was having a church wedding with bridesmaids and groomsmen! Beyond seeing my family and so many friends were there, it meant everything to me to have the blessings of my parents on the renewing of our vows.

My daughter, Stephanie, who was my *maid of honor* and my sister, Carole, my *matron of honor*, walked down the

171

aisle ahead of me. The *flower girl*, Shandee, and our two young *ring bearers*, Mason and Christian played their roles perfectly. I could see Mike, so handsome in his black tux, waiting for me at the end of the aisle with his best friend, Rich Hardesty standing up for him, and our son, Mike, as his *best man*.

I was fully present the moment the double doors opened. Denise finished singing, and everyone immediately stood to honor the bride. *It was me!* I felt the vibrating of the organ underneath my feet as the traditional wedding march began to be played. I took my dad's arm, and the dream became a reality. I was being walked down the aisle on the arm of my dad. I remember trying to look into the eyes of as many guests as possible and smile as to say, "This is my day! This is the day the Lord has made especially for Mike and for me!"

As we got to the end of the aisle, Pastor Dick and Edie, who were performing the ceremony, began to thank God for all He had done in our lives over the years. They made a comparison of how things were quite different now than they had been for us 25 years ago.

My dad, hearing these words, began to weep as he was pulled back in memory and emotions to the night Mike and I came to announce our engagement. Everyone thought my sweet daddy was weeping tears of joy at all God had done. But, I instinctively knew he was remembering how I broke his father-heart that night so long ago. I remembered that night, too. I remembered how after we had announced our plans to marry, my dad had me meet him at the church, and how he begged in deep sobs for me not to marry.

As Pastor Dick continued to share of God's faithfulness, giving glory to God for calling us into full-time ministry, and for the effect our lives had on others, my dad sobbed harder, now his whole body shaking.

I leaned over and said into his ear in a weeping whisper, "I remember that night, too, Daddy! I'm so sorry for how we did things, but look at what God has done!" It was a surreal moment for us both. It was a moment where God brought us full circle from sobs of sorrow to weeping for joy! God used a perfect opportunity to unearth an old wound that had been buried and needed healing. With my arm still in his, God took the pain of that memory from the heart of both father and daughter, wrapped it in His grace found in forgiveness and carried it far, far away.

Pastor Dick then asked, "And who gives this woman to be united again to this man." My dad, with joy in his voice, answered, "Her mother and I!' Daddy put my hand in Mike's, and we continued with a beautiful ceremony.

After communion, we were re-pronounced "husband and wife," and Mike kissed his bride! As the music began, Mike and I walked back down the aisle, with my arm in his. We greeted each guest in the receiving line and enjoyed hugs and lots of laughter.

After lunch was served and the cake was cut, the microphone was opened for tributes. Oh, my gracious. We heard testimony after testimony of how we had impacted their lives and many shared words of their love for us. The time of tributes culminated with a standing ovation. We were humbled and honored.

I didn't want the day to end. I purposefully lingered inside talking and taking a few more pictures so not to end this extraordinary day.

As we finally exited the building, I was shocked to find most of our loving family and friends still waiting there. They all shouted out to us with happy voices of congratulations while simultaneously giving us a loud applause! Everyone had waited, wanting to see us get on the Harley! It was parked just down the steps with a sign taped to the front windshield and the back boot that read, "Just Married—Again!"

Yes, Mike in his tux and me in my wedding dress rode the Harley off for our "honeymoon." The helmet went on my perfect hair, and off we rode with pipes roaring, leaving behind waves of goodbye and shouts of "We love you!" Pictures that captured this perfect departure still bring a smile to my heart!

We road home where we traded the bike for our car and drove up to spend the night in a beautiful hotel in Old Sacramento. As I lay in bed in the arms of my love, I realized that every moment of the day had fulfilled my little girl's fantasy of a "wedding dream come true." It didn't matter now that it was a mere 25 years later.

There had been one thing missing in Virginia City the day we eloped so long ago without my family or his. But, today it had appeared. In fact, interwoven through every moment of the entire day was the "holy" in matrimony. Our holy Father in heaven was our invited guest of honor! He not only came but was the One who had been at work in our hearts for years to make this a perfect day!

Story 23:
Clouds or Ceiling

Decisions can be difficult to make. Especially the decision to give "the gift of life" to a stranger by donating the organ(s) or tissue of one's loved one. It requires great emotional strength.

If the decision was not previously thought through, discussed and documented by the would-be donor together with their family, so that there was no doubt lingering of their wishes, it becomes much more difficult. It is a generous and noble act. Most understand if one can't give the gift. But the thousands who do each year, earn our deep gratitude!

At the beginning of the year 2000, we lived every day in the hope of Mike's liver transplant. I remember us struggling with the thought that someone would have to die so Mike could live. We realized that the number of days God gives a person will be complete, and then one of two things will occur.

He or she will have thought it through and decided with their family, or with an organ donation center, to will their organs to another who needed them. Or, when they died, their family would look past their sorrow, and honor the life of their deceased loved one, by donating their organs as a gift of life to another.

We were thankful not to know that we would still have to wait until the end of that year to receive Mike's transplant. As we looked ahead to the year's ride season, Mike did not consider himself on sick leave. But, we both needed much prayer for strength and support. Mike needed it as the one who was sick; I needed it as the caregiver.

I am so thankful for those times when God puts a burden of prayer on someone's heart to pray for another. These calls come from God's Spirit with an intention that this one will pray through the burden until it lifts and peace is felt.

My mom, Dorothy Smith, was a woman who prayed these kinds of deep prayers for many years. She would give countless nights into the wee hours of the morning "praying through" for someone God put on her heart. The location is unimportant in prayer. Oceans are crossed, and unknown souls are brought to peace by the prayers of an intercessor. Prayer has diverted untold tragedies and canceled many crises. I would come to find out that my mom gave of herself, on our behalf, on one of those nights. It brought me to tears.

At that time, she was 83-years-old and suffered a chronic, increasingly painful condition. God had mostly lifted her late-night prayer assignments because of her age and poor health. My dad was to be at the hospital at 6:00 AM the next morning for an angioplasty, so they were planning to be up at 4:30 AM. That night, of all nights, the call came.

It was midnight, and the burden was heavy. One o'clock – Two o'clock – Three o'clock passed. She labored in prayer so hard she thought she might die from the weight of

178

this and would have if that's what it took. She knew she *would* pay in extreme pain and fatigue the next day, yet she pressed into the call to pray. Finally, at four o'clock, the victory came—the breakthrough when she knew in her spirit that Satan's plans had been defeated in *this* situation and God would have His way!

When we learned of her sacrificial gift, we were humbled and awed at the ways of God, that He would break our heart to honor us with this intercession prayed with great personal cost. I believe now that God was using her prayer to rewrite overpowering illness with strength to persevere.

As Mike and I made it through the year to the month of June, God continued to surprise us with blessings. It felt like Christmas in June! Some friends took our Harley in for a minor tuneup, and to replace a few worn parts. But in reality, the bike was actually getting a complete makeover! All the pin stripping was removed, and it was repainted totally black. The chrome was all powder coated. The carburetor and ignition were upgraded and could it go!

Now the "new" black bike fit Mike's title of "Midnight Mover for Jesus" that our good friend, Robert Carrillo, had given him the year before while we were all at Sturgis. The following year Robert had a patch made for Mike's motorcycle vest with that title because of his late-night encounters at Sturgis, and other biker events.

We were tentatively making plans for the Sturgis Rally in August. It would be the 60th Anniversary Rally, and there was expected to be 700,000 bikers there. Our Sturgis fund only had $140.00 in it, but, regardless, we believed God would make a way. He had done it every other time.

We had been asked to speak at our *Northern Christian Motorcyclists Association* (CMA) Rally by our new Regional Evangelists, Joe and Judy Maxwell. We accepted. God graciously spoke through us, and His presence and anointing were there. At the end of Mike's message someone yelled out, "Can we take an offering for their Sturgis trip?!" When all was said and done, we were given $1,640.00, which was enough to pay our gas in the motorhome and all other expenses. What favor God gave us through our friends!

God's protection, power, and purpose were felt every day and in every encounter on this trip, even as we limped our motorhome to the home of our friend John in Elko, Nevada. We had a major fuel problem. Rich and Jennie felt God's assignment to travel with us and thankfully so. Rich managed to get the problem diagnosed and, after a huge repair project, got us back on the road in a couple of days.

Once we arrived in Sturgis, we were thankful Mike was able to ride the bike back and forth from Main Street to the *Calvary Baptist Church* where several of us were allowed to make camp. The church provided us with electricity so we could run the air conditioning to keep Mike cool during the day. We worked the hospitality kitchen in the church basement. It was being run by our friends from Sacramento, Robert and Beverly Carrillo of *Feeding God's Children Ministry*.

We visited a dear Sturgis friend, who had been unable to attend church since December, and served her communion.

We worked the CMA booth in the evenings, handing out tracts and Bibles. We passed out 40 Ladies Travel Bags (with toiletries, tracts, and prayers tucked inside) made by the *Pricilla Circle Women's Ministry* of Elk Grove First Baptist Church.

We handed out many Death/Life business-sized ministry cards and also handed out coins donated by our friends, Bill and Barb Engvall. Both the cards and the coins had John 3:16-17 printed on them:

> *"For God so loved the world that He gave His one and only Son, that whoever believes in Him shall not perish but have eternal life. For God did not send His Son into the world to condemn the world, but to save the world through him."* (NIV)

Coins were popular and well received by the bikers as "good luck." We would tell them, "This coin will keep you safe clear into eternity—if you read the inscription and do what it says!"

I handed out more than 20 Women's Gift Bags with a CMA Hope Bibles, tracts, poems that I had personally written, and our testimonies on cassette. We added to the top of these bags fun hair accessories and perfume to act as "bait" so that these gifts would be accepted.

The gift bags were the response to an experience I had during our first trip to Sturgis back in 1993. We were at a gas station, just hanging out. I saw a group of bikes pull in to get gas and a man got off his bike that had a woman sitting on the very tiny back seat. There was a dog collar buckled around her neck. He had a leash he attached to it and, as he was putting gas in his tank, he led her off the bike. In front of us and others standing there, he purposefully degraded her.

Seeing the look of shame in her eyes, I determined then and there that I must bring something with me the next year to offer hope to women like her. I knew it must be something that the men would allow their "ladies" to have. I saw myself handing women a gift, where hair ties and jewelry could camouflage the true purpose of sharing hope with them through the gospel of Christ's love.

For the next ten years, on our trips to Sturgis, I brought 20-25 of these gift bags with me. I would wait for my heart to hear, "Give the gift bag to this one." These gift bags, with items hand-selected, beautifully packaged, and prayed over, would be treasures in their darkness.

Every evening after sitting on the bike on Main Street until midnight, where the mural on the back boot opened numerous witness opportunities, we rode over to where I first saw that woman. That Amoco Gas Station became our hang out from midnight until 2:00-3:00 AM; and many midnight encounters happened there. We became the answer to many mothers' prayers whose sons and daughters were far away from God.

Our trip was a success! Mike had given of himself above and beyond what anyone thought possible, but we all saw the physical toll it took on him. Was it worth it? He said, "Yes!"

Once back home, we received a letter from an out of state friend, whom we had known since he was a younger teenager. We were shocked and deeply humbled as he offered to be a living organ donor to Mike. He was offering him a part of his liver. From his heart, he shared he had prayed about it, counted the cost and was willing to do whatever it took.

But, as we prayed about it, we could not find the peace to proceed officially. Mike was not willing to jeopardize Jeff Shreve's life, even if it meant he would lose his. Both men had the heart of Christ, each willing to lay down his life for the other. There will never be enough words to say thank you for this offer, but I believe this is one of the times that, though it did not happen, God will count Jeff's reward in heaven as if it had.

On November 12th Mike downgraded quickly into a high toxic coma. Thankfully, I managed, as before, to get him into my car and drive him to San Francisco. This time the doctors said they were going to keep him hospitalized. We prayed he would get a liver in time.

We spent almost six weeks there, but, as you would know, God redeemed our time. Living at a hospital allows you to get to know the doctors, nurses, and staff on a much more personal level. Your "neighbors" in the other rooms become your new friends.

I was asked to pray for a woman's dying sister who also had liver disease. As I prayed, I made sure to include the opportunity for her to ask Jesus into her heart. We wouldn't know until we reach heaven if her spirit was responding when her body could not.

We were thankful that I was allowed to sleep on a cot in Mike's hospital room. The weeks passed by. We spent Thanksgiving there and believe me, we were thankful. Then, one normal hospital morning the Physician's Assistant came in with a smile on her face. They had a donor for Mike, and the transplant would take place the following morning, December 14th. That gave plenty of time for the family to come to the hospital for the surgery and our long-awaited miracle!

We were all very excited, yet our hearts could not forget there was another family whose hearts were broken. A young, 14-year-old girl had been in a car accident. Her family's willingness to give the Gift of Life to a stranger in the middle of their great tragedy was the highest form of love I could think of. I am forever grateful and will forever remember this young girl, who lost her life while adding seven amazing years to Mike's.

I looked at Mike and kissed him as he was about to be wheeled down the hall on the hospital gurney. It was a very emotional moment, yet Mike said for us all not to worry. He said confidently that all was in God's hands, and that one way or the other he was going to wake up. He said, "I will wake up seeing clouds, or wake up seeing the ceiling!" His natural humor proved his peace.

The surgery had been more involved than expected, but after an 8-hour vigil with updates along the way, we received word that he was in recovery! I struggled with my emotions as they flashed back and forth between happy tears for us, and tears of sorrow for the other family "out there." I knew I was going to have to either release this family into God's care and comfort, or let their time of sorrow overtake our time of joy.

The desire of this family was to give what they wish could be given to them. There is a season for all things. This, their season of grief, was our season of life. With respect and honor for them, I chose to release my stress that had been building for years and to receive their gift with joy without measure!

The family's gift, passed on to Mike, was first given to them by God at the birth of their lovely daughter. Now, through the doctors' God-given knowledge of how to transplant organs, they had passed on God's gift of life to another. I want to end this story with a soul-searching request. Will you consider and pray about becoming an organ donor?

Giving your heart to Jesus in this life is the *utmost important decision* you can ever make because it affects where you spend eternity. Becoming an organ donor will not only give another person a second chance at life, but may give them an opportunity to make that *most* important of all decisions!

Story 24:
The Other Side of the Miracle

Living in what has been promised to you is what I came to call "the other side of the miracle." Making it through all the crises, when the odds are totally against you, cannot be chalked up to happenstance, but must be credited to God's deliberate intervention! It is a sweet place that has been dreamed of and hoped for; where we live today in what was promised yesterday.

The other side of the miracle began for us while Mike was in recovery from his eight-hour liver transplant surgery. From September 1996, his first hospital stay that revealed his cirrhosis of the liver caused by Hepatitis C, to this moment, our journey had taken four years, two months and 15 days. It was December 14, 2000, and we had arrived!

We were beyond thrilled. I tried to express it by saying I knew what it felt like to *fly*! Even though Mike was still hooked up to life support, it was as if I "took mount" that late afternoon, soaring into the heavens as our eyes met in the recovery/ICU room immediately after the surgery. It was a shared moment in time between us and, at the same time, us with our God. We realized He had led us into our Promised Land, the land of fulfillment. "It's happened! We are here! God's promise has come! We are on the other side together!"

We could not remember a time so solemn, yet so joyful! We felt His glory. We relished those first hours and days immediately following Mike's surgery thanking God for His faithfulness in getting us here.

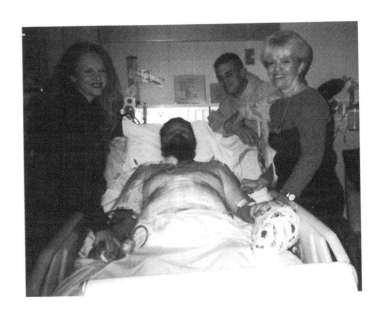

We permitted ourselves to enjoy life, pushing back the thoughts of life with the need for immunosuppressant medication and the reality of the Hepatitis C virus that was still active in Mike's bloodstream. We knew this side would present its challenges and perhaps even changes, but we knew, too, whom we would continue to trust. He would be the one constant, the One who never changes. We would stay in Jesus, enjoy the now and walk forward into this new season He had given to us.

As Mike's health continued to improve day by day, he gained back lost ground. The first time his blood test showed liver function in the normal range, we felt like having a party.

We stayed in a hospital-owned apartment complex across the street from *California Pacific Medical Center* until Mike was officially released on January 18, 2001. The cost of that stay was paid for in full by friends of our ministry.

Several months before, God initiated a phone call to us from a friend in CMA. In our conversation, he pressed me to know details of our financial needs. I told him that very morning there had been a voicemail left us from the hospital. They wanted a confirmation from us that during Mike's recovery phase after transplantation, we had the money in place to be able to stay for 4-6 weeks within a short driving distance from the hospital. The voicemail said they would call back the following day.

Then John Finan said, "When they call back, tell them you have the money. Mary Ann and I will put a check in the mail first thing tomorrow morning." Again, God's provision came totally out of His Blue.

Our stay there went smoothly, and it wasn't until we were back at home that a complication appeared. The top of the incision looked like it was healing, but underneath bacteria had gotten in and an infection was brewing. Mike had to go back under anesthesia, have the wound re-opened and cleaned. The first time the incision area needed to be repacked I was shown how to do it. I was a little apprehensive as they handed me the gauze and 12-inch Q-tip instructing me how to pack the wound opening.

My "nurses" training over the past four years kicked in, and I did it like a pro. The gauze was meant to keep the area dry which promoted healing. At first, I needed to use an entire roll of gauze three to four times a day, but eventually, it became once a day, using only a small 1-inch piece folded in half and put on with a band aid.

Watching this deep incision heal little by little, slowly from the inside out, has become a powerful illustration of how many of our life wounds heal. Left unaddressed bacteria, the effects of sin, multiply and can affect our whole life. Addressing our inner wounds, and then packing and repacking them with God's love and His specific word to our need, allows us to heal little by little and from the inside out. The scar remains, but there's no more pain.

In March and April of 2001, with the liver transplant now behind us and with Mike's health status continuing to do so well, we began to ask the Lord, "What now? Where are we and this ministry headed?" We needed to know if His plans still include Mike's "dream" of having a biker style club house?

As Mike prayed about this, he felt a strong confirmation to move forward. But, I was not quite so ready to jump into such a huge project. I wanted Mike to take some time to recover fully. Feeling wonderful, after so many years of illness, he was chomping at the bit to work hard in God's Kingdom. I was feeling exhausted from all the responsibility involved in four years as ministry overseer and caregiver. Rest sounded good to me. I wanted quiet normal ministry stuff. Couldn't we just enjoy the place we were at for a while longer?

The clubhouse was all Mike could talk about, and he started looking for property or a building every spare moment he had. He would call me and say, "Honey, I found this building, come see what you think," or "I found this piece of property, come look. It would be perfect!" Truthfully, I didn't want to look. I didn't want to do this at all. Not yet. Not now. All the memories of our life in business were stirred up. All the detail involved, from the first permit to the final responsibilities, went rushing through my mind. It all seemed overwhelming to me.

Mike's heart was set. He was excited. I knew I needed to face this and have a meeting with God. I had to hear "yes" or "no" directly from Him, and I had to hear it out of His Word. Otherwise, I could not see how I could get behind another building project.

Very early the next morning I went into our home ministry office, and sat down at my desk, desperately wanting, to be honest with God. I poured my heart out to Him, expressing all my concerns and list of reasons I did not want to go down this road. But then, of course, I prefaced it all with, "But, it's not what I think. It's what You want. If this is Your plan, You know I will do it, so I'm asking You to please show me. I must have a confirmation from You."

Immediately, in my spirit and almost audible, I heard "JOSHUA 1." It caught me by surprise. I took my Bible and opened it to that passage. My eyes immediately fell on chapter 1 and the last part of verse 14 (NIV), *"The LORD your God is giving you rest and has granted you this land."* My eyes about popped out of my head!

I went back up to the beginning of Joshua Chapter 1 and read it all. *"...The LORD said to Joshua...Moses, my servant, is dead." (v 2) "I will give you every place where you set your foot, as I promised Moses." (v 3). "Be strong and courageous because you will lead these people to inherit the land..." (v6) "Be strong and courageous. Do not be terrified; do not be discouraged, for the LORD your God will be with you wherever you go."*

Oh, my gracious. There it was in God's Word, printed in black and white. God was going to give us land! And what, also, stood out was that God had just changed our "character" or the "role" we had been in the Bible. We had first been as the children of Israel being set free from years of bondage, then in this last season we were Moses watching God part our Red Sea, and now we were Joshua, who led the people to inherit their *land*!

Here was another example of God showing me where I was in His Word! This always gives such understanding and direction to my everyday life. I continue to depend on this type of revelation and feel lost if I do not know "where I am," or "who I am."

Just that fast, my attitude changed. This was God's plan, not just my husband's dream. I couldn't wait for Mike to wake up so I could tell him, "I don't know how God is going to do it, but He is going to give us land!" Later, God confirmed to me again that Mike was anointed to build, and I did not need to worry or be concerned. God would be in control of this and would oversee both Mike and the needs of the building. He would anoint Mike to oversee the work.

Mike was more excited than I was, yet this Word changed his behavior. He said, "What the receiving of this word has done is relieve me from the pressure to be on a constant search to find land or a building suited for the clubhouse. Now, instead, I can check out leads, yet be at rest and wait on God for His direction and provision for the right place."

The old was gone, the new had come. Death no longer was crouching at our door, and life was full of expectancy waiting to give birth to a new dream. Our role as Joshua held many adventures ahead for us. Joshua had not only been Moses' aide but was the one who had brought back a good report to Moses declaring the Israelites could *take the land*. We would be a Joshua to the best of our ability.

Though at the time, life was good, the next six years would require perseverance with a different focus and faith, not only for property but once again for life itself. We would desperately need for God to add His blue pen into our stories on this side of miracle and on the land where we would be living.

Story 25:
The Promise Comes to You

Promises are words that fill us with hope. When someone breaks their promise to us, we feel let down and disappointed. When God gives a promise, it is unbreakable. That is why when we have a promise from God on a personal level, we feel assured of a definite outcome. God tells us in 2 Corinthians 1:20 (NIV): *"For no matter how many promises God has made, they are 'Yes' in Christ. And so through him, the 'Amen' is spoken by us to the glory of God."* We find great comfort holding to His words when our days are hard and difficult, and circumstances are not encouraging, but we hold to our promise, we believe, and we wait for the fulfillment.

A promise of God never changes, but sometimes it does require us to relinquish our interpretation of the promise and to be content in the truth that God always knows the beginning from the end. We are quick to process what our spirit hears through the lens of our "here and now." If the promise is not fulfilled exactly how we perceived it would be, we could lose confidence in the Giver.

Therefore, we must guard our heart against deeming our finite minds fully capable of understanding an infinite God. When our promise plays out differently than we imagined it, we should be encouraged when we realize that any confusion is *because of us*, not in anything God has or hasn't done. There are actions yet to come into play and events only He knows about that can change the landscape of what was known to us at the beginning. If we will stay attached to Him, and not leave the conversation or the relationship, we will find that He always fulfills His promise in a perfect way.

One morning as I was just waking up, and with my eyes still closed, I heard the words, "The promise comes to you." Then came the continuing thought of, "We don't go to the promise; the promise comes to us." God *sends* His promise to us. This was true in how Jesus, sent by the Father, came to us. We could in no way go to him so, at the appointed time, He left heaven and came here! There are, of course, things that we must participate in as we wait for the promise, but the timing and arrival of the promise are God's to give and his to send.

Just as God had promised us on April 4, 2001, he gave us land. When Mike told one realtor how much he would offer for the land, the realtor laughed out loud. But, now, here it was, and right on a busy thoroughfare for bikers.

This property was a long narrow piece of land owned by the railroad in the small town of Victor, three miles east of Lodi on Hwy 12 East. Mike knew it would work perfectly for what he saw in his heart that he was to build. We closed escrow on December 12, 2001, with its appraised value at more than six times the price we paid for it! ($30,000)

Mike gave the property its name. It would be called *His Place*. We all thought it fit perfectly.

Before we bought it, the property was being used by an adjoining business. They had no rights to the property, but their pallets and other equipment spilled over onto quite a bit of the area. Before we closed escrow, this business offered us $30,000 if we would walk away from the sale. They would have deposited cash into our account, and then they would have bought the property for another $30,000. It would have been "free money" to us. Mike knew we could not find property the size of ours on a highway again for that price. We had to consider it, and Mike joked we could buy a brand-new Harley, but we knew this was the land God had given to us. It was not for sale.

When we purchased the land, we agreed that they could continue to use the area and pay us rent. This rent money paid our property loan payment. With this added financial responsibility covered, it would enable us to stay in the home we were renting as we began the mounds of paperwork and building prep it would take to begin actual construction.

We were just in the beginning months of what became an almost 5 ½ year project. We would continue to attend biker events and some campouts throughout this entire time. With a bit of sadness, we both sensed in 2002 that our phenomenal ten years Sturgis Season had come to an end. We attended that last rally with bittersweet emotions as we turned our hearts to our new focus and to what would become Mike's last season.

We knew that a project this big was not going to be an easy task. We took things as they came and tried not to be surprised at the struggle, and sometimes blatant opposition, we faced from the beginning. We had built homes before, but this project, because it was commercial, had additional requirements. We launched our search right away for a construction loan but found that banks were not so willing to give a ministry a construction loan for the commercial property. It would take us about a year to find one.

We simultaneously began to make our way through all the red tape for our planning application to be approved. As we did, we were told that we had some zoning issues and would eventually need to apply for rezoning to accomplish our full dream. We would proceed and cross that bridge when we came to it. We were very grateful for two men who offered to donate their time and ability to provide us with our engineered plans, but they had full schedules. Doing our plans on the side meant we had to wait months to get them completed. In that first couple of years, we grew in patience due to not having control over the time factor of banks and agencies.

Our greatest challenge came in 2003 as Mike's latest follow-up doctor appointment revealed he was back at stage 3 fibrosis in his new liver. I was beginning to see some familiar signs of health issues but was not prepared for that diagnosis. We fought off discouragement and remembered that phrase God had spoken: the promise comes to you. Mike was more determined than ever and even felt God added to the intent and purpose of His Place, as he had a dream one-night seeing food distribution as a part of God's plan. We began to call our facility *His Place Food Distribution and Care Center.*

God gave us another one of His miracle coincidences as we met personally with a group of men who we had no idea owned the bank that had just turned us down for a construction loan. Friends, Gary and Irene White, had set up this appointment for us and they were all, also, unaware of the connection until we put the pieces together during this meeting. After hearing Mike's testimony and his vision for His Place they made an executive decision that only the owners could make. They went over their loan officer's head and said, "Give them the loan!" We signed papers on October 15, 2003, and the money was deposited into our account on October 22nd, a GodThing!

We held our Ground-Breaking Ceremony on October 25, 2003, under a commercial canopy set up on the property.

We had a great turnout of bikers, family, and friends. Excitement ran high. Don and Vaughnda Griffen, Rich and Jennie Hardesty and others helped us get everything ready. With gold painted shovels we turned over the dirt symbolically stating, "Let the work begin!"

Soon after our ceremony, a lady in Victor filed a protest against us, requiring a hearing with the building department. She feared His Place would bring an unwanted element into their little town.

In the months ahead, I prayed daily for her, as I looked out my kitchen window at her house across the street. The day would come when she would walk across that street to invite Mike and me to their home for a Super Bowl party. We accepted her invitation and brought cookies to share. Regardless to say, her protest had been denied, and now she had seen proof that our building *added* a positive element to the community.

In June of 2004, with the challenges of the past three years behind us, we finally had the stamped and approved plans in hand, but during this time Mike progressed to "extensive bridging fibrosis indicating early cirrhosis." It was devastating news. At first, it felt like we were right back in the same place we were before his transplant. Then I realized we were not in the same place at all.

Our faith had grown and our lives with it. We were in a different place spiritually and on our life journey. We didn't know, without a miracle, exactly where the progression would lead us, but we believed in miracles. What was "the responsible" thing for us to do? Was Mike going to have the strength to handle this huge project? Should we purchase the building permit at the cost of hundreds of dollars knowing, if we did, there was no turning back? I wrestled hard with these questions.

God sent His Word to me twice to answer them. The first Word came through the Old Testament story where Abraham was instructed by God to go to Mt. Moriah and sacrifice his son Isaac on a pile of wood. God was not only foreshadowing the death of His Son on a wooden cross in this story, but was also testing Abraham's faith. Abraham was willing to trust that God would somehow raise his son from the dead, but, instead, God provided a ram whose horns were caught in the thicket. That ram became the sacrifice instead of Isaac.

As I pondered this Old Testament story, I desperately searched for where the relief would come in Mike's resuming health crises. It seemed that in the past year, we had walked the long, slow journey to Mt. Moriah. As Abraham felt the death sentence for his son, I remember feeling the death sentence for Mike. God had provided a ram for Abraham. I wanted to know where "our ram" was *this time* on Mike's behalf. Stopping by to receive a second signature on a check, I wanted to grab Pastor Dick's shirt at the front of the collar and desperately ask, "Where's the ram?"

In sharing this with Pastor Dick, he calmed my frantic heart with a simple and profound answer. He looked me straight in the eyes and with a calmness that transferred into me said, "Sherri, the Ram is seated on His Throne at the right hand of God." It was a simple, yet profound truth that went directly into my spirit. God was in control, and He would continue to bring the promise.

The second word of the Lord came through a new friend, JonJulienne Peters, who I met at a *Christian Motorcyclists Association* women's small group. I had just given a short message to their local chapter's wives and single women and had mentioned Mike's recurring illness. JonJulienne walked up to me and simply said she had something she needed to share with me. My spirit leaped, and I immediately discerned that she had something significant to tell me from the Lord. I was initially stunned as she began to talk to me about a health product called *Reliv*.

Normally I would have been polite and listened with no intention of purchase. However, because my spirit had responded to her invitation to present this nutritional product to me, I knew I was to pay attention, and that this was God's direction.

Within a few weeks of Mike taking the *Reliv* products, I witnessed his strength and stamina dramatically increased. He was strong enough to go out and work for 6 – 8 hours at a time on the dirt-mover tractors, as real work began on God's place! I believe the *Reliv* product helped to counter the effects of the Interferon treatment he had been put on by his doctors to try to stop the fast progression of the liver failure. It wasn't a cure, but I know this product improved the quality of Mike's life.

With peace and this new product, a double confirmation, on July 14, 2004, we purchased the building permit for His Place! Everything in us knew that choosing not to purchase it would kill all possibilities for God to prove

Himself mighty in this situation. We could not and would not stop what God had started. If God stopped it, that was His to do. We would go forward.

The actual building phase officially began on July 31, 2004. We were excited to finally begin! Walking forward into this unchartered territory every day was a step of faith. When Mike's next liver biopsy showed another downgrade, I prayed for the heaviness to leave and pushed back fear. I had always felt safe in God's promise, but, now, somehow things just didn't feel quite so safe anymore.

I knew all of this had been building an even deeper relationship between God and us. We were fully dependent on Him as our trials provided grounds for the testing of our faith regarding our future. We were passing our test, not perfectly, but passing. Our obedience in perseverance was its own reward, and our sacrifices for His Place were given without regret. We saw it was all for the cause; His Place in the small picture, God's Kingdom in the large. But, I began to realize there was one more question, for which I was not sure I was prepared.

I felt God knew we had given Him a pledge of our love, and were committed to being disciples, planning to serve Him together for our entire lives. But, now He was taking it a step further. It was as if I could see the test question printed out and it was not a multiple-choice question. It was a simple "true" or "false," "yes" or "no."

"Do you realize that I want you to entrust not only your life in service to Me, but literally your breath, as well?"

What? Seriously? This entrustment seemed to hold the possibility of risk, and I knew not to answer lightly. I chose to put Mike's life, my life, and even our children's lives on the altar that night. Life here may be unsure, but life in heaven will be everlastingly secure.

By the end of October, Mike took our motorhome to the property to sleep there because of all the material on the site. The foundation for His Place was poured November 6, 2004. The steel structure went up with the help of Jim Lyons and many others. We officially moved out of our house on Locust Tree Road and onto the His Place grounds in February of 2005. Though it was hard to leave what had been our home for ten years, once done we never looked back. This was a forward movement for the Kingdom of God.

We would stay temporarily in our motorhome until the double-wide mobile home, sold at cost to the ministry by Sam and Karen Knapp, could be delivered. I watched it arrive in two pieces and was excited to peek through the windows and imagine our life being lived there. The septic system was a huge endeavor during our construction. It was an awesome day when it passed inspection, and we could remove the portable outhouse!

The final on the mobile home was received in June of 2006, and its 1,500 square feet never looked so spacious. With discounts, we could do some upgrades in the carpet and install hardwood floors in the kitchen. Our friend, Johnny Benson donated all the inside paint to give it a custom look. In fact, he not only did the painting, but handed us $400 cash to help provide whatever else we needed.

As our daughter was in a serious relationship with Larry Haley, Mike built a wheelchair ramp to give Larry full access to the house. He also built a hall closet with shelves and put in ceiling fans in every room. I would sit on my couch and look across my living room to my white kitchen table and chairs sitting on a large zebra print rug and inhale pure joy! It was a lovely home, and I had decorated it with grape décor, a spiritual theme of "much fruit!"

The 4,000 square feet of warehouse still had much work to be done. Little by little, one baby step after the other, we moved forward. Day after day I watched Mike commit to "the promise." There is a memory etched in my mind. I had come out to ask Mike a question and remember being struck by how tired he looked. He walked toward me having just bumped his arm against something. It had torn the skin open, but he was giving it no priority. He wiped the blood on his pant leg so he could answer my question and get back to what he was doing. God's word says, *Greater love has no man than this: to lay down one's life for one's friends."* (John 15:13 NIV) Mike gave every bit of his strength to this call that dominated his every waking moment. He was compelled to keep working when he felt weak and to keep looking up when there were long delays. He kept motivating others to help and kept believing when we ran over budget.

One day our friend, Dan Randel, while driving to work felt compelled by God to turn around and drive straight to His Place to share a verse of Scripture with Mike. He knocked on our door, came in and sat down, opened his Bible to Philippians 1:6 NIV and began to read:

"I thank my God every time I remember you. In all my prayers for all of you, I always pray with joy because of your partnership in the gospel from the first day until now, being confident of this, that <u>he who began a good work in you will carry it on to completion until the day of Christ Jesus.</u>"

When he finished reading, he prayed a short, powerful prayer and said, "I've got to get to work!" And he left. But, the life of that Scripture lived in our hearts and on the wall of our home until the day I moved out.

It would be impossible to share all the details of 2005 and 2006. At one point, we began to earnestly pray for help and then watched God answer in abundance! "They" began to come. Jack Harper came to hang sheetrock; a group from the *Christian Motorcyclists Association* (CMA) came to paint parking lines and install the handicap marker. *First Baptist Church* in Elk Grove, CA took our breath away with over 100 people coming for a "Serve the City" day. They helped do plumbing, electrical, work on the block wall and put in a sprinkler system, as well as to provide $25,000 to purchase materials and landscaping needed. Their staff of about 25 people came on a separate day just to plant!

Our church body, *Zion Christian Fellowship*, rolled out grass turf one hot Sunday afternoon. Individuals and groups came with shovels and hammers and helping hands. Bill Engvall would come and, as Mike sat too sick to work himself, he would do whatever Mike told him to do. Gary White and his team worked on the air-conditioning and heating and built our back porch. Jerry Blakeney and his company, J.B. Electric, did all the electrical work throughout the facility. Kent and Linda Textor provided carpet. Kevin Woods gave countless hours in devotion to Mike and God's promise and without his ongoing supervision and being Mike's hands and feet; we would not have completed our project.

Money from individuals, groups, churches and organizations arrived "out of God's blue" in small and large numbers. Secular bikers and Christian bikers, the Body of Christ and our local community volunteered. It would be impossible to name everyone who gave their time and their money. Much slower than we ever imagined, but one day at a time, the promise took on the structure as the Body of Christ, with God, built His Place together!

In 2006, we witnessed God come through for His Place over and over, even as Mike's health dropped lower and lower. I did not want Jesus to call me *"you of little faith"* so I fought hard not to allow my emotions to pull me into fear and unbelief. We had to live with reality, but I learned to guard my faith and my emotions. I often had to keep them separate.

Faith taught me that by letting God's dream be placed on top of mine, I would discover *that* I could trust His dream as I released my own. Faith allowed me to surrender my understanding, including my *need to know why*. Why was this taking so long? Why was Mike getting sicker? My emotions constantly wanted to control my heart, but faith would pull out the Sword of God's Word and keep them in their place. Journaling helped to give my emotions a voice, and at the same time, it gave my spirit an understanding of God's truth as I prayed and processed on paper.

February 13, 2007, at 8:50 AM, we experienced moments that will remain in my heart forever. They were "holy moments" as the inspector officially signed off on the needed final document on His Place! The Certificate of Occupancy was in our hands!

We took pictures at the signing of the Certificate to capture the moment. Then, Kevin, Mike and I went into the building and had a victory prayer! We prayed, "O God, we did it! You and us, and *your* people! It is *finished*! This is *Your*

209

place, built for *Your* glory and we lay it at *Your* feet, finished. We have completed the task. *You* called us to. Now, all that is in *Your* heart to accomplish here, *do it*, O GOD! Perform *Your* mighty deeds in the hearts and lives of men and women!"

A day or so before we got that final document, I was praying in anticipation of the "end of the race." I felt as if we would be coming before the Lord weak and very weary. I pictured us crossing the finish line with it taking every ounce of energy we had left. We would fall to the ground, scratched up and scathed. We had often come to "very tiny passage ways" on this nearly six-year journey, and it would seem there was no way around and no way through. In those times God would say, "Keep walking. Keep trusting me." As we did *somehow* (GodThing!), we *would* get through the lack of finances or the long periods of time with no one coming to help. I saw myself apologizing to the Lord for it all taking so long and for us looking so "badly."

But, God's Word says (Paul speaking), *"That is why, for Christ's sake, I delight in weaknesses, in insults, in hardships, in persecutions, in difficulties. For when I am weak, then am I strong."* 2 Corinthians 12:10 NIV. Immediately I heard in my spirit, "No, look at yourself again." As I did, I saw us *stepping* across the finish line and standing there in a victor's stance *strong, healthy and whole*. I felt God's presence and His favor. He said, *"This* is how *I* see you!"

I was blown away. God did not see us having lost strength, but having gained it! I was so encouraged by this picture the Lord gave me! The long journey had made us strongly dependent on God's promised provision, and He was pleased. Let me encourage you: Don't give up. Keep pressing through. In your weakness, He is made strong!

In my journal, the morning after we had received the Certificate, I wrote:

> There are yet a few details of painting and wallpapering to complete. Glena Ezell, Kristy Rego and I picked out the wallpaper Monday. We chose motorcycles for the men's bathroom and zebra/leopard shells for the women's. And for my office wallpaper... zebra in brown and black!
>
> Kristy ordered and paid for my beautiful office furniture!
>
> We still have some cleanup, then the setup and a date to pick for the Grand Opening!

And then I wrote:

> The *joy has a buffer*... Mike's physical place. He's so sick. He looks so very sick: thin... sunken eyes, hollow... sick. He needs a miracle. He can't do much at all. But, his heart is full of hope and expectation that God will yet come and heal him. And so am I.

Mike was admitted to the hospital two days later with overall degrading health and ascites, which was fluid buildup in his abdomen from liver failure and high toxins. Spiritually we had the faith Mike would be healed, physically we were losing ground.

We chose April 21, 2007, for the Grand Opening of His Place. We put our trust in God that Mike would make it that far. We would trust that the good work God began, and now completed, would be able to be honored with Mike in attendance. We prayed that Mike would be granted the closure of his life journey with a glorious celebration of the opening of His Place, even as we wondered what would become of the promises.

Story 26:
His Place Grand Opening:
Balancing Belief and Grief

Belief and the anticipation of grief may seem incompatible. They are not. It is possible to look expectantly for God's healing miracle, while at the same time, embracing the beginning processing that this could be the end of life here on earth for someone we love. Faith does not demand that we live in denial and lose the opportunity to prepare effectively. God's grace gives us emotional strength *and* eternal hope to balance them both, and not fail at either.

With receiving the Final on His Place, we began to make preparation for our Grand Opening planned for April 21, 2007. For the next two months, the seesaw ride was emotionally stressful and physically draining. We would plummet down on this ride, as I would have to make another rushed trip to the hospital in San Francisco with Mike. We would refuse to stay down and so, with God's Word and our faith in His promises, we would push ourselves back up where His peace and better perspective could be found.

But, then, we would fall back down, feeling the hard jolt, as severe toxin buildup from Mike's failing liver would rule his days and rob the carefree joy of our celebration plans.

We managed during all this, with the help of many men, to move all that was in our storage over to His Place. Mike was there to give directions on what was ours, but he was so frail he barely made it from the car into the building without severe nausea that demanded a response.

Mike's 57th birthday was March 9th, and we planned a big family party for him with everyone knowing this would possibly be his last. He was lavished with gifts for his office and the bike shop as if he would use them both for the next 30 years.

My April 7, 2007, Journal entry reads:

We have and hold on to hope. I would rather, after Mike's death, look back on hope lived than to have his healing happen and have to look back on unbelief or too soon grief.

An entry made as a prayer:

I feel so detached. I do not like this! O God, I want to go through this with You—the best way possible. I want to protect Mike—to veil him from people's shock at seeing him and from their comments. O God, overshadow us. I ask for Your glory to be seen instead of his very sick eyes and body. Lift all oppression. Any grief that is seen or felt may it be "holy grief." Cover us and make us holy. Make this season to be mighty. Display Your presence.

I take my stand in what will be holy grief—face to face—with my Holy Heavenly Father, with my LORD and Savior, Jesus, and the precious and powerful Holy Spirit who is the Great Comforter.

Another journal entry:

O God, I love and worship You with all my heart and soul and mind and strength. Please show me any sin that lies between so my heart can be pure. Please allow me to walk uprightly before You. The way ahead I can't see—is Mike in it? This I know: You are in it...and so all is good and under Your divine care. Today is Good Friday, and I remember Your grief and surrender to Your Father's Plan – for You—for us—for me. I, too, surrender all—all to You my Precious Savior—I surrender all.

The scenarios of Mike's illness had become routine occurrences with increasing severity. I was so thankful that I was with Mike every step of the way. I had driven him back and forth to San Francisco countless times now for 11 years, always able to stay by his bedside. I felt I could almost qualify

215

as a "gastroenterologist" regarding the liver disease, understanding Mike's blood level readings and his medications.

With just a few days left before our Grand Opening, we had to take yet another trip to the hospital in San Francisco. Mike seemed gravely ill. In many ways, it felt as if we were entering the last pains of labor to deliver this child — His Place.

I prayed for warring angels to be sent to fight the enemy if this was an attack or attempt to rob us of Mike being able to attend the Grand Opening. As it turned out, Mike had a severe reaction to a new medication. Adjustments were made, and we were sent home with 36 hours to spare before the big day!

Our Grand Opening on April 21, 2007, was wonderful! We had over 350 people come—family, friends, our CMA bikers, church friends and secular motorcycle friends. It was an amazing and incredible day! We had great bands playing and solo artists singing. We barbecued and had more than enough food and dessert.

It was everything we hoped for, and more. Everything looked so nice. The biker décor was perfect! The pool table was in its long-awaited spot. Antique biker memorabilia outlined the ledge at the top of the walls and Sturgis and Redwood Run posters hung throughout the community room. The bike shop was in immaculate order. Kevin had put every tool in the exact drawer and compartment as Mike gave direction to fill the brand-new rolling red tool box.

Kevin Woods had set up the food shelves, and food had begun to pour in to fill them. How thankful we continued to be for Kevin! He looked at Mike as a mentor, and very best friend and Mike loved him like a brother. Without him, none of this could have happened.

Our offices were stunning! Mike's office was all in biker décor from lamp to wall hangings, and mine was in "Zepard," my name for the balanced combination of zebra and leopard!

Everything was perfect that day, for those moments! It was as Mike had dreamed for years it would be. We shared a dedication statement, and our Pastor Dick Paterson prayed a powerful prayer over Mike and me. Our hearts were full of joy, and our spirits were again soaring in the heavens. We felt

God's pleasure at our presentation to Him of our beautiful gift.

Three days later Mike personally handed out His Place's first two boxes of food to two different families in need. The goal of performing that small act had kept him going for months. His dream now lived out meant the promise had surely come!

That same weekend our church family was ending a 40-day time of prayer and fasting with Mike being #1 on the prayer list. So many of our family members were in town for the Grand Opening on Saturday. On Sunday, Mike and I and our son, Mike, and daughter, Stephanie, went to church together as a family for the very last time. It was a special time of honor to Mike. We were also able to dedicate Mike's baby nephew, Blake, to the Lord that day.

The next few days after our grand opening, Mike became so ill, he could not even go out into the His Place facility. I was distraught and did not know what to do. I received a Scripture about going to the mountain of God, and then advice from a friend to take a break and go to the cabin of our friends, Bill and Barb Engvall. So, with a heavy heart, I put a "CLOSED until further notice" on His Place, and we took our last trip away together. Though Mike was there in body, he was too ill to enjoy our special get-away place. He could barely eat and the hours passed with him asleep in his chair, leaving me to watch DVDs alone and without his usual interaction and laughter.

When we returned home, and at what would be his last hospital visit, the evidence before me, clearly and heartbreakingly showed that the doctor's efforts were immediately overtaken with the advanced effects of Mike's Hepatitis C-induced cirrhosis of the liver disease. The doctor's defenses were no longer able to do any more than what I could do at home. I felt overwhelmed as I was told that Mike's lifespan was certainly within the parameters of six- months, which qualified him for hospice care. These facts forced me to begin the extremely difficult process of making the agonizing decision to move Mike from curative care to comfort care.

Mike no longer had the energy to shower or give himself proper care. I wanted to do what was best for him, and what might relieve him from unnecessary use of his treasured, yet extremely limited, energy. I wanted to provide his friends and family with the best possible access to him, and him to them.

I knew it was time for a very serious discussion with Mike about his life, but it must be shared from that faith perspective that God was still a part of our story. We would do this with both truths. Grief was hanging heavy in my heart, yet there would always be a window of hope left wide open, hope that Jesus would yet come to heal.

God's promise to give us land, and the strength for Mike to build His Place on it, was complete. Now, it was time for God's plan that would carry us both into our designated future. God was still in control, and we would never give way to anything less than that unshakable belief.

Story 27
Sand Storms and Saying a Long Goodbye

Strength for our weakness and His courage to replace our fears are exchanges God generously offers us throughout the living stories within His Word. He *knew* their physical and spiritual lack and *saw* their fear-based emotions, yet He would boldly exhort them to *"Be strong and courageous!"* His written Word becomes our Word, too!

If we embrace Jesus, take on His strength that will sustain us as His courage challenges us, we will have all we need to press through difficulty into deliverance. As we strive for this exchange, in the process, we will gain a revelation that our commitment to His cause and His Kingdom is at the core of everything that matters.

It was Sunday, May 21, 2007, and this would be my last Sunday in church for about six months. I needed to be by Mike's side while he was in his last days, and then, as I would begin processing my life without him. It was just too difficult to be anywhere but at home.

As we sang worship songs, I felt strongly the presence of the Lord. I had one of those moments when I felt the stirring of the Holy Spirit within me, and I knew He wanted to say something. I thought maybe it should be shared with the congregation, but when there was no appropriate place to speak it, I sat down and wrote it out. It was not a word for them. It was a word for me. These words would carry me through months of loss, letting go, and loneliness--the greatest of my entire lifetime.

I will only share the first sentence of God's message to me in this story because it was this that I would cling to for the next four months. I will share the full message in the story entitled, "It's Not A Tomb."

That first sentence was, *"Be strong and courageous—and hide—in the cleft of the Rock, Christ Jesus."*

Later that day I transferred the entire word God gave me into my journal. There was no way, at that point, that I could have fully grasped the complete meaning or power it held.

That first sentence, as I began to ponder it, sounded like an oxymoron, *"Be strong and courageous... and hide."* But, with the revelation came life-giving wisdom as only God can give. He did not minimize the challenge lying ahead for me, or the requisite strength and courage I would need. He gave the specific direction of where I would find it. I would find it by hiding in The Rock, Christ Jesus.

The Rock became my high tower, my place of refuge; a place to go to get away from the extreme stress and sorrow of watching my Mike's life ebb away right in front of me.

I shared my lifeline phrase with many, and when anyone would ask, "How are you doing, Sherri?" I would always answer, "I am hiding in The Rock." God knew to find me there as well.

My friend, Cheryl McEachron, told me one day she was crying out to God for me and said something to the effect of, "God, please be with Sherri! She is in a living hell right now!" God responded, "No, she's not. She's hiding in the Rock!" Cheryl delighted in the correction!

I was grateful that God saw me there and knew how dependent I had become upon Him for His shelter in this raging, life-taking storm.

Mike had worked long and hard to finish the construction of our ministry facility, His Place. Now, he was gravely ill, His Place was empty, and I felt helpless. People would excitedly ask, "How is the ministry going now that you're open?" I could only cry out to God asking Him what to do. What was I to say? How could I share how desperately sick Mike was now?

I knew it was a very little thing for God to add an hour to Mike's life (Luke 12:22). As He had done in the past, He could do again. So, I would give my answer: "We are standing in the presence of the Lord. We are hiding in the Rock until this storm passes." We had no choice but to wait and let God lead us as to what to do next. I knew Mike would experience God's resurrection power one way or the other.

It was time to ask for help and to seek options. I reached out to my family, my pastors and close friends, and all confirmed the next step should be to bring in home health care. Mike was reluctant at first, denying he was at that stage, but after prayer and a few heart to heart talks, we agreed this would provide him with the optimal comfort care we were pursuing.

During one of those talks, my heart broke when he laid his head back in his chair and said, "I want to live, but not this way." Then in direct response to my question of whether he agreed to call hospice, with a heavy sigh, he just solemnly nodded, "yes." It was then my difficult responsibility to call each family member and a few close friends to confirm our decision.

Home health care sent a nurse to discuss with us the parameters of hospice, and for Mike to sign the paperwork. It was a Friday, June 1, 2007. I expressed my experience of that day in an email sent to my friend, Cheryl:

> Hospice was here this morning. The meeting itself went fine. The social worker and RN explained how it all works and I signed consent forms.
>
> There will be one of two nurses that will be coming out twice a week, but are available 24/7 if needed. Tomorrow they will send out a hospital type bed and all the comfort meds including oxygen. A nurse will come out on Monday. There will be a social assessment done in the middle of next week, and we will meet the chaplain next week as well. There are home health aides and volunteers to sit with Mike, if I

want to do errands, etc. He isn't to be left alone at all.

Mike is processing it all. I just keep trying to reassure him that *God alone* holds his life and his time of death in *His* hands...not hospice. He said to Phil (Fugate) this afternoon when he and Doreen came by, "God is on the Throne and I'm on my way Home."

Afterward, Mike wanted to go to Denny's to eat. Of course, I took him, but, by the time we got there and sat down, he was *sick*. He only could eat three bites. It broke my heart. He looked so ill.

I choose now to run to the Rock where there are hope and peace. The day feels like it's been raining sand. I know that must sound strange, but that's what it has felt like...like it is raining sand, and I'm going to suffocate in it if I don't hide...

I needed to say this to someone. I know Jesus heard me, too, and so I lay my head on His strong shoulder. Thanks for your love and letting me express my heart.

That outing to Denny's was Mike's last time off the His Place property. I do not know how to adequately share the events of the next 3½ months. In the first few weeks of those months Mike's mom, Angel, and stepmom, Virla, came and stayed about a month to give him their love and to say goodbye. Our church coordinated dinners to be sent every night for that month, overseen by Karen DeHart. She had walked a similar journey. She knew. What a blessing that was to me! I could never thank everyone enough.

Mike became increasing immobile and would go for days without eating. I think I counted 18 days at one point. We held prayer vigils on more than one occasion. A friend, Virginia Miller, came with a very gifted and loving family member, Brian Besser, who sang beautiful worship songs over him.

Kevin Woods, Rich and Jennie Hardesty, Bill and Barb Engvall, Jeff and Cheryl McEachron, Pastors Dick and Edie Patterson, John and Mary O'Mara, Joe and Judy Maxwell, John and Bobbe Addington and family, Mike's family, my family, and so many came that I couldn't begin to name them all. During this time friends, Rusty and Peggy Henkens, came to visit and out of the blue handed us a check for $5,000--"blue money!" God knew how desperately we needed that money. It proved to us, again, that God was our provider.

As time went on and visitors came, Mike usually had no idea they were there. Our hospice nurse said he defied all the boundaries of her personal nursing experience as he clung to life, and fought to live. More than once we would be told, "it's likely he will pass today," but then he would rally, insisting on sitting up, as he would do his best to eat a bite of food.

Our daughter, Stephanie, took leave from work so she could help care for her dad, and give support in numerous other ways. Our son, Mike, who lives out of town, drove the more than four hours more than once to be near. My stress level and fatigue were off the charts.

Hospice aid came twice a week to give Mike personal care and to change his sheets. On the day's hospice was not scheduled to come, I had no choice but to give Mike his personal care. It's not that I didn't do it lovingly because I did, but I remember feeling that when this responsibility was added, I identified with the Israelites when Pharaoh told them that they now had to make bricks with no straw provided to them. Their predicament went from bad to worse as this added labor dramatically increased their work load. I did not see this added care as punishment, but with everything else, it felt impossible to manage.

My friend, Kathy Binkley, would give me short reprieves as we would meet at Starbucks so that I could decompress. We continue to meet to this day. Our "mocha time" paved the way for a deep friendship. We have had hundreds of conversations throughout the years and have always carried one another's burdens through prayer and support.

One of my "holy moments" during this time was when Cheryl came to visit. As she prayed for Mike and then for me, she shared what the Lord was showing her. She saw God come to minister to me in a physical way by serving me communion from the tables of heaven. This holy act added literal strength to my body. This strength gave way to courage which enabled me to continue pressing forward to Mike's finish line.

Mike was now only in the hospice bed, and I was sleeping alone. One night I was so lonely that I got up out of bed and went into the living room where Mike was. I gently scooted him over so I could climb up on the bed and lay next to him. He felt my presence enough to put his arm around me and held me tight as he had done through so many beautiful nights. I will never forget that special moment as Mike responded to me in genuine love for that very last time.

Another very sweet display of Mike's gentleness and love for me occurred as I would try my best to understand what he was whispering. I would get very close to his face and listen intently, and he would spontaneously kiss me! And then he always mouthed, "I love you."

Two visits also stand out in my mind during his last days. One happened on a Friday evening when the *Modified Motorcycle Association* meeting was being held at the "Know Place Bar" across the street from His Place. One of Mike's long time outlaw biker friends, "Animal," walked over and knocked on our front door. He had a few of his club's prospects with him.

Mike had been non-communicative for a few days. But, when Mike heard Animal's voice, with all the life that he could muster, he rallied to greet his friend, who represented to him the bikers he so loved and for whom he had built His

Place. Kevin and I were shocked to see the visible display of love between these two friends.

The second visit happened one morning as a friend of Mike's, and his son came to visit. He caught Mike on a morning, during a small window when he was "alert." Mike insisted on taking his friend on a tour of the facility. We tried our best to talk him out of it, but Mike would not relent. So, Kevin and I got Mike into the wheelchair and wheeled him out for what was to be this man's first look at His Place... and Mike's last.

It was exciting to have Mike out there again, yet heartbreaking to see in his eyes all he knew he would be missing. If faith alone were the ingredient needed for physical healing, it would have happened that day. All the faith held in all the prayers of all those who loved Mike would have been enough to dissipate the horrid Hepatitis C from his body.

On top of all we were going through at the time, with Mike's health steadily declining, my mom had a brain stem stroke on her right side requiring her to be in a rehabilitation center for several weeks. I was only able to visit her a couple of times, and it was difficult to see her so weak. I wanted to bring her to my house and take care of her along with Mike and even discussed it with my family, but all knew, better than me, I was in no condition to take on another "patient."

At the advice of my Pastor, I knew it was time to move the ministry forward. Mike would also want that. Kevin Woods was appointed Assistant Director in charge of overseeing Bike Ministry, Food Distribution, and Ground Care.

We knew it was a matter of time before Mike would be in heaven. God's grace came as we finished up arrangements at the funeral home; I wanted as much done ahead of time as was possible. As her dad laid mostly unresponsive in his hospital bed in our living room, Stephanie began to pull out pictures and assemble them for a power point presentation of his life that would be shown at his funeral service. It gave her something productive and honorable to do, as we waited.

I had tried for weeks to hear a Scripture of confirmation that God would heal Mike. Every day I asked God many questions, not in anger, but in a search for His plan. I would hold out for God to take His opportunity to answer, and I reasoned that He might just be silent now so not to spoil the surprise! I chose to embrace contentment in my heart. I prayed desperately for faith and stated that when I got to heaven and had a chance to talk to Abraham and Moses, I would say to them, "Me, too!" as we shared of how faithful God was to keep His promises to us! I expected the best and prepared for the worst. There it was again, the balancing of belief and grief with each asking for impartial courage and equal strength.

Story 28:
Chariots of Fire

Death is only acceptable theoretically. In our youth or when we are healthy, we usually speak of death lightly, and though we may sing about it as a beautiful experience when it comes down to it, we fight it and often fear it.

Everyone wants to go to heaven, just not today. When "today" has finally arrived, we struggle to let go. For the Christ follower, however, the curse of death *has been removed*, and our comfort comes through the authority of the Word of God that assures us that our loved one or we will be in the presence of the Lord. Friends can comfort us in our sorrow, but they are not capable of touching our true need. For that, we must have the active, living Word of God.

Hebrews 4:12 (NIV) tells us, *"For the word of God is alive and active. Sharper than any double-edged sword, it penetrates even to dividing soul and spirit, joints and marrow; it judges the thoughts and attitudes of the heart."* The Word reaches where no man can.

The day turned out to be an incredible day, but it didn't start that way. It was Saturday, September 22, 2007, and Mike had now been 3½ months in hospice care. He had experienced

233

extremely high fever for the past couple days… up to 105.8 degrees. I knew this was a signal that his body was about to give up. I was mentally, physically and emotionally exhausted. I didn't know what to say, what to think, what to do, or even what to pray.

Stephanie was planning a three-day spiritual fast to begin on Monday for her dad. I was debating if I should join her. I wanted to ask God to let it end, but I didn't want to risk asking Him to shorten the test—lessons were being learned.

I felt confused and was truly struggling. I didn't know what to do anymore. Stand firm? Pray? Ask? Believe? Submit? Surrender? I knew I had done all those things and would face the end without regret. Feelings of anxiety tried to set in. I asked for strength and courage to stay hidden in the Rock. It was getting harder to see Mike suffer.

My thinking was not clear. My questions and concerns and even fears on this day were largely a result of exhaustion. God, in His love for me, knew it was time to intervene on my behalf. He knew exactly what would bring me peace. I had to have His Word. Let me share how He ran to me with it.

I fully released Stephanie to leave about mid-afternoon to spend time with Larry, and I knew she would be gone until late that night. My emotions began to peak, and I felt they were ready to break. I had fought so hard for so long.

At 6:14 PM I sent a text to my friend Cheryl and said,

"I know it's because I'm really tired, but I am having a hard time tonight. I'm alone, and my emotions want to release the floodgate. If I do, will it take with it the belief [that I have stood on all these months]? Will I compromise [and God see it as unbelief]?"

I could not stop crying. I was looking for something in the Bible to read, but I was so distraught I was just fumbling pages. At 6:25 PM, before Cheryl could respond to my text, I received a text from another friend, Sonja Johnson, who, by the way, is also now with the Lord. Her text simply read, "Psalm 20, NIV."

"May the Lord answer you when you are in distress,

may the name of the God of Jacob protect you.

May he send you help from the sanctuary and grant you support from Zion.

May he remember all your sacrifices and accept your burnt offerings.

May he give you the desire of your heart and make all your plans succeed.

May we shout for joy over your victory and lift up our banners in the name of our God.

May the LORD grant all your requests.

Now, this I know: The LORD gives victory to his anointed.

He answers him from his heavenly sanctuary and with the victorious power of his right hand.

Some trust in chariots and some in horses, but we trust in the name of the LORD our God.

They are brought to their knees and fall, but we rise and stand firm

LORD, give victory to the King! Answer us when we call!"

At 6:28 PM another text came through. This was from another good friend, Barb Engvall. Her text simply read, "2 Kings 6:17 and Psalm 125:2."

"As the mountains surround Jerusalem, so the LORD surrounds his people both now and always" (Psalm 125:2, NIV).

"Then the LORD opened the servant's eyes, and he looked and saw the hills full of horses and chariots of fire all around Elisha" (2 Kings 6:17b, NIV).

At 6:46 PM I received Cheryl's response to my text to her:

"Remember, Jesus wept too. He will come and hold you. To let some of the pressure releases will free more room. You are full of late nights, phone calls, taking care of everyone. *You're full* of faith, perseverance. *Run to Jesus*! I will be praying!"

At 6:58 PM my response back to Cheryl,

"HE ran to me! As I was crying out to Jesus what to do, He had Sonja and Barb text me scripture. My tears are flowing, but He has sent His *Word*. I am *not* alone here tonight. My God has come."

Through three dear friends, God sent words of comfort and Scripture that spoke directly to me. God's Word absorbed the floodgate of emotions, extreme fatigue, and out of control grief that was set to overtake me because of Mike's grave illness. God's Word brought a powerful promise that God saw me in my day of trouble and distress, *and* God's *Word* covered me in holy moments that lasted throughout that entire evening.

I wrote a detailed breakdown of each Scripture in my journal, how it had affected my walk during these past months. I believe the enemy, Satan, had sent his horses, chariots and a great army to surround and overtake me that night with an emotional breakdown. But, my God sent His Word! He opened my eyes to see that He, too, sent His chariots of fire in my defense and there were many more than the enemy's!

From that night on, I felt God's chariots of fire surrounding His Place in the heavenly realm. It was as if I could see them with my spirit eyes! I knew they were there to keep back the attack of the enemy against me and I knew, at God's appointed time, that one of them would break rank and come to take my sweetie on the ride of his life through Heaven's portals, straight into the arms of Jesus!

That night I was able to speak to Mike with his understanding one last time. I told him, "Fear not, for God is here and has surrounded you with His horses and chariots of fire! Be at peace because our God is in control." I didn't know if he would suddenly sit up, healed, and say, "I'm way to thin, get me something to eat!" But this I knew, it would be God's will for us both.

I felt God close as I shared with Mike and believed he did, too. He was in pain, so I gave him some medication, and I encouraged him to sleep, which God enabled him to do.

I had total peace from that point on. I knew if God came for Mike it would be because His appointed time for Mike's numbered days of life had finally been fulfilled. The enemy could not and would not invade with any takeover plan.

The next morning, I awoke still feeling the love and presence of God from His Word He had sent the night before. I heard Him call me "His bride," and it made me smile because Mike always introduced me that way.

That Sunday morning God sent His Word in one more text through yet another friend, Linda Textor. It read, "Isaiah 41:10, 13, NIV."

"So do not fear, for I am with you; do not be dismayed, for I am your God. I will strengthen you and help you; I will uphold you with my righteous right hand... For I am the LORD, your God who takes hold of your right hand. And says to you, Do not fear; I will help you."

God, again, confirmed His Word to me! I knew what He was saying. He was telling me He would hold my hand and be with me when Mike was gone. He was telling me that I would not be alone. He was preparing me because in less than 48-hours He would be releasing one of those chariots of fire, the Harley looking one with the biggest flames (smile) to come and carry my beloved husband into the glory of His presence—Mike's eternal home.

The rest of that day, and into the next, Mike's heart rate increased. Stephanie began her fast on Monday seeking the Lord's will. I determined I was not going to be on a death watch, but on a "God watch." God was the One we looked to in life. Now He would be the One we would look for in death.

Story 29:
5:55

5:55 - Whenever a clock reads 5:55 my heart remembers. There are those moments that are frozen in time forever within that secret place in us where all that is life-changing is held. One of those moments was September 25, 2007, 5:55 AM.

The night before, on September 24th, I had quietly shared with Mike that his time was near. I had sat in the chair next to the love of my life, as close to him as I could get, holding his hand, wondering what it would be like to never touch him again. I remember saying, "I'm here, honey. You are not alone." I wanted to prolong every minute of that night that I knew would likely be our last night together here on this earth.

As I write of these emotions now, the tears fall fresh. Death is so tragic and tearing because it was never meant to be. Death became a sentence upon mankind back in the Garden of Eden. God had told Adam that if he ate of the tree of the knowledge of good and evil, he would surely die. After Adam and Eve had disobeyed, it grieved God deeply to pronounce within the curse, death; not only upon them but on the entire human race.

Our Heavenly Father's love is so intense toward us that He would send His Son to be our reconciliation, and whose blood would not only become the payment for Adam and Eve's sin, but for the sin of every generation afterward, right down to the sin of my beloved.

Jesus' resurrection ended the curse of death and is our *promise* that we, too, will rise again! Jesus' resurrection gave Him back the keys of hell and death, and now, we have no need to fear either. If we have accepted Jesus as Lord, and have asked Him to forgive our sin, when death comes, we are *immediately* with our Father in heaven! Mortality takes on immortality!

For those who depart, death is awesome! For we who remain, death is tragic, even though we will grieve with the hope of seeing them again.

My heart was heavy, yet part of me ached for Mike to be free from this world that now only kept him in pain and darkness. Though I longed for his morning of freedom to come; I knew that when it did, my night would begin.

There lay the love of my life. Was this happening? Was this his time? I sat there next to him as long as my body would take it, and then moved to the couch next to his bed. My eyes closed with tears fresh on my pillow, but sleep would not produce rest.

I set my alarm to wake me every two hours. There was nothing I could do for *him*, but for the feeling I needed to do *something*, I would take his blood pressure and run the thermometer across his forehead.

I stood over him about 3:00 AM, and I could hear his heavy, labored breathing. My senses were shocked as I lifted his arm. They felt unusually light, even feather-like. This shook me to the core, and I was instantly *awake* as a deep sadness swept over me, declaring in its unspoken words that Mike's day to ride a chariot of fire was about to dawn.

I began to speak to him softly with a gentleness you would speak to a child. I didn't know how long he had. Minutes? Hours? I wanted him to hear what was yet in my heart to say. I told him how much I loved him, and how much I would miss his love and laughter. I brushed his hair and pulled the sheets up tight around him, wanting him to look his best to exit my world and enter into what my dad had said we as Christians wait our whole lives for.

I kissed his mouth and his cheeks, then his lips again. Our lifetime together passed before me. Though he wasn't awake that I could tell, I know our love exchanged one final goodbye embrace as I felt the first chilling wave of grief wash over my body, soul, and spirit.

Exhausted from weeks of intensive caregiving, my body forced me at another attempt to rest. I remember hitting the snooze on my alarm a couple of times. But, then, suddenly, my eyes sprang open! I believe an angel leaned over and whispered into my ear, "Sherri, get up!"

I was groggy, but went to his bedside fearing I might have let too much time pass since my last monitoring routine. It was then that I believe I recorded Mike's spirit leave his body as the first blood pressure reading spiked and read

"Error." I retook it, and this time the reading plummeted and displayed "E" for error again. Later I would reassign the meaning of that "E" to "Eternity."

I let out a loud call for my daughter, and she was there within seconds! I was so thankful that I was able to be *with* Mike as God came and *took his breath away in a majestic display of all that awaited him!* I could only imagine *the thrill* Mike experienced as his heart stopped beating and his spirit eyes opened to see a *chariot of fire* waiting to transport him to heaven, to be *face to face* with His God!

Mike's body lay quiet. Though death had come, all time and eternity were now his! His spirit was free, and He was fully alive! But, for me, the clock read **5:55**.

Story 30:
Day One, Minus One

Days when life's road is smooth, and we travel in relative comfort are those that are easily embraced as God's blessing upon us. It's easy to say "yes" to God's plan for our future until we bump against an unknown outcome, or we need to surrender our hopes and dreams in exchange for unchartered territory. Then we have a decision to make as to whether we will lay down our first-choice destination, and allow God's plan to override ours.

Our all-knowing God has our best outcome wrapped in His strategy which always includes a deeper relationship with Him. I have come to call this "God's First and Best Plan."

It is by our free will that we stay under God's destiny for our life. If we choose to remain, then at the end of every day, at the close of every season and especially upon our life's completion, we will have no regrets. We will have experienced a lifetime of knowing Him and the proof, as His Word states, that He is our great reward.

It was day one, minus one. Mike had left for heaven on the first day of fall. My season in life changed that day as well. Necessary phone calls were made, first to our son, Mike, and then to other family members. Stephanie called a few friends. Some of those we called came and were still there. I was thankful for all of those who helped us through those first few

245

hours of loss. Because Mike was under hospice care, we did not have to call 911. We could take our time and call the funeral home to come within an acceptable timeframe. I was so grateful for that extra time. His body lay there, free of pain while he, his true self—his spirit, was in the presence of God. I knew for him it was all joy, but it was hard for me to imagine he could be fully happy there without me. That was a grief emotion that God would help me work through in time.

I could hear muffled voices in the kitchen from my bedroom as I faced my first moments alone. I tried to lie down as others had suggested, but I knew sleep would not be found. So, I got up, took a shower and then went to the chair that would become my "grief chair" during the months to come. I opened my journal and wrote my first sentence. I needed to make my declaration to God in answer to the question I had left hanging as I made my journal entry at 11:35 PM the night before.

I had written:

"I just can't believe this could be it. The biggest and obviously most serious crisis we've been in is here, yet we have been through so many it doesn't seem real. Nothing seems to be crises anymore.

Steph went to bed. I sent out text updates. Cheryl offered to come, but if this is the night, then I know we want to be here alone with him in those first moments.

246

I did talk to him and shared his crises. I hope he heard me. He is unable to respond at all. I just want him to rise and sit up—to get up and come to me—to hold me and hug me and tell me he loves me.

O God, I know I am not alone here now… and I am not afraid… but I am sad… and I'm waiting and watching to see which way we go here—which plan is revealed… What is your *First and Best Plan*? I trust you with all my heart."

So, now, six hours into fresh grief, I simply wrote:

"O God, Your First and Best Plan has come, and my precious sweetheart is in heaven with You. Thank you, thank you that you waited for me and Steph to be there when you came for him. It's you and me now—just me and you."

My coined phrase, "God's First and Best Plan" came out of a prayer I had written in my journal after I been reading out of Isaiah 38, the story of Hezekiah having 15 years added to his life.

If God could add 15 years for Hezekiah, He could do it for Mike, right? As I did a short study on Hezekiah, I found that Hezekiah could not trust God's plan for him. Fear caused him to beg for his life. But, what came of God's extending Hezekiah's life was that a son was born who grew up to bring idol worship back into their nation. How sad is that! So many would now live in darkness because of Hezekiah's fears.

I did not want to pray out of fear. I did not want to beg for Mike's life if this was his appointed day and *God's best plan* for him.

On July 10, 2007, I had written in my journal:

"God gave Hezekiah the incredible sign of turning the sun backward 10 degrees! But, what is incredible about God turning back time or adding a day to a life? (Luke 12) God called that "a little thing"!

O God, again I come before you and know you have heard the cries of many for Mike who are asking and believing on his behalf. But, My Father, I pray again that you act on *your first—best—and perfect plan*. Do not act on the innocent love and short-sighted petitions of we who pray out of our desires. *You* choose, O God—and I will *know* it is *good*."

From that time to this very day, I have continued to link arms with hope, and to feel the most secure when I ask God for His First and Best Plan.

That morning, September 25, 2007, was day one, minus one incredible soul living here on earth. But, for heaven, it was day one, plus one, for one amazing man who would now ride his "chariot of fire" on streets of gold, and sing with King David, "Oh How I Love Jesus!"

By my choice, I stood present as the funeral home personnel came to take Mike. I looked again at the clock, and it was 11:35 AM. As I marked another moment in my heart, I knew my watch over Mike was over. I felt such great loss. It was the beginning of sorrow as I had never known.

What I did know was that I had trusted in God's First and Best Plan for Mike and I would trust in God's First and Best Plan for me; now, in my uncertain tomorrow and for the rest of my days.

Story 31:
Not "The End."

Relationships with others produce some of our most cherished treasures in life. When someone we love passes away, breaking off that relationship is extremely difficult. Where we once enjoyed the loving interaction, we now have silence. The pain of experiencing a permanent interruption of our communication with them leaves us feeling lost and lonely.

Memories bring comfort, but at the beginning, they are superseded by our sorrow in our inability to make more. We are challenged to bear grief that overwhelms our souls. Many try to bury their grief rather than bear it, but that only brings a false release—denial. Without an outlet, the pain festers and debilitates the healing process.

What *will* bring relief? The One who knows how to help us process our loss, who relieves our pain, and gives divine aid and direction, Jesus, our Shepherd. He will lead us out of the valley of the shadow of death.

My living relationship with Mike was over, and to me, my future looked dark. I could not imagine ever feeling happy again. My only true comfort was to have a strong and active relationship with my Heavenly Father. He *was* my Shepherd, and I knew His voice. I had not left my place of hiding in the Rock. In the middle of my emotional stress, God would tenderly lead me, and His rod and His staff would comfort me in the days ahead.

I would like to let you read a couple of excerpts from my journal before Mike passed away on September 25, 2007, and then one shortly afterward. The first two entries will show you how God began to prepare my heart a full year before Mike's passing to be at peace *without* knowing the answer to the question, "Why?"

Then I will share a journal entry from a few days after Mike's passing. You will see how God immediately began to tend my heart.

August 23, 2006, Journal Entry (13 months before Mike passed away):

"Yesterday at Tuesday morning prayer, as I was praying for Mike, I believe I heard God say:

'Moses died honored in my sight [without entering into the Promised Land], and it was not the end of my plan for the Israelites.

David died honored in my sight [without being allowed to personally build my Temple], and it was not the end of my plan for my Kingdom.

John the Baptist died in his prime after being the Way Maker, and it did not stop the plan of God to continue to unfold.

Paul died at his appointed time, honored in my sight, and it did not stop the spreading of the Gospel.'"

My journal entry continued:

"I was going over this in my mind when a friend, Jeanne Wichman, came and began praying over me. It was a gentle, refreshing prayer as she prayed over me the 23rd Psalm. I cannot remember the exact words she used, but I knew her prayer was on behalf of my heart that would soon be walking through the valley of the shadow of death."

"The LORD is my shepherd; I lack nothing.

He makes me lie down in green pastures; He leads me beside quiet waters.

He refreshes my soul. He guides me along the right paths for His name's sake.

Even though I walk through the darkest valley, I will fear no evil, for you are with me; your rod and your staff, they comfort me.

*You prepare a table before me in the presence of my
enemies.*

You anoint my head with oil; my cup overflows.

*Surely your goodness and love will follow me all the
days of my life,*

and I will dwell in the house of the LORD forever"
(Psalm 23 NIV).

"It has been ten years since Mike's very first
crisis, and it was *this* scripture I feared God
would give me if I asked Him where we were
going and if Mike was going to die. I feared the
valley of the shadow of death. Now, ten years
later, have we come full circle?

Back then God said we were to stand as
Moses did [with his rod over the Red Sea] and
see the deliverance of the Lord our God. Is God
preparing me [now for Mike's death] or testing
me [in my faith]?

I must not listen to the voice of my
enemies but come to your table that you have
set for me in their presence."

August 19, 2007, Journal Entry (One month before
Mike passed away)

[I had been desperately asking God, "What am I going to do if You take Mike to heaven. How am I going to raise the His Place ministry alone?"]

"It's 3:45 AM. Mike did not have a good day.

I've been up and down with Mike tonight, but I have been having dreams. One of the dreams was that a group of us were trying very hard to get a huge white blimp off the ground. We tried unsuccessfully to pull it forward thinking if we ran very fast it would rise to the sky [as one would try to fly a kite]. At one point, I had us all stand in a circle saying, 'On the count of three we will all lift it using all our might!' We could not even budge it.

Then different ones began to ask, 'Where's Mike?' Someone said, 'We need Mike to get this off the ground. He is the only one who knows how to make it lift and fly!'

As I pondered this dream (awake) I asked the Lord, again, however, would we get His Place lifted off the ground—up and functioning—if Mike were not here to do it? [My heart is aching with this question.]

As I lay on the couch next to his hospice bed a song, an *old hymn, 'Love Lifted Me' began to* sing in my spirit."

"Love lifted me; love lifted me

When nothing else would help, Love lifted me"...

(Author: James Rowe, Composer: Howard W. Smith)

LOVE!—The Love of God. That is what would lift His Place!

I closed my eyes and "saw" the blimp *high* in the sky! Many people were on the ground, and all of them were pointing to the blimp, to His Place, saying, 'Look at the Love! Look at the Love!'

And then I remember hearing a strong voice in my spirit that said, 'No man can lift a ministry.'"

September 29, 2007, Journal Entry (Four days after Mike passed away)

Tomorrow will be Mike's viewing, and it is going to be a very hard day. But, You [God] said something to me today. You said that as You reveal truth into my places of deep grief, to *allow it* to bring healing to that area — to not go back to question again and again.

You have highlighted three areas for me already:

1. *Mike's perspective of dying* taken from his prerecorded video, to be played at the funeral: "I haven't passed away. I've graduated!"

   So, I see him now being able to take his gifts to the highest level! Heaven!!

2. *Mike's view taken from that video of him not being at His Place* to be a part of the ministry phase: "His Place is still here to be used by who it was created for...

3. *Your word to me yesterday saying, "Mike knows!"* Mike knows the how and why of Your First and Best Plan, and He agrees with You that it *is* good! I find *great* comfort in this.

If I had constantly tried to reconcile the original call to build His Place and the fact that, upon completion, Mike was taken out of the picture, I would only be thinking in circles. I knew I had much grief ground to cover and I wanted to begin it walking forward.

Yes, God held the answers to all my grief questions, yet I realized that He often withholds detailed answers. Some questions He may answer over time, some not at all, and some differently than the way we would want them answered. His ways are higher than our ways, and so I prayed to know what I needed to know and what I could understand. I would find my peace in His Sovereignty.

Now with Mike gone just a few days, I did not have a clue what to do. In the next eight stories, I will share of His Place in the context of my journey and struggle to move forward without Mike. All the miraculous that became a reality and that brought His Place into existence would continue to be present to help me let it go. It's true. God gives, and God takes away. In time, we come to understand that in both, He is multiplying His goodness in our heart.

In these next stories, I will share my journey of learning to live again without Mike. I will share amazing "blue stories" of my living experiences that are now among the best of my entire life!

Mike was living his first glorious days in heaven, and I was living the first of my hardest of days on earth, but this was not the end. Mike was in a new beginning, and so was I. God would care for me like no other. His voice would be the only voice that could console me. He would run to me again and again as He saw my tears, and His peace would fill my heart, fulfilling our covenant relationship.

Story 32:
The Miracle of Metamorphosis

Determination to face the difficulty of grief by staying engaged with God, grants us access to supernatural intervention and divine insight. However, that will not make the journey easy or take away the pain of loss.

When we want to be brave, yet the debilitating emotions blindside us, we will have One who sees through the storm and leads us to safety. He will show us how to be active in our faith, yet not suppress our sorrow. God will speak hope and new promises, yet encourage us not to understate the magnitude of the grieving process. God will give us the courage to embrace our journey because He knows that is the road to healing.

I knew my life had changed forever. I knew grief would be a journey like I had never been on before, and I did not want to muddle my way through it. I decided right away that I would require myself, with God's help, to know where I was. I might not like it, but I had to know at least what stage or phase I was in and how the process worked.

In the beginning, it all seems surreal. Your mind knows that there is a gaping hole in your life, but, as a buffer, you live in short term denial. Your pain is numbed to help you in those first days of doing the next required thing. That usually means phone calls, visits to the funeral home, writing the obituary, overall planning and then attending the funeral service. There are often guests to host. It was that way for me.

Mike's service was everything I wanted it to be and more. For as long as I had known him, Mike had always said, "I'm going to preach at my own funeral." So, about a year before he passed away, he made a video that we hoped would be tucked away for years to come. I pulled it out to view ahead of the service and was so thankful that we had made an effort to do this. It would have been one of my great regrets not to have followed through.

There was a funeral home visitation the day before Mike's service. I stayed the entire day. It was the last hours, this side of heaven, which I would ever have with him, and I had no desire to be anywhere else. My son and daughter were with me, and it was at the end of this long emotional day that we each, alone with him, would say our final goodbyes.

The next morning, before the service began, the casket remained open for those who had been unable to attend the viewing the day before. I stood there to personally greet each person who came early to pay their respects.

I chose for the casket to be closed at the beginning of the service because I did not want to go through another emotional goodbye, yet I wanted our family to have the opportunity to give him one last tribute of love. Mike's mom and stepmom, my mom, my daughter, my son and I each had a rose and, one at a time walked over to Mike and laid it on his chest. After I had laid mine down, I bent and gave him his last kiss. I remained there as the casket was closed to silently display my final act of love and in the symbolism of being with him to the very end.

Beautiful tributes and letters were shared, including one from my daughter, and one from me. A video picture tribute of Mike's life produced by our friend, Ted Bobrow, was shown. It brought both tears and laughter from so many of the memories we had experienced living with Mike.

As it was time for Pastor Dick to share a short message from God's Word, instead, another video began to play. There was Mike, sitting in his chair; his voice projecting out, "I know you all thought you'd heard the last of me!"

After the shock of hearing his voice speaking directly to them, everyone sat mesmerized listening as if he had walked into the room and sat down for one last chat with us all. There were laughter and tears in every eye that was now glued on the man they had come to honor!

Mike, in all his wit and wisdom, shared his love of life and his heart for everyone there. He would be proud to know it had the exact effect he had envisioned. I know it left a lasting memory of the final testimony of a 1% biker becoming a 100% follower of Jesus Christ. They had heard it before, but this time the impact had the weight of Mike's being in heaven behind it!

In the days following Mike's service, I waited for night to come so the tears could flow unrestrained. Grief came in waves, hard and frequent. With every wave of grief that came crashing down on me, I felt I would drown. And though at my core I knew it wasn't true, I could not yet acknowledge that Mike was truly happy in heaven, because I was not there with him.   That was one of the last things he had said to me, "I want to go to Heaven, but not without you." One night, as I sat alone in my room, I began to pray and take my fears to God in my journal writing:

> "October 8, 2007, 11:22 PM. O God, please don't let me get lost... I don't know where I am... I need You. I know where Mike is... he is with You, but me... I'm lost..."

I stopped writing and let the grief roll through me as I prayed. Then I wrote:

> "12:07 PM. God just whispered to me "You're in The Rock." Yes. Yes. O God, I am in Your love and place of safety. We will go together through this dark place."

It was during this same period, just a couple of weeks at best into my grief journey, that God gave me a new visual of where I was and of what was happening to me. It was morning, and I had come out of my room, poured myself a cup of coffee and sat at the kitchen island on one of the bar stools. Grief was very heavy on me that morning. I had woken myself up crying.

I knew I had been grieving for about a year before Mike passed away. Now, I realized it had been anticipatory grief. This, without trying to be over dramatic, felt like I was the walking dead, unable to breathe in life.

I spoke to God at that moment as if He were next to me. I said, "I feel as dead as Mike. So, You might as well take me, too. I feel as if I am in a tomb."

As soon as I expressed those feelings, I heard God's loving correction in my spirit. He said, "You are not in a tomb. You are in a cocoon."

Instantly, my thoughts went back to those words from God that I had written down the last time I had attended church before Mike was put on hospice. Hope, like a shock wave, vibrated through me, and I immediately went to my journal to find them in their entirety.

As Mike's body had slowly shut down over the last four months, I had found strength and courage again and again by fully embracing the first sentence of that Word of encouragement God had given to me. Now I needed to understand this hiding place at a deeper level, and this message was going to show that to me in a profound way. Here is the full Word God gave me:

"Be strong and courageous... and hide in the cleft of the Rock, Christ Jesus.

Let it be as a cocoon. For it is a birthing place for your new calling to become anointed and to be given wings to fly! To fly high above the circumstances and to soar into My Presence for your daily renewal and divine charge to be given."

I was overwhelmed by God's personal interaction with me. I was at one of my lowest points, and God had just revolutionized my understanding of where I was! I was not in a tomb, but in a place of transformation, a changed identity and destiny, as a caterpillar within a cocoon.

A cocoon is small and dark inside. Once encased within the cocoon the caterpillar changes into a pupa. The pupa gives off digestive juices that are meant to destroy all but a few cells of the pupa. The pupa must feel as if it's dying. It is disintegrating as the cells change. But then, restructure begins as the few remaining cells begin to grow and multiply, feeding on the nutrients of what was once the larva. The timeframe for this process varies, but for each species, there is an appointed number of days.

This process, called metamorphosis, is a miracle in the making! Although change like that feels like death, it is birthing new life—a butterfly! When the appointed day arrives for this new creature to exit the cocoon, it will find it has wings to fly!

God had just given me a beautiful picture of how my days of sorrow would end. I was not in a tomb. I was in a *cocoon* of change. Okay, I could breathe now. I knew where I was. I didn't necessarily like it, but this revelation enabled me to see that this was part of God's First and Best Plan, and I spiritually understood that it was going to transform and position me for a new life. Somehow, at some point, God was going to reveal my new calling and with it, provide me with wings to fly. It put hope on the horizon, even though my heart could not begin to relate to the idea that a new day would dawn.

My church's women's retreat was held each October at Old Oak Ranch in Sonora, California. My daughter Stephanie and I were encouraged to come, and we were offered a special room with a private bath where we could be together, and feel a little more secluded in our time of grief.

We agreed to go, and though I felt much love during the weekend, it was difficult for me to be there. At past retreats, I was in leadership and often one of the speakers. I would look forward to praying with others and interacting one on one.

This year, instead of the welcome weight of God's Presence upon my heart, I felt that I brought with me the unwelcomed elephants that sat on my chest. Grief was all around me, and I was concerned that I was tainting the atmosphere with the heaviness of sorrow. I sat in the back and was unable to sing or even really grasp the flow of the messages. The women were wonderful, and a few looked for a right moment to speak sensitively to me about Mike. I ached to talk about him, and this gave an opportunity for needed expression.

At our retreats, we always found a Scripture on our pillow, along with a special little gift. Dianna Patterson would spend hours handwriting Scripture verses in beautiful calligraphy, and sometimes she would spend months making lovely handcrafted gifts for each woman to take home. This year she had crocheted each of us a scarf, and with them, she had bought beautiful pins for each of us. They were butterfly pins!

I asked Kristy Rego, my daughter's best friend, who is like another daughter to me, if she would pick one out for me. I wasn't up to feeling excited about much of anything, and I couldn't bring myself to go to the display table to choose one. She brought back a pin that had the wings similar to leopard print! It could not have been more perfect because of my zebra/leopard taste, and she knew it. It brought a smile to my face as she said to me, "This one is *you*!

I looked at that pin and was immediately reminded of being in the cocoon. How could I wear this pin as the other ladies would? I couldn't. I was *not* a butterfly. I was "disintegrating." So, instead, I conversed with God. I confirmed to Him that I knew I was in a cocoon of His choosing, and that I had no clue how long it would take for Him to change me into a butterfly with wings to fly. I continued my prayer by saying, "So, I am not going to wear this butterfly pin until You tell me to. When it's time to emerge from the cocoon, and I have wings to fly, then You tell me, and I'll put it on."

I took the pin home and put it on top of the decorative box on my bathroom counter. I looked at it every day. I would often state out loud just the two words, "One day." I knew that one day I would wear the pin, and I wondered who I would be on that far away day.

Getting ready to return to my room at the retreat, a dear friend, Linda Gaetke, came over to give me a hug. As she did, she prayed for me and said, "Sherri, God has much to say to you about your future, but right now your heart is too full of grief to hear it." Then I understood why I felt so out of place among so many friends, and it calmed me to know God was going to speak more to me. He was respectful, in love, holding His words as He gave precedence to my time of sorrow.

As we were about to part, Linnie, as her friends lovingly call her, whispered a beautiful truth in my ear. She said, "Grief is a tribute to the one we love and have lost. It is an expression of *your love* for Mike." Her words penetrated through my cocoon and went straight to my heart. It took all I had to hold back the deep groans fighting to be released. I would cry, but I would somehow manage to hold back the full release of what needed to come forth for a few more days when I would take my trip to the cabin where I would be alone. I will share that experience in another story.

I wrote this poem on November 15, 2007, just under two months after Mike's death and on the eve of what would have been our 33rd Wedding Anniversary:

CHANGE

A caterpillar I am – a butterfly to be?

How can this change possible take place in me?

A cocoon – A Rock – only darkness surrounds

In this place of death can transformation be found?

My mind and emotions long for the Light,

But my heart is alone in its darkest of nights.

Perhaps little by little, too small to see now

Hope will become wings, and then I'll know how.

Seeing grief as a tribute to Mike because of my love for him, not only gave purpose to my days spent in this inconsolable pain, but it also assigned a priceless value to my tears. There was now a strange beauty to this journey.

I would entrust the creation of my wings to God and to His ability to form them in the secret place. I knew I was in the early hours of what was going to be a long night. I would walk the journey looking for His promise that He had sent with confirmation, and I would surrender to the process with an even greater determination.

Story 33:
Intentional Grief

Intentional is not a word we might associate with grief. That is because no one would choose to be in a situation that resulted in great sorrow. But, once in that situation, what if we realized there was an advantage to heading straight out into the deep waters of grief, rather than lingering on the sidelines in shallow water?

The shallow edges may *feel* safer, but the danger of hopelessness lurks there. The waters need to be crossed. Fear of sorrow's pain and facing an unknown future has kept many missing out on God's individualized involvement. His interactions would be as paddles propelling us forward and His insights as our lifejacket protecting us in rough waters.

When I looked at my future, all I saw were question marks. I could not imagine my life on the other side of grief, but my main goal, my true desire in learning how to live without Mike was that I would gain an intentional life to be used for God and His purposes around me. I knew I needed to jump into the deep of grief and face my sorrow. I chose to go up to the cabin where I felt safe and would be alone to let my journey finally begin.

The cabin belongs to dear friends of both Mike's and mine. We met Bill and Barb Engvall somewhere around 1995 through the *Christian Motorcyclists Association* (CMA). They were riding with the Sierra Saints, a local chapter up in the foothills of our area and our respective chapters intermingled at various poker runs and CMA events.

By now Mike and I had been up Hwy 108 to their cabin several times. To this day our picture is on the refrigerator door along with many others who have visited there over the years. They use the cabin as a retreat type get-away for family, friends, and people in ministry.

Although the cabin is within a gated community, it looks exactly like what one would visualize when hearing the word "cabin." It is surrounded by tall pine trees. The sliding glass door in back leads out onto a large deck with table and chairs, and a barbecue pit.

Beyond the deck are the woodsy unfenced backyard, where you often see squirrels scampering about and various birds in the trees. There is even a small group of turkeys that roam the area. More often than not, you can hear a pin drop. Inside, the décor features bears, moose, and everything that screams "cabin." It has every imaginable convenience; all you need to bring is food and your personal items.

There is one noticeable thing that is lacking. There are no cable TV or internet service, *but that is on purpose.* The cabin it is meant for you to leave technology and your world of emails, texting, and Facebook, and retreat to the world of "yesteryear." There are a VCR/DVD player and six shelves full of family-friendly movies to choose from.

Nine shelves of books hold everything from novels and health books to study Bibles and concordances. There are comforters to snuggle up with and a front deck to enjoy the quiet of a summer morning. The cabin can be a hideaway of solitude, or it can pack in a larger group if some don't mind using a sleeping bag on the floor.

It has access to its own community lake, or with just a short drive, you can enjoy lakes in nearby little mountain towns. Bill and Barb never charged us when we came to stay, and they often blessed us with "Blue Money" to make our time there even more special.

Mike and I loved Bill and Barb as dear friends. I still do! They have true servants' hearts, and they still bring honor and beauty to that gifting in a multitude of ways. Barb has a gift of encouragement and uses it often by giving Scripture to others that turn out to be a perfect match for their need. Several times Barb wrote her notes with Scripture on behalf of her and Bill to both Mike and me and then, after Mike was gone, to me. Her notes were always as God saying, "I see you!" and her Scriptures as *"apples of gold in settings of silver,"* as described in Proverbs 25:11, NIV.

I always knew that their cabin would be the place I would want to be if God took Mike and I needed a place to grieve. I arranged to come the week after I got back from the women's retreat. I knew Jesus would meet me at the door and send angels to watch over me.

It was there that I had my first stop at "still waters" in beginning my journey through the "valley of the shadow of death." It was there, for three days, I felt safe and alone enough to allow the floodgate to open, and to release what I'd been holding back for at least 16 months.

Remembering that moment of release and the hours of agony that followed triggers emotions even now. Love was spilled out.

I brought with me items that I knew would easily open the double emotion of love and loss giving intentional opportunities for my tears. I brought pictures to help me process, journals to read, our Travelog Ministry Newsletter Binder that dated back to 1993, and even Mike's recent medical logs where I kept a record of his declining blood pressure and escalating fevers. I also brought the Memorial Book with all the signatures of those at his funeral, the sympathy cards I'd received so I could read them again, Mike's DVD picture tribute that was shown at his service, as well as his final message on DVD played as a surprise to everyone. And I went through every one of them.

I counted and verified those who had attended Mike's service. There were extra chairs brought in, and still, there was standing room only. There were 20 different secular biker clubs, including a few outlaw ones. There were, also, three distinct Christian motorcycle ministries and at least 12 *Christian Motorcyclists Association* chapters.

To review the names of the clubs and ministries, along with the scores of names of just family and personal friends, as well as all who came to His Place afterward to eat and celebrate Mike's life was like wrapping a warm comforter of love around my heart. I had made it a point to speak to every person. Mike would have done that if he could have been there.

I planned "sessions" of what I would look at, and how much I would cover in a day. It was during one of these intentional grief sessions that I did the calculations from the first day we met to the day Mike went to heaven. It was a total of 12,195 days spent together—241 "dating days," and the 11,947 days we were married.

There were just seven days from when we met to our first date, and then life took us on a 33-year journey, minus about three weeks. I wanted to have just one more day, to make it 12,196 days together, but I knew that, then, I would want just one more. I wept over my realization that there would be no more days.

By the time I left the cabin, I felt as if I had cried an ocean of tears, but knew I had, with courage, turned my ship's rudder to face head-on the black storm of grief. I survived what we all don't think we possibly could, because God was with me. He had made my time productive.

I returned to the cabin about a month later, but this time I made a choice to focus on heaven. I brought books and music CDs and felt they allowed me a glimpse into eternity. One book that brought joy was given to me by my mom. Although now out of print, it awakened my spirit to heaven as none I have ever read. The book is entitled "PARADISE, the Holy City, and the Glory of the Throne," by Rev. Elwood Scott. As I processed thoughts of Mike being in heaven, I felt as if I was standing behind a fence peeking through a knothole, privileged to view where Mike was *living*.

During that stay, Bill and Barb took me to dinner the evening of what would have been Mike's and my 33rd wedding anniversary. I like to think that perhaps Mike asked God to arrange that dinner together so rather than me being alone on that night, I would be with friends who would care for my heart with sweet friendship love.

I would return to the cabin several times over the next few years. I wrote "Grief as a Sea" during one of those first cabin stays. In fact, I wrote much of this book while at the cabin, and you are reading the fruit of my first intentional steps.

I could not have survived those initial deep waters without Jesus. How thankful I am that God did not leave me to wander aimlessly alone on the shore. He had a purpose and a goal in mind. His loving invitation to change me was intentional.

Grief as a Sea

The deep level of grief is extremely hard to live in;

Those moments when the waves come crashing over you.

You see it coming, and it's as if they swallow you.

You experience a sense of drowning—loss saturating every molecule of your being.

Sorrow fills your whole world, and all you can see is murky waters,

and you are sinking to the bottom.

The waves continue to crash over you— exhausting you as you cry,

and groan so deep no sound can be heard.

When you think you, too, will die in this sea of deep sorrow,

Jesus appears – walking on water with eyes of love, with arms of help and with a word to 'come.'

The waves subside—your heart responds to Him alone who has the power to comfort your grieving soul.

He is your peace, and as you lay your head upon His chest, the pulse of peace in His heartbeat somehow is transferred into yours.

And it calms your raging emotions.

He holds you for as long as you need to be there.

(1-16-08, Sherri Sumstine)

Story 34:
How to Empty the Cup of Grief

"Call to me, and I will answer you and tell you great and unsearchable things…" (Jeremiah 33:3 NIV). Whatever we need to know, and all that is in our heart that needs an answer, God wants to speak to us about. God loves to help us understand. His answers come as a revelation as if a "bell of truth" is rung in our spirits.

I saw my grief as a huge cup that was with me everywhere I went. It always filled the room. Whether the room I was in was small or large, the cup of grief stood from ceiling to floor and wall to wall. When I was outside, it filled as far as my eyes could see and reached to the clouds and beyond. I think you get the picture.

I had no choice, but to carry it with me. The sorrow and loss I experienced following the death of my husband were more difficult than anything I had experienced before. It weighed heavy on my heart and blocked my view of all normal life and activity going on around me.

I didn't want to go out much because the cup of grief would have to go too, and it was exhausting to carry it. I would look forward to going somewhere, but as the day and time to leave approached, I would feel overwhelming and painful apprehension that the cup would spill over while I was there.

Even when I did go, I often found I could stay only a short time. The grief would overpower me and mar any possible enjoyment I might have tried to receive from the event. I didn't have control over this cup and its contents. My life was radically changed, and I didn't know how I would ever be able to normally function.

One evening I was on the phone again with my friend, Cheryl McEachron. Our conversations, from the beginning of our friendship back in the early 80's until now, were 90% about God and our relationship with Him. We love it, and we love each other.

That night I had attempted to unload some of my grief to her on the phone. I told her that I felt detached from life, and was unable to concentrate on any Bible Study as had always been my practice. I described how I walked in a fog, and then shared my analogy of "the cup" to try to help her grasp the deep sadness and pervasive grief that was upon my whole being.

Cheryl was one I could be real with. She knew me at my best and my worst. She gently reminded me that God was with me and that if I didn't go through this part of grief, I would not be ready for what was next. She agreed that we would have wanted this cup to pass, but it didn't. So, as counsel to her friend, she encouraged me, in the best way she knew how to find a way to drain the cup.

Desperately wanting to accomplish this, I asked Cheryl how to drain the cup. She promised that as she prayed for me, she would pray for answers. As we hung up, I continued the conversation with God and asked Him my desperate question, "However do I empty this cup?"

His response was immediate. I heard Him answer in my spirit, "You have to drink it." And with His simple answer came the revelation of why. It's because the cup held precious content. I could not just dump it, as might be my first self-preservation tactic.

I instantly knew that to drink the cup meant that I was to fully process all the aspects and each of the multiple levels of my grief. I had to face my losses and allow God to bring me new promises. I could expect the taste to be salty and bittersweet, as my tears mixed with the years of love and memories Mike and I had together.

I also perceived that as I drank the contents, the cup would shrink in size, smaller and smaller as the disabling aspects of my grief were healed; causing the cup to become lighter and to demand fewer tears from me with time. Eventually, the cup would become small enough that I could set it inside my heart, where it would remain forever.

I remembered that Jesus had described his having to "drink a cup" in the Garden of Gethsemane. (Matthew 26:36-56) It was in great anguish that He asked His Father if this cup could pass from Him. It held the contents of His brutal death. His love for us won, and He drank His cup.

Jesus tried to share the grief and anguish of the cup that lay before Him with three of his closest disciples, but they could not grasp its magnitude. When we have a friend, who is in grief, it would be wise for us to pray and ask for understanding. I shared the revelation of my cup with my family and close friends, and it helped them to understand my grief, and became an effective way for me to let them know I was having a hard day. When someone would ask me how I was doing, I would simply say, "I'm drinking from the cup today." They understood without me having to explain.

Following the example of Jesus, I knew I must be willing to drink my cup. I drank of my cup for days and months to come, but I never drank alone. I always invited God's presence to come, and we shared many intimate conversations as we processed together.

Today, I consider myself on the other side of grief, and the cup now sits in my heart, as foretold. The cup that once filled every room and space no longer dominates my thoughts. But, there are certain times, important days and random ambush moments when, in great respect, I am compelled to stop and remember the taste of love and loss. It brings me sweet joy to remember Mike and the life we shared.

I have let go of pain, but I hold on to love. I have released sorrow, but retain memories of gold. My heart is aware of the cup's presence and feels honored to be its special hiding place. It's more of a resting place, where this small memorial is tucked away in wait for another tribute's call.

Story 35:
Holiday Survival Surprise

Celebrating the Holidays, as usual, is often overpowered when one is in grief. Our normal gatherings of Thanksgiving and Christmas celebrated with family and friends, now feel lonely and sad.

We feel robbed of our normal Christmas traditions. Instead of sending Christmas cards, we find ourselves handing out a "grief letter," to make others aware of our limitations during this season. We are invited to parties, but because of ambush tears, either we can't go, or we can't stay long. Lights and decorations are going up all around us, but their beauty is shadowed, and our excitement dulled.

While our friends bake sugar cookies, we try to process questions of life and loss, and the purpose of both. We are acutely aware that our personal world is tragically different. We feel as if we are standing outside in the cold, watching others through a closed window, who are safe and warm inside.

As grief pulls our focus to death and loss, we wonder if there is any source of joy to be found during the holidays. Yes, there is. If we can refocus more diligently than ever before on the "reason for the season," the birth of Jesus, we will find a hidden gift.

That gift is Jesus Himself. This baby would grow up to be the sin sacrifice for us all. His life would end in death, too, but His *resurrection would change everything*! It would give all of us who grieve *real hope* to see our loved ones again. Jesus, the Reason for the Christmas Season, promises us eternal life where death and tears are no more. Even for the griever, *that* is worth celebrating!

I could celebrate very little the holiday season of 2007. I was painfully distracted from the usual festivities of lights and parties during my first holiday season without Mike. I wasn't surprised that I was not looking forward to Thanksgiving or Christmas Day. I knew that even once I got through both of them, I still had to face, what was to me, the hardest holiday of all: New Year's Eve.

Thanksgiving arrived, and our family gathering was at the home of my brother and sister-in-law, Stan and Karen Smith. Karen always goes above and beyond to have their home decorated beautifully, and the table setting is always perfect for the occasion. That day was no different.

My heart was thankful for God's faithfulness to me, and I was trying to focus on His promise that one day there would be no more tears. But, I wondered during our meal and throughout the entire day if anyone could hear my constant silent calling out of Mike's name.

I would purposefully refocus my thoughts heavenward over and over. I was practicing my hope. The pendulum would balance out in time, but I savored those moments when it swung to heaven's side, and my heart found relief in the promise that the birth of Jesus brought.

On Christmas Eve Day, my son, Mike arrived, driving down from Fort Bragg, California. My daughter, Stephanie, and Mike planned for us all to go to dinner together so I would not be alone. Our dinner was enjoyable, yet I was very aware of the unusual setting for this special night and that the usual life of the party was starkly missing.

When we finished eating, with our blessing Stephanie excused herself to spend the rest of the evening with her boyfriend, Larry Haley. We knew they wanted to have some special time together to exchange gifts.

My son couldn't hold in his news, even for two minutes, after she left. He proudly shared with me that Larry had asked him for his sister's hand in marriage and that a proposal was pending! I loved that Larry followed the "old fashioned" custom and I was ecstatic at what was about to unfold for them!

I joined in to celebrate with my son at the honor he was given to say "Yes" to Larry, while at the same time holding back a huge wave of grief from washing over me. Her father should have been giving her away. I waited to be alone to weep. I grieved for his loss in missing this once in a lifetime opportunity to be the one to give Larry and Stephanie his blessing. And, I grieved for Stephanie who would have to feel the loss of realizing her daddy was not there for Larry to ask.

Sure enough, Stephanie called later that night to announce to her brother and me that she was engaged! Larry had given her a beautiful diamond ring! I could not have been happier! Marriage would be a greater commitment to them than most because of Larry's life in a wheelchair after a trampoline accident when he was 16 years old, but I knew this union was of God's design. God had assured me from His Word, early in their relationship, that theirs was a Joseph and Mary story. There was a divine element in their God-arranged relationship. It would be lived out before others, their story written in blue, as they faced uniquely difficult circumstances with ever-increasing faith.

On Christmas Day, I was drawn to stay close to my mom. This was her fourth Christmas without her sweetheart, my dad, who passed away in September 2004; and my instinct knew she understood my loss. Though she was 89 and frail and I was 56, I felt like her little girl, and I needed the comfort and strength that I felt coming from her. Just the year before she had given comfort to my sister Carole, who lost her husband unexpectedly on September 28, 2006.

Now, mom would comfort her second daughter. There we were; three widows, each almost one year after the other. Death kept shrinking our family. And we had no idea this would-be our mom's last Christmas with us.

It was awesome for Stephanie and Larry to make their engagement announcement just before we sat down for our Christmas dinner. We were all thrilled and welcomed Larry into the family with love and open arms! I shared with Karen later that for the past few years our highs of His Place's progress always came with our lows of Mike's poor health, and all the "what ifs."

But, today, the low of Christmas and life without Mike blended with the high of Stephanie and Larry's engagement. I was so grateful for the wedding planning, and preparations that I knew would soften the hard year that lay ahead.

We enjoyed our Christmas Day together as a family and because of so much loss over the past few years I think we were a little more mindful of life and the value of family love.

As our day drew to a close, Karen, out of concern for me, asked about my New Year's Eve plans. I began to give her my answer, but was interrupted by my tears. I braced myself to keep from being carried away by the undertow of unexpected grief. I managed to regain my composure quickly, apologized though no one expected it, and told her that, by my choice, I would be alone that night.

As New Year's Eve approached, it was almost as if I was on the countdown to doomsday. New Year's Eve represented not only facing the coming New Year without Mike, but it also meant me facing my future without him. Unknown to me, God already had His pen out and was going to add a remarkable "blue story" to alter my perception of what this was going to look like.

The day before New Year's Eve, the Lord spoke to me as I made up a grocery list for the week ahead. He said, "Be sure you have grape juice and bread on hand." Then He added, "We're going to have communion tomorrow at midnight." I was completely caught off guard and felt a quiet excitement sweep through me. I knew I had just been personally invited to a New Year's Eve with a featured event!

The afternoon of New Year's Eve I began to wonder what cup I would use to take communion in that evening. I went to my small china hutch to see if I had something there to use. I heard God say, "I want you to use one of those" as my eyes fell on our 25-year Wedding Anniversary goblets. Mike and I had used those at our vow renewal celebration where we had toasted our future with sparkling cider. Now they sat, side by side, on a silver tray as a glass monument to our broken dreams.

As I remembered that special anniversary day, my heart was flooded with memories. I would have never had reason to use those glasses again, but God specifically chose them for our night of new beginnings. I felt anticipation bubble up. My dread had been that I would drown in my tears that night, but God had a rescue plan in place.

On New Year's Eve, I started my countdown to midnight with prayer and then I went out to my His Place office where I looked at countless pictures stored on my computer. Photographs were always a grief release for me. Your images give a tribute to yesterday, as they tell you that today is different. I played Mike's "I know you thought you heard the last of me" memorial DVD to hear his voice, and to allow his perspective to help me get through the night. There were tears, but I was pacing myself and watching the clock.

I came in from my office to my room and sat in my special chair, the chair where God and I often met. I read the Bible's three different gospel accounts of The Lord's Supper. I loved the one from John 13 through 16 the most.

I especially noted John 16:12-13a; 16:22 NIV spoken by Jesus after that first Communion He shared with His disciples:

> "I have much more to say to you, more than you can now bear. But when He, the Spirit of Truth, comes, he will guide you into all truth.... Now is your time of grief, but I will see you again, and you will rejoice, and no one will take away your joy."

Those were the very words the Lord spoke to me at our women's retreat! A strong presence of His peace filled my heart, and I knew, as I read them that night, they were especially for me. The Holy Spirit of Truth was confirming that He would, in time, tell me all I needed to know about what was to come for His Place and for me.

At 11:57 PM I put in a CD on which my sister had recorded specific songs. I set it to play the song "Wish You Were Here," by the Kingsmen Quartet; and then I listened as if Mike were singing to me.

Just as the clock turned twelve midnight, the music transitioned to playing what had become one of my favorite songs, "My God and King" by Terry MacAlmon. I took communion savoring the meaning of the bread and juice.

As the song continued to play, and I had finished communion, I heard the Lord say, "Now, shall we dance?" As I stood to "take His hand," which I knew was extended to me, I stepped into one of the most real experiences of my lifetime. The lyrics played softly:

My God and King

To You alone, I sing

You're the face I seek

For all eternity

You'd be my dream come true

Just to be with You

How I'd see brand new

With eyes for only You

My God and King

Through the storm, I sing

Covered by Your wing

This song of love I bring

You are my dream come true

Just to be with you

Now I see brand new

With eyes for only You

I closed my eyes, and my feet began to move, as being led in a divine dance. My heart felt the closeness of One greater than I. We moved gracefully in a small circle as if on a cloud, and I was enthralled in holy romance dancing with my King. At that moment, I realized *He* was my dream come true, and I was His.

I was astonished at how the evening was brought to a special climax. What had been full of sorrow, became an incredible night. I reflected on the featured event of communion. What a gift! The bread represented the body of Jesus that was given for us, and the cup represented our covenant in His blood. Both made all things new for mankind.

I felt joy in knowing Mike's sin was paid for and he was with Jesus in heaven that very New Year's Eve. New life had already dawned for him. Then I saw it! There it was— grace and the promise of a new life for me, too.

I *experienced* the reality of holy moments with God who took my dread of the future and added hope into my 25th Anniversary Cup. He had transformed it into a communion cup of promise. I knew Mike's future. I knew God knew mine! It was as if we had shared our toast to that tomorrow.

I still had a long journey ahead of me, but I could say "Happy New Year to 2008." I didn't yet know any real details of how, but by faith and because of God's personal visit with me that night, I knew there was a blue-filled future I could look forward to celebrating.

Story 36:
Back to the Chapel

Direction to some seems to be inborn like that of a homing pigeon, but that would not be me. I say with a chuckle that I am directionally dysfunctional, and so I do not go very far out of my comfort zone without accessing Sofia. Sofia is the name given to my GPS, and it means wisdom or wise. Sofia tells me the name of the street to correctly make my next turn. I trust her tracking, and even if I've driven for a while in a travel daze, all I do is press Sofia's VOICE button. She will announce how far away I am, and reestablish my bearings.

A grief journey needs wisdom as well. There is no higher authority to listen to, and to follow than God's Holy Spirit. We should want Him to be our travel guide and companion. He is the VOICE of truth that will direct us to our next destination with accuracy. He will tell us when it's time to make a turn.

It had been seven months into my grief journey, but it seemed like an eternity. They had been long and difficult months emotionally for me. One evening at our Women of Light Bible Study Group, my friend, Linda Gaetke, asked me how I was doing and if things seemed to be any easier. I answered her honestly by saying, "No, *not at all.*" I shared freely with Linda that I still felt just as depressed as I had at the beginning. I told her that every day I waited for evening, so I could shut myself in my room where I would grieve and pour out my pain to the Lord.

I expected my friend to offer me her sympathy and perhaps offer to pray for me, but her response was, "Oh, Sherri, you are giving Mike such a *beautiful* tribute!" I was taken back by her insight. What she saw was my love for Mike. She understood and by her choice of words, validated that my heart had to express in its entirety the loss it had experienced. There was no calendar time, period.

Too many times well-meaning people want us to just get over it. We feel pressured to move on, and so we stuff the sorrow, not realizing that because our tribute is incomplete, it will eventually pop up later in our life. The tribute of honor needs to be given permission and encouraged to be expressed in whole before moving on to the next phase of grief. Though I wanted it to be over, I knew to hold steady and ask God for His direction.

The book, "Through A Season of Grief" by Bill Dunn and Kathy Leonard was my main resource for the first two years of my grief journey. I used it daily as a devotional and as a "mini journal, " and I would date my short remarks on each page to keep a log of my thoughts and progress.

I flipped back and forth through the pages never reading in sequence, but always searching for the topic that seemed "written in blue," perfectly written for me in that struggling moment. I read them over and over allowing their healing balm to be applied to my open wounds. One of the writings shared about taking a determined step forward to *let go* of what was now the past. God began to prepare my heart to make my first big step.

I knew what the first "let-go" would be. It would be a symbolic gesture of letting go of Mike's hand. I had been holding Mike's hand from our first date to his last day here on earth. Throughout our marriage, we held hands like we were teenagers, anytime and anyplace. In my heart, I was still holding it with all my might. However, I knew if I was going to heal, the time was coming when I must let go.

God gently brought it up several times over a period of a few weeks. At first, I couldn't even discuss it. To do so brought me deep grief. I believe God understood the tearing that was going on inside of me, and He was patient with me to come into that agreement with Him. I knew I needed to do it. However, I did not know how, nor did I want to. It felt dishonoring and disloyal.

I opened my journal and began writing to process my emotions. I had no idea that on the pages of my journal God was about to give me a golden "blue opportunity." It was as if He put His hand over mine with both of us now holding my pen. Through my journaling, He took me back to a long-ago memory, to a familiar place where He would now help me to let go of what He had, then, put in my hand to hold. This new vision would ask for the answer to a very big question.

April 22, 2008, Journal Entry

"I just took the ring that Mike gave me at our 25th Wedding Anniversary celebration off my left hand and put it on my right. I don't know why. Maybe this symbol of love and marriage relocated will help me process the pain I'm feeling in knowing I must let go of Mike.

I've been so emotional this evening feeling anger at needing to face this next step and realizing how easily it could lead to bitterness. I don't know how to let go and receive the healing and the new.

Prayer: O My Father, You are my hope. I don't see how, but by some way, unknown to me, my life will become new and good again. You see my tears and how my sorrow rejects those words "letting go," but I speak now out of my spirit: Enable me by Your grace to do what, to me, is not only not desired, but not possible. I can do anything through Christ who strengthens me. I can. I will let go by that strength. I want to want to. Help me, please.

It has been a hard "grief session" tonight, but I feel calm and that God has tended to my heart.

Today I give Mike to God. I know he is already with Him, but I need to say it:

Father, I give my beloved, my husband to You. The vision You gave me so many years ago—the wedding setting—when the minister asked, 'And who gives this woman to be married (joined) to this man?' I looked at who I believed was my father, but then I saw that it was You, my Heavenly Father, and You said, 'I do.' You put my hand in Mike's, and it's been there ever since!" (Reference Story "A Supernatural White Wedding")

Then, there it was: God's divine opportunity! Suddenly, I was very aware that God had entered my prayer and He was taking me back to the place of another holy experience so many years ago. I continued with my prayer journaling:

"Father, tonight I see Mike and I standing again in that same chapel. It is another wedding setting, but this time, looking directly at me, *You* ask, "And who gives this man to be united back to His Creator and His God?" And I see that I am to give the answer…"

A lifetime of love and marriage memories flashed through my mind. I immediately discerned that God had prepared this opportunity for me to "let go" by simply answering "I do." Every cell in my body ached with the knowledge that when I did answer, my words and God's power would unclasp our hands and release Mike from me. But, I knew this was God's time, and if I took it, a transition would happen on my journey.

I continued interacting in this holy transaction through my journaling:

> "...and so (*I took a deep breath*) I put Mike's hand in Your hand and say, *'I do,'* as... I... let... go...
>
> Though it will always be cherished, let the soul tie be loosened and broken.
>
> I believe it has begun."

Our wedding vows stated, "Until death do you part." The literal day of parting had already come, but that night, almost seven months to the day, the seal on our vows was removed in my soul.

The *very next day* I felt the profound impact of my experience the night before. The heavy deep grieving I had for seven months had lifted. Not that I never cried again, but I never returned to that place of prolonged despair.

God had visited me in my struggle and asked a question, knowing it would be one of the hardest I would ever have to answer. He helped me face what must be done and then He gave me strength to follow through. I took a sharp upward turn in "the valley of the shadow of death." God could now begin to heal my broken heart. I felt growth in my cocoon.

I didn't know then that this would only be the first of *many* "let-goes." This phase would take the longest on my journey, but, as I purposed to travel forward, I would learn that my course was already set by the One who would order every step.

I would struggle deeply in what I yet had to release, often confusing letting go with disloyalty to Mike. I constantly listened to God's voice. More than once, as He did in this story, God came in an amazing visitation. He influenced my choices and circumstances with His Word that would be a light to my path, and with His trusted voice to give me clarification. He would teach me how to live in today, instead of leaving me in my unproductive attempt to hold on to yesterday.

His plan was to deliver me safe and sound to my new destination. My plan was, at all cost, to trust His voice and follow His direction.

Story 37:
Identity Clarity

Identity speaks to the core of who we perceive ourselves to be. And, at the core, our true identity can only be found when we are spiritually born again and adopted into the family of God. It's there that we become our Heavenly Father's sons and daughters. That identity fully completes us, and it can never, ever be taken away against our will.

With that real identity firmly in place, there are other positions in our everyday life that seem to suit us perfectly and help to give us a place to function in this world. We feel secure within our labels of being identified with a certain sports team, a business organization that provides growth into a career, and even cherished roles as a spouse or parent. But, what happens when one of our life's titles is suddenly gone? It can invoke a major makeover process.

Though it will often take time, if we can hold tightly to the Father and embrace faith, we will discover that God has a new charge to give us, and though it won't replace the loss, it will, once again, be a perfect fit.

One day in late May 2008, I stopped by my Pastor's home to take them a Reliv Nutrition order. This quick stop became a two-hour divine appointment as Pastors Dick and Edie both, first separately and then together, shared a matter with me they felt was from God's heart.

They both expressed the deep love they always had for Mike. I had no question about that. They were present as God had redeemed our lives and called us together into biker ministry. They lovingly prefaced what they wanted to share with the statement, "Upon Mike's death God's purpose for him on earth was obviously completed, but you are still here, so God yet has a purpose and plan for *your* life." What was so strongly in their heart that afternoon to share with me was that they felt God wanted to move me forward by taking me back, back to where I was in His plan before I met Mike.

Pastor Dick said that God used all my life with Mike to shape and mold me—nothing was wasted—but he felt that my new identity would be traceable *back* to His original plan for me, which was in His heart from the beginning. Pastor Dick and Edie said that His Place must now come under *my* vision. I should no longer feel bound to what had been Mike's.

Pastor Dick restated the fact that years ago I had yielded to Mikes' vision. It was true. I gave up my desires in ministry to the deaf to answer God's to join Mike in biker ministry. His Place was 100% Mike's God-given vision to be used as *Mike's* platform to spread the gospel to bikers.

Our conversation took on a prophetic tone as my Pastors shared that God wanted to give me my own vision. We talked a little bit about that, and I shared how as a young woman I felt called to the nations as a missionary; to Africa in particular. The prophetic voice continued as one bringing me a Word from the Lord to give me permission to make changes and to catch a glimpse of who I was now, of who I would *become*.

I realized I *had* been trying to function out of Mike's vision, under his call, and on his platform. Doing so was like David in the Bible trying to wear Saul's armor to go out and defeat the giant Goliath. The armor didn't fit. David recognized he could not function under the King's plan.

I was trying to wear Mike's armor. It was heavy, and the weight of it took all my energy. I was trying so hard to honor Mike, but the vision he had for His Place was not a fit for me at all. I was a biker because he was a biker and God had called me to join in with his calling. I was not going to buy a motorcycle and ride. I felt a fresh wave of grief wash over me, yet it also seemed to wash away the denial that the vision must change.

What was *my* vision? What was *God's* vision for me now that Mike was gone? What was God's vision for His Place, and how would I lead it to a new purpose in this new season?

This discussion initiated a long heart-wrenching search to find God's answer to these questions. I hadn't recognized yet that this letting go was a phase of its own on my grief journey, and it would encompass many areas.

I felt as if I had been standing guard over Mike's His Place vision. Now in a similar way, as when I let go of Mike's hand, I was to let go of Mike's long-standing dream that he and I had shared together. God had been preparing my heart to remove the guard that was protecting the vision of the past.

301

I prayed, "Father I step out from under Mike's vision and trying to fit into his calling." Though I didn't know anything about what the new vision was to look like, I knew it would be different.

I took this release very seriously and was acutely aware of the weight of my new responsibility for His Place. I felt, now, like a single parent watching over this "child." It was mine to protect, with God's help, of course. I would wake up mornings with my spirit crying out for God's plan. In one of those times, I felt God quiet my heart and say, "It will be a process, and for now you are to wait. Just wait." That was not the clear answer I was wanting, and I can't tell you how many times I would run back to God asking again only to hear Him repeat that instruction. Waiting is difficult, but I would trust that there was a reason for the wait.

God's reason, at large, was about my need to heal, but it also was about overall timing. It was His love and mercy to give me time to make my way through the dark, winding roads of grief while He was preparing others to cross my path at His choice moments in my future.

I came to understand that waiting takes strength and that it is not a sign of indecision, as some might presume. When waiting is obedience, it is a sign of faith. If I had faith, which was the one thing I knew I possessed, then in God's time, all would be well.

It had not even been a year since Mike was gone. I was in a very slow turning curve on my road of life. I still missed him with all my heart. God was giving me much grace and no demands. He knew I had to process every small change and every new decision after filtering it through a grief sieve. Was this thought grief talk, or was this God? Was a particular opportunity being taken in a grief reaction or was it God's new road? This was all hard, but normal "grief work."

In my prayer time one afternoon I felt at some point in the future that God might lead me back to the deaf community, and to the place where He asked me to lay down my dream to serve them... that He might again give me eyes to hear and hands to speak, a silent voice to a people He had put in my heart to love because He loves them. I even wrote it in my journal. If not, there would always be a prayer in my heart for them.

I did not know what surprises God might yet have in store when my road straightened, and my eyes adjusted to seeing life in a different light. He is the God of change. Where I was, was not where I would always be. Yesterday, God had given me the adventure to be a biker. Today He was giving me the grace to take it one day at a time. My heart believed God had already written a beautiful new story for me. It would have His blue signature color all the way through and was just waiting for me to be ready.

I wondered what my new assignment would be and how He would unfold it to me. One thing I knew, my arm was in His, and He would walk me into my new season. He would hold the door open, and I would step across the threshold. I would still be me, but a modified version. Though my days would play out differently, all would see one strong similarity: God was my forever identity.

Story 38:
Enlarge Your Tent

Goals remind us that we are actively participating in a planned endeavor, which will take time to accomplish. In my heart, I knew that from the beginning of my grief journey I was continuing to adamantly pursue one goal for one purpose: a healed heart so I could be active and effective again in service for the Kingdom of God.

God has planned goals for us as well, and to effectively share them, He often communicates with us in a variety of ways. He spoke in parables to His disciples. He uses visuals and graphics to make it easier for us to grasp a truth that He sees vital to our understanding of healing and recovery.

He loves to use His Word, the Bible, to reveal a new vision that He wants to birth in our hearts for our future. He sometimes employs symbolism to represent a process He is taking us through. He often chooses something tangible to express the intangible truths of hope and promise.

I do not know how I could have managed at His Place for those first two years Mike was gone without Kevin Woods. He and his wife, Serina, moved on site in their 5th wheel for about a year as we began the search for God's heart for His Place.

After I had experienced God's release from trying to function under Mike's vision, I felt the Lord tell me it was time

305

for Kevin to move into what would have been Mike's office at His Place. I had already appointed Kevin as Director of Biker Care and Food Ministry, but he was working at a desk out in the food room. Up to that point, I just couldn't allow him to use Mike's office.

Unknown to me, I was beginning to make it a shrine, and God did not want that false holy place in my heart. I understood, for a season, it had to be grieved, but to keep his office untouched for too long would become unhealthy grieving and would stunt my growth within the cocoon of change that God had me in. Kevin being there would become a daily visual to us both that Mike was not here to lead us anymore, but the most important One was our Father in heaven. We were asking for His Place and His will.

It had been a while since I had attended any of our biker events because I hadn't been able to bring myself to go without Mike. Then, there was the real issue of my not feeling comfortable to go to the hard-core club events alone. I was concerned with what was happening now with the spiritual seed Mike and I had planted in so many biker hearts over the years.

One day while at a prayer time in Sacramento, God specifically comforted my heart as He addressed this issue through a young man, who came to me and said, "You are *not* to worry over the seed that you and your late husband planted. It is *His* seed, and He will watch over His seed."

I felt a mixture of relief and sorrow. I loved that God reassured me that He would send others to work in the fields of their hearts. I felt sorrowful because I realized that after years of labor I would no longer be engaged in "front line" duty with our bikers. I knew that God was ordering my steps. I had to trust it would one day all make sense.

On August 15th, 2008 after a morning of glory in prayer and God's Word, I heard the Lord tell me to drive to my mom's house in Stockton. I was to have her pray for me and spiritually impart to me her call of prayer and intercession. This impartation was the first place my spirit affirmed a connection with my new emerging identity. I was awed to realize that a spiritual mantel was being handed down. It was God inspired and a precious mother-daughter experience that I will forever cherish.

I would soon realize that it was precisely timed. This impartation was one generation passing the baton to the next. It was my turn to run in prayer. Only God knew that my mom had six weeks left of life on this earth. In my journal that day I wrote: Time will reveal that this *is* the stepping into the "new."

My "new" emphasis on prayer was expanded on my birthday in September 2008. My heart-friend, Cheryl McEachron, gave me a very special birthday card. First, the Lord had instructed her to include in the card a $100 bill with a Word from Him to me that said: "Tell her, I will take care of her."

When she delivered those words, my mind went to two places at once. It raced back in time to how, with a $100 bill, God had confirmed that He would take care of me if I would quit my job with the deaf students, and join Mike in biker ministry. I also remembered the stash Mike always hid in his wallet, that $100 bill, that he would pull out to bless me with a cute outfit or piece of jewelry that had caught my eye.

God had given me "blue money" in that birthday card, and I heard His promise of a Husband's provision.

To add to the visual promise, written in the card was a Scripture that would prove to be a prophetic Scripture for me. God had spoken it to Cheryl right after Mike passed away, but she had been waiting for God to release her to give it to me. The scripture was Isaiah 54:1-5 (NIV):

> *"Sing, O barren woman, you who never bore a child; burst into song, shout for joy, you who were never in labor; because more are the children of the desolate woman than of her who has a husband," says the LORD.*
>
> *Enlarge the place of your tent, stretch your tent curtains wide, do not hold back; lengthen your cords, strengthen your stakes. For you will spread out to the right and the left; your descendants will dispossess nations and settle in their desolate cities.*
>
> *Do not be afraid; you will not be put to shame. Do not fear disgrace; you will not be humiliated. You will forget the shame of your youth and remember no more the reproach of your widowhood.*

For your Maker is your husband – the LORD Almighty is his name—the Holy One of Israel is your Redeemer; he is called the God of all the earth."

My spirit validated it as another connecting piece to God's plan for me and the nations. As my mom's impartation affirmed a prayer assignment, this Scripture gave insight into my destiny. At that point, I was still in the cocoon, and I knew it, but to receive these glimpses of where God was taking me brought excitement and wonder.

This year was playing out to be a mixture of emotions. There was sorrow for Mike, the expectation of new promise for my future, and great joy as we planned my daughter's wedding. Laced in with our loss, there had been bridal shows and showers. God's blue money enabled me to dress the bride in her gorgeous gown, lovely veil and perfect shoes.

I had given Stephanie the $100 bill I found tucked away in Mike's wallet in a special presentation done in front of her bridesmaids. I shared how happy her dad would be, knowing that his secret stash would be used as his last gift to her to pay for her wedding day jewelry. Larry's parents had enabled them to plan for a dream come true fairy tale wedding. My son, Mike, was honored to be asked to walk his sister down the aisle in her dad's place. Mike's leather motorcycle jacket would be displayed in the seat next to me. It would be a visual memorial to her father who would be missing on the most special day in her life, and it would announce him as still very much present in our thoughts and her heart.

As the wedding approached at only three weeks away, on September 24, 2008, the eve of the one-year anniversary of Mike's passing; my mom was diagnosed with end stage liver cancer, and we brought her into my home to be put on hospice care. I wondered how we could celebrate a wedding with this unexpected shadow of death now hanging over our joy.

Everyone was shocked at my mom's fast declining health. That next day, the Bible Study group that she still led every week came and circled her in the tightest possible way so to be as close to her as possible. She spoke encouragement and hope to each of them! Two days later she couldn't sign her check at the hairdressers. That evening she missed Stephanie's bridal shower that she had looked forward to attending.

I began to wonder if her body was shutting down so quickly because of the medication changes we had agreed to. The next morning, I cried out to the Lord about my concern that it was my fault in allowing those changes. His voice broke in to stop my lament. With a soft tone of great love to express His deep longing for her, He spoke into my spirit and said, "Stop. This is her *time*. Let *My bride*, come to *Me!*"

God chose to speak to me in "wedding terms" to reveal what was going on from His perspective, knowing we would immediately relate. Just as Larry was ready and waiting with great anticipation for Stephanie to be his bride, so it was with Jesus for my mom. Neither He nor Larry wanted to delay one more day than necessary the event that would bring their bride to them.

Mom's lifetime here was complete and her eternal life ready to begin! This fresh word from heaven gave us all peace beyond explanation. It gave us an understanding and a visual of two weddings that were about to take place: grandmother and granddaughter would both soon be dressing in white wedding gowns.

It was only six days from my mom's hospital release to her heavenly wedding reception. She entered eternity and the arms of Love in the early morning hours of October 1, 2008. This could have been sorrow upon sorrow here, with enough tears to ruin a wedding day, but God's amazing grace put a special banner of His love over the next three weeks. There was time for her funeral service and with two weeks left to let our hearts fill back up with joy for a bride and groom, whom the Lord wanted to join for a lifetime here on earth.

On October 25, 2008, we all held our breath as a stunning bride, dressed in pure white, was escorted across the garden lawn to her waiting groom! We beheld on their faces the future glory of our eternity with Christ, the one that her grandmother had just entered. We watched God display heaven's view of *holy* matrimony through Stephanie's and Larry's Wedding Day.

It was another "perfect day" as I remembered to wrap my sorrow of Mike's absence in God's grace, and set it outside this day's story. I chose to allow the power of love to overrule the evidence of a missing father and now a missing grandmother as well. I chose to feel the pure joy of a new "son" gained. I wanted to remember my daughter's wedding day as one without blemish. And I do.

I had already made the decision to remove my wedding band on that night of Stephanie and Larry's wedding. I had transferred my 25th-anniversary ring to my right hand six months prior, and when I had let go of Mike's hand at the chapel visitation, the seal on our vows had been removed in my soul.

I knew, to continue my progress of healing, it was time to permanently take off my wedding band, the symbol of our vows spoken 34 years before.

This is a personal choice for each person following the death of their spouse. I had decided I would continue to wear my wedding band for a full year in honor of Mike and our life together. I chose my daughter's wedding night for a couple of reasons.

First, I wanted to wear it for the wedding itself. I wanted the ring on my finger to represent Mike and me together as her parents one last time. Second, I liked the symbolic picture: Stephanie putting her wedding band on as a commitment to a new life beginning with Larry, and me taking mine off. My vow to Mike of "To have and to hold from this day forward, for better, for worse, for richer, for poorer, in sickness and health, 'til death do us part" had been fulfilled.

When I got home, there in my room with my Mother-of-the-Bride dress still on, I repeated the words out loud, "Til death do us part" as I removed my ring and said, "It is finished. I'm not married anymore. I am a widow. I am single now." Then came my tears in a brief tribute to say goodbye to a 33-year marriage that had been made beautiful by the love we were able to give each other and because we had embraced the love God gave us.

My "letting-go process" was developing a pattern. A particular issue would rise to the forefront, and God would give me time to process it. When I could make my decision to follow through and "let go," I would immediately feel the release. But then, a few days or a week down the road, I would always stop and look back at what I had let go of. I would have to strongly resist the urge to pick it up again. I knew if I did, I would only have temporary comfort and then I would have to release it all over again.

Once I made my decision final to move forward, God could begin preparing my heart for the next release. I knew that every letting go brought me closer to crossing the finish line and reaching my destination of "acceptance" on my journey from the past to what was still my future.

As the holiday season of 2008 was coming to an end, I wanted to continue with what God had started the year before: communion at midnight on New Year's Eve. This year, as I was grieving the death of my mom, as well, I felt to use one of the tea cups that were given to her and my dad on their actual wedding day of June 11, 1949. It was a 59-year-old cup, beautifully designed, that would represent my mom in her new life, and what I'd spiritually inherited from her.

In early January 2009, I felt impressed to apply for a passport. The prompting alone excited me as I thought about the possibility of one day taking a trip to a faraway land.

Our *Christian Motorcyclists Association's* Regional Evangelists, Joe, and Judy Maxwell came by for a surprise visit. They wanted to ask me to accept the role of "Women's Ministry Advisor" in their five-state region. I still had many friends in the Association and was thankful that they were pulling me in and giving me a place. When I told Judy that I had applied for my passport her eyes lit up, and she began listing off some mission trips CMA was doing.

In the spring of 2009, I received a call from Donnie Henderson, a dear friend. She and her late husband, Wayne, had been our CMA Regional Evangelist before Joe and Judy. She had continued to serve God through taking teams of women on mission trips. She asked if I would join her team to Nicaragua that September. I was ecstatic! God did have a plan to use my passport!

The year continued to bring more change. My Pastors, Dick and Edie Patterson, retired in June of 2009 and their grandson, Jason McEachron, would step into the role of pastor. Jeff and Cheryl McEachron, co-pastors with her parents, would resign to give way to the new vision their son had for the church. Though not directly related to my grief journey, this brought on another major "letting go" as I said goodbye to their almost 30 years of pastoral leadership and the one major component in my life that had remained the same.

My brother-in-law, Ted, called the evening of July 18th, 2009 and after our conversation, he prayed for me. In his prayer quoted Psalm 2:8:

"Ask of me, and I will give you the nations for your inheritance..."

After his prayer, he said, "By the way, that Scripture was a word from the Lord for you!" After he had hung up, I felt the Lord say to me, "I'm going to send you on your feet, where your mom went on her knees." I would not share this with anyone for a while because I did not want to sound like

I was grandiose, though it would prove to be a true word and another piece of my new life puzzle.

That year the Lord also opened doors for me to speak at two different women's retreats in early October. I was looking forward to my upcoming mission trip and now these two retreats; one for a group in Washington State and the second one in Utah. I began to pray that God would grant me confidence and effectiveness in His Kingdom in each of these three events.

One afternoon, I was praying while driving and I wondered aloud to the Lord if He might tell me that it would be time for me to wear my butterfly pin by the time I spoke at the CMA Women's Conference in Utah. He immediately responded to me, "No, you are to wear your butterfly pin to Nicaragua!" I think I gasped at this word, then inwardly screamed with joy!

Remember that butterfly pin? (Read my story entitled *The Miracle of Metamorphosis*.) I had been given this pin at a women's retreat shortly after Mike passed away. I knew that God gave me this pin as my symbol of hope. When I felt I was in a tomb with Mike, the Lord had sent a word of promise that it was not a tomb, but a cocoon where my new calling and gifting would be given wings to fly!

I had looked at that hope every day for almost two years. To wear this pin would mean I had made it through metamorphosis, and that I now *had* wings to fly! It would mean that I had emerged from my cocoon, a butterfly! I could not have imagined back then what I would be doing the day

I was told to put on that butterfly pin! As I put it on that morning of September 4, 2009, I felt ecstasy! I was wearing my pin as I was leaving on an airplane to *fly* to Nicaragua!

As the plane took off at 6:20 AM I looked across the aisle and out the window. We were ascending upward, and I caught a glimpse of the huge morning sun just beginning to rise over the eastern horizon. I heard God's voice declare to me, "Your new day has dawned!"

It took everything in me not to break down in sobs. I sat there trying to absorb the reality that I was heading for my first time to a foreign land… short term, but as *a missionary*. I was seeing the fulfillment of "enlarging the place of my tent (heart) and stretching my curtain wide."

I received some beautiful words of affirmation from my team members after I spoke to the women in Nicaragua. One of them said to me, "I see you as a good partner to Donnie, being mentored by her. You bring a calming presence to our team. You are capable of being a leader yourself. We see you as confident, lovely, and in charge!"

That was more than a compliment. It was confirmation that this was God's direction to pursue. The day I arrived back home, I received a call from a friend who asked if he could come by. When he did, he wrote me a check for $1,000 toward my next mission trip, wherever that might be!

This was just the beginning! God was going to provide for me over and over again! This first blue mission money was ten times the $100 in that birthday card promise. God was making His point loud and clear! My heart was being healed, and my service for God's Kingdom was being activated in what I knew was God's first and best plan! It was exciting to realize that God and I had the same goals!

Story 39:
The End Begins Again

Omniscience is a divine characteristic of God alone. Possessing the attribute of being all-knowing gives us full confidence in God's divine wisdom. God can be trusted because He knows all things. God can be trusted with our lives because He knows everything there is to know about us. Who else can that be said of?

Our Omniscient God has gone to great lengths to share with us who He is. He has designed a plan for us to learn about Him. This plan is unfolded within the experiences that we have as we walk with Him through our life's journey. As we engage with Him through His Word, He shares His wisdom with us in every season and gives us the revelation of His ways. This revelation changes how we think and act. If we release all resistance against Him and embrace His precepts, we will arrive at the end of life knowing so much about Him. We will know that He is the LORD.

As I worked toward writing the last couple of stories for this book, I knew I needed to share the outcome of our facility, His Place, and the way I was led to know God's will for it.

Truthfully, I became a bit overwhelmed as I read through my journals, newsletters, and notes for these remaining years. I still had before me the years of 2010, 2011,

2012, and beyond. There was so much in the day-to-week-to-month happenings that I have chosen to condense and share a few of the best stories.

God was going to settle it, as you will see, but I was still on that curved road during those years. I kept trying to see the end vision for His Place. I assumed it was supposed to be part of my life. I was making every effort to fit my new puzzle pieces of prayer and mission ministries into the big picture, but no matter how hard I tried to make them the honored corner pieces of the His Place puzzle, I could not get them to fit.

His Place was Mike's dream, and God blessed it. That's just all there was to it. As Mike held the puzzle pieces, they all fell into place. When God took Mike to heaven, He knew how tied I was to the dream, as well. I knew things would be different now, but God knew that because of the level of my commitment, I would never quit without His direction.

I felt the love of our friends and fellow-bikers. Everyone was giving me much grace with no voiced pressure. They rallied around me and showed great support as I took on the role of Director of His Place. However, I was harder on myself than anyone else could have been. Though heartsick with grief, I took my responsibility to have my own vision for His Place seriously. Everyone's expectation was that I *would* step up and carry His Place forward. People had invested much time and finances to build it. All their resources could not be left idle. I didn't want to let them down. I didn't want to let Mike down. I didn't want to let God down.

I was a leader in my own right, but I couldn't seem to connect to the same type of authority Mike had held in sharing the vision of His Place. I prayed that God would bring everything together and make things happen the way I thought they should. However, *His* ongoing plan was already set in motion, and it would prove to be nothing like what I expected. God continued to show favor with "Blue financial provision" as He purposefully began what He knew would be for me the most painful step yet: to show me His Place was not mine to lead, and that I was to let it go, too.

God had spoken to me about a year or so after Mike passed away that my grief was going to be a five-year journey, and that I was to pace myself. To some, that may have sounded overwhelming, but it brought me great peace. It told me to take a deep breath and not be in a hurry. It validated to me that God saw every day of those five years ahead and I could trust His plan for His Place and for me. I just had to walk it out.

God was the ultimate Divine Director, and He would oversee the fading away of the old that would have kept us each tied to our past identities. He knew how to redesign His Place to take it on to its second step, and He knew how to transform a woman still within the small quarters of a cocoon through the process of metamorphosis.

In early 2010 I was asked by my brother-in-law, Ted Rose, who was the current California State Coordinator for the National Day of Prayer Task Force to join his team as Assistant (California) State Coordinator for Christian Motorcyclists. He wanted to mobilize prayer on behalf of all Christian bikers throughout the state of California to *pray* for every biker ministry and for every unsaved biker to come to find Jesus as their Lord and Savior. I had released all Mike's and my biker ministry seed to the Lord to watch over, but now I felt like He handed me back a *prayer watch* over them.

Ted Rose resigned his position about a year later which meant my resignation as well, but, I am thankful for the prayer card that was under development and carried forward into Ted's new ministry focus, the United States National Prayer Council. Together we created a "PRAY for BIKERs" 3x5, glossy, full-color prayer card to help mobilize prayer for bikers. The cards hold 10 points for prayer focus with Scripture to reinforce each point. Mike's picture is on the front and back of the card. As he sits on his motorcycle, it displays a memorial to his love for the bikers and his call to serve them.

http://www.usnationalprayercouncil.com/members/pray4bikers.html

With Kevin Woods' help, I continued to push forward in my desire for His Place to be a resource in meeting the needs of others. We wanted to provide boxes of food and give spiritual and emotional support to those in need. We wanted to remain "biker friendly," and to encourage bikers to help with food distribution and for them to make use of our planned support group opportunities. Our plans were good, yet I couldn't help but noticed that God's hand seemed to withhold productivity in these areas. I would feel concern over this unfulfilled vision while, at the same time, delighting in my heart as God opened another door for me toward missions.

In April of 2010, God gave me my lifetime dream of going to Africa. There was so much I experienced at the *Longezia Mission Base* near Sinazongwe in Zambia. There were eight on our team, and we each participated either on the medical team, teaching at the Bible School nearby, helping with the children's ministry, or providing sewing classes to the women on the hand-powered machines purchased with funds that had been raised for this trip.

I witnessed a desperate mother bring her severely malnourished 19-month-old daughter for help. I heard the women singing and sewing as they learned a trade that would bring in a few extra dollars to add to their far below poverty incomes. I saw Tonga men, women, and children walk for miles on primitive dirt roads to fetch water and wood for fuel.

They live in communities of tiny huts that house broken families and orphans who had been disregarded by their culture. I touched the amazing ancient Baobab trees, and every so often saw wild monkeys in them. I was thrilled to attend church in an African thatch hut, and our team held more than one service in modest brick churches that used tree limbs as pews. Vibrant and heartfelt singing came from within them both.

I had the privilege to share my testimony with a group of the Tonga people of how I received Jesus when I was 11 years old. Over 50 children raised their hands for salvation that night.

We saw animals in the wild, including lions, giraffes, *zebras*, and elephants; as well as the one that knocked me to the ground! Not many people can say they have been thrown to the ground by an African elephant, but I can!

There is a particular zebra story that happened as we were leaving Zambia that you must hear.

As I sat back in my seat on the huge airplane that was transporting our mission team back from Zambia to our stopover in London, I smiled and thanked God for saving the best for last. I was referring to my having visited the Safari Park and the zebra blessing!

On our last day in Zambia, the missionary we supported there took our team to the Safari Park for the day. He asked each of us what animal we hoped to see "in the wild." My special animal was a zebra! Every team member saw their special animal, but me. There were just no zebras to be found. We even stayed out a bit longer looking for them.

When we returned, the missionary realized one of his team members had not seen their desired animal. I saw him go over to a group of tour guides who had gathered to talk and ask them if any of them had seen any zebras on their excursions. One guide's group had seen them out in a meadow earlier.

Our missionary "interceded" on my behalf, and the result was that we all climbed back into the safari jeep and were driven out to that meadow where we found an entire herd of zebra grazing! There were 10 to 15, including foals (babies)! The tour guide shared with us details of their species and life. It was awesome! And yes, *I took pictures.*

So, that next morning, as we felt the thrust of the airplane taking off, which by the way is my favorite part, I was thanking God from the bottom of my heart for this amazing dream-come-true mission trip, *and* for saving the best for last the day before! In thanking God, I said, "You knew all day that I was going to get to see a zebra in the wild. You let me take pictures of the zebra pictures hanging on the wall inside the Welcome Center at the resort, knowing all along what was yet to be. *You saved the best for last! Thank you!*"

Then God surprised me by interjecting a statement that caught me totally off guard. I heard a quiet voice say into my spirit, "I saved the best for last in your life, as well." I was stunned at His unexpected comment. I guess I thought I needed to correct God because I responded by saying in my heart, "Oh! No. It's OK. I've already experienced the best!" I was referring to Mike and our life together. But God replied, "Yes, I know. It was the best *for then.* I am going to give you *the best for now!*"

Oh, my gracious! God did not discount my life with Mike at all. He validated it and then gave me a promise that embedded itself deep in my spirit! It would also be from this experience that I would, some two years later, take my new ministry name, *God's Best for Now Ministries*!

In May 2010, I began to attend a new church plant, *Real Life Church* in Galt, California, pastored by James and Chris Seiler. After attending there for a year, I was asked to serve as the church's mission director. It was a perfect fit to my very own puzzle-picture God was creating.

During June 2010, I took a second mission trip back to Nicaragua, as the Holy Spirit continued stretching and enlarging my heart to hold within it God's love for people of every nation. I knew the Holy Spirit wanted my discipline to be in the school of prayer, and to be involved in "hands-on missions."

At the end of June 2010, I was invited to be a charter member of the newly forming *Christian Motorcyclists Association* (CMA) International Intercessory Prayer Team. We would focus prayer for the sensitive needs of the over 32 nations that CMA was currently involved in.

I was also asked by our CMA Regional Evangelists, Joe and Judy Maxwell, to become their Regional Prayer Leader. My role was to coordinate prayer for CMA leaders in five states, and the bikers they served. That year God began to set a new course in my life through prayer and world missions.

I continued to struggle to fit His Place into my life's picture. The counseling plans I had hoped would happen within the facility were set aside, as those who were to help in leadership were led by God in different directions. Food distribution had become low key. I began to be aware that His Place seemed burdensome, and that I was struggling in my CMA biker ministry prayer times. I felt confused with His Place's failure to thrive, and in my separation from it.

I constantly brought this before God who, unknown to me, was using these very circumstances to prepare me to fully let go of both CMA and His Place; ministries that had been a natural outgrowth of my life with Mike. God knew the time was right for Him to help me release these two ministries into which I had invested so many years, and to take hold of what was to become my *best for now*.

I attended a National Day of Prayer luncheon, and while there I became engaged in a conversation with Arlene McElhenney, a woman who had known Mike better than she knew me because they had prayed together weekly on the steps of the California State Capitol Building. I trusted her spiritually, but her words were hard for me to hear as she told me that I needed to "lay His Place down, and see where God might take it." Had His Place become to me, as Isaac was to his father Abraham, something God was instructing me to lay down?

She also told me there was *still* some "untangling" that needed to be done with Mike and our life and ministry together. My spirit recognized it as a deeper letting go, but my heart just felt the pain of more loss.

I wept as I drove home from that luncheon knowing the cords that were once tied together of God's design would choke out His best for now if I did not relax as He worked to

329

separate them further. Inside I wondered if God was asking me to give up His Place. I could feel the stirrings inside of my spirit and recognized His voice, but I could not yet acknowledge it as a reality.

This began a six-month encapsulated grief journey for His Place as I could feel the cold wind's effects of God's whispers saying that His Place was not mine. It was as if denial wrapped a coat around me in a futile attempt to keep me warm and take off the chill in those first few months. God was so patient, so loving, as I scolded myself for not trying hard enough to make His Place succeed.

In that denial and determination to try harder, I appointed an advisory board for His Place and wrote out a vision. Our first meeting was scheduled for late July of 2010. I knew that this new board would expect me to "cast the vision," and set plans in motion. But, I was sick inside. I was heart sick and could not find peace in my soul. I felt paralyzed when I went out into the His Place facility. I was beyond upset and full of anxiety. I knew this should not be.

The day before the first advisory board meeting I found my fingers dialing Pastor Dick's phone number. He is like a dad to me, and I felt safe with him. I knew he would have my best interest at heart and would discern what was going on with me.

After pouring out my heart to him, he shared an analogy with me. He said there was a harbor that was particularly dangerous because of unseen rocks beneath the water that would cause great damage to any vessel that struck one of them. Three lighthouses were built with the intent that as the ship came into the harbor, the captain knew he was in safe water if the three lighthouses lined up as one.

Pastor Dick went on to say that we, too, need three "spiritual lighthouses" to know we are safe in our direction decisions. One lighthouse alone is not enough as it would be easy to unintentionally misread God's set course for us.

The three spiritual lighthouses Pastor Dick spoke of were:

1. The Word of God (Scripture) given as a confirmation.

2. The unction of the Holy Spirit's affirmation by feeling the peace of His Presence deep in our spirit.

3. Clearly seeing what the Hand of God is doing. If God's hand is opening the door, then we walk through. If things seem to be closed, then we must take another look.

None of these three lighthouses, regarding His Place, were lining up for me. With divine wisdom from the Father, Pastor Dick said, "What Mike did in building His Place was an offering to the Lord. The Lord doesn't feel obligated to Mike. Mike gets his reward no matter what!"

Pastor Dick did his best to relay to me that I was not bound to stay at His Place, nor was I obligated to make it work. He said that God, very likely, had different paths for His Place and me. His words brought me tearfully to an *unexpected comfort*. It was that unction of peace from the Holy Spirit that Pastor Dick had just referred to.

I talked to my family first, who came in agreement with me. Kevin took it hard, but he knew, as well, that God had been leading us to this for a while, and that God had a different plan for His Place, for him and me. It would not be long until Kevin would resign from his role at His Place, and return to the Salvation Army where he had worked for 15 years before leaving to help, first, in a men's home ministry and then to help Mike at His Place.

Kevin and Serina sold everything they had and entered a Salvation Army College for Officer Training in Southern California to complete a two-year program. They are both currently Lieutenants happily and effectively overseeing a Salvation Army Post in Alaska!

At the advisory board meeting that night, instead of casting the vision they were all expecting, I dropped a bombshell. I told them that I knew in my heart I was not to lead His Place. I shared my agonized pacing I had done for weeks, not knowing why I was feeling so separated. We discussed options of other ministries coming to help or even take over, and even the possibility that we might need to put it up for sale. It forced each of us to face the reality that we must let go of Mike's dream. As the meeting ended, all were in full support of me and how I felt God was leading. I called a realtor to inquire, and to have them come out to view the property, but I was not ready to sign.

About a week later God would give me what my heart was crying out for. It was a word from Him straight out of His Word. There was another of Pastor Dick's "lighthouses" lining up. Oh, how I love when God's Word comes to confirm! There is *nothing better* than finding your current story right in the Living Word of God!

In early August 2010, I was getting ready to have my quiet time with the Lord and to read His Word. As I prayed, I saw "First Samuel 1" in big bold letters in my mind. So I turned there to read. It was the story of Hannah grieving for her barrenness and making a vow that if God gave her a son she would give him back to the Lord. The priest Eli saw her anguishing in prayer and thought she was drunk in the temple. After she had explained to him that what he saw was her great sorrow and her desire for a child, He blessed her, and she went home and conceived. She had a son, and named him "Samuel."

True to her word, when the child was weaned she took him to Eli, the priest and gave him to the Lord. God used Hannah's hopeless situation to produce such a desperate prayer from her that it became an opportunity for God to set apart a young boy who would grow up to be an honored prophet to His people.

What stood out to me as I read this story, were the words, "Hannah gave Samuel, her child, to the Lord." His Place was as my child. I guarded it, protected it and would lay down my life for it.

333

I had thought I was in an Abraham/Isaac story. But now, having read this word, was God saying that I was as Hannah, to give my child to another? Was this His confirmation to sell?

A day or so later God, again, spoke to me unexpectedly. He said, "You are not Hannah. Mike was Hannah." That revelation caught me by surprise as I realized that it was Mike who made the vow to give this "child" back to God, just as Hannah had made it before Samuel's conception!

Mike desperately wanted to give birth to something (in his case to build something) that He could give back to the Lord as an offering. I think deep inside he always knew he would never raise "this child." God had sent me to First Samuel 1 to help me let go of this land as profoundly as He did when He sent me to Joshua 1, almost ten years previously, when He revealed we were to take hold of the land God would give us.

On September 21, 2010, twelve members of the *Jus Bros Motorcycle Club* rode into His Place. They had not heard that we had canceled the 3rd Annual Mike Sumstine Memorial Run, and in their minds, there was no way they would miss it. As I went out to greet them I felt the honor they gave Mike by coming, and their respect for me. Mike loved these bikers, and they loved him. It was reminiscent of old times seeing twelve bikes lined up and parked in a row on our grounds. And then, almost with a jolt, I recognized it. God had sent them as a final biker farewell to His Place.

Within the next two years, I saw God sovereignly rescue His Place three times. Twice there was a viable plan in motion to allow others to take the lead, but neither proved to be God's first and best plan. Brian and Kristy Rego were used by God for months to be the financial bridge that held everything steady until that third and final redemption when God came in with the last minute miraculous *monetary miracle!*

At that holy moment, I had the joy of putting the His Place property and facility, my and Mike's "child," in the hands of Sandra Dykema, the new director of a growing ministry, *Second Step Living*. As Mike had already done in his heart, I physically gave His Place as an offering to the Lord.

There was an agreement of monthly ministry support to be shared with me, but within just a few months the Lord instructed me to release His Place from all financial commitments. I was to trust God alone for my support as Mike and I had always done.

His Place would first be housing and a care center for those who were struggling with and coming out of lifestyle dysfunctions and addictions. God would take them beyond salvation and into the Second Step Living adventure, learning who they are in Christ by providing them with godly mentorship and Christian counseling. It currently houses a ministry named *Building Blocks* and serves the community with food distribution and household needs as they have them available.

Mike and I could not have imagined this journey His Place would take. There is One, however, who looked upon an obscure half-acre and said, "I choose *this* land, and I see a man and woman who I will commission to develop it for Me. I have plans for it to bring honor to My Name."

I have tried my best to share the story of His Place. God has been beyond faithful to His land. I do not regret a single day of the journey that He chose for us to walk together. Of all the days combined, the most special was the day I gave it away on behalf of Mike. It truly was set apart as an offering unto the Lord; but not only our offering. It was the offering of every person who had invested their time or money in it.

For me, it was the end of an incredible "Blue" story. However, in God's seasons, the end of my assignment was the beginning of another's. God knows the history of His Place, and what His destiny is for its future. I have no doubt that God will impart into the new directors' hearts His first and best plan; as He is doing for me in my new season. They too will find their sufficiency in Him who is omniscient.

Story 40:
God's Best for Now

Signs are necessary. They are markers that alert us to something important. From customized signs that offer direction, to street signs posted on every corner that state our location, we depend on them. Signs are typically posted by someone in authority, so we trust them.

From the creation of the world, signs have appeared on the pages of history. Signs show the way so that in the future, others can follow the same signs to believe and find their faith in God. They come as a warning, as a promise, or as a confirmation that His Word to us is true. God's signs validate the experience of a person's encounter with the presence of God.

Probably one of the most marked signs in the Bible is found in Luke 2:11-12 when angels appeared near Bethlehem, to shepherds watching over their flocks, and announced good news for all people, saying:

> *"Today in the town of David a Savior has been born to you; he is the Messiah, the Lord. This will be a sign to you: You will find a baby wrapped in cloths and lying in a manger."*

God still communicates in signs, and word pictures today. His signs in our stories are intricately planned, and they are too amazing to be considered coincidences.

These last pages of my book will cover my journey after His Place. I would like to share some insights that God gave me and then a surprise series of personal signs He revealed to me in Israel. I hope these will encourage you to listen and look for God's active participation *with you* on your journey!

I moved off the His Place property on March 1, 2012. As I drove away, I stopped to look back one more time. The name of the place would soon change to fit its new role, but in my heart, this would always be His Place.

I was excited to move to a small apartment in Galt, California where I still reside. I have decorated it throughout with my fun "Zepard décor," zebra and leopard print. Every room makes me smile! I have designed my tiny back porch into a lovely private garden while making sure my neighbors can still share a morning chat by peeking through the Jasmine vines and flower pots. This little community has become my home and a place where God remains my provider.

My home church, *Real Life Church* of Galt (www.rlcgald.com) is called to serve our local community and to take Jesus from its neighborhoods to the nations. I continue to serve as Mission Director and am getting ready to take a team to Mexico where I pray God will put the world in their hearts as they hold an orphaned child and work on behalf of those who have so little.

I have facilitated eleven *GriefShare* 13-week support group cycles over a six-year period, plus five of *GriefShare's* special one-night events called *Surviving the Holidays*. *GriefShare* provides support to those who have lost a loved one in death, and though I am not currently facilitating their groups, grief support will always be a part of my heart and one-on-one encouragement to others.

I have remained in full-time ministry using the name, *God's Best for Now Ministries* (GBFNM). I am still under the covering of *Outreach Ministries International* and Pastor Dick Patterson, who continues as its President. My dream is to see GBFNM support one missionary on every continent (then two per continent, then three...) and to bring an on-site prayer team to each of them!

My call is to give prayer-care, mission-care, and grief-care to the nations. I am called to pray for the persecuted church, and for those who are deceived from believing in our

Triune God. I also share *Heart2Heart* mentoring with other women, and occasionally speak at events.

God gave me a renewed word in January 2013 for this revised season of my life. He sent me back to His Word in Joshua 1:1-6, where we read, *"After the death of Moses the servant of the LORD, the LORD said to Joshua son of Nun, Moses' aide: Moses my servant is dead. Now... I will give you every place where you set your foot, as I promised Moses... Be strong and courageous because you will lead these people to inherit the land."*

At first, my mind went back to when God gave this Scripture to Mike and me at the very beginning of our His Place journey, but then God explicitly said, "Mike is not Moses is this story. Your mom is."

With those words, the Lord *confirmed* what He had spoken to me almost four years earlier when He said, "I will send you on your feet where your mom went on her knees."

How many nations did she visit on her knees in her 70-years of intercession? My mom left me a legacy of a life committed to Jesus. I want nothing less for mine.

In mid-2013 God released me from my positions in the *Christian Motorcyclists Association* (CMA), although I remain a forever member! My struggle to feel at peace and to fit in, even with the prayer emphasis, was validated as God said to me, "Your struggle is because your season as a biker is over." It was another one of the "letting go" surprises God purposed for me in His redesign of my life.

I remain deeply thankful for the hundreds of friends I still have with CMA and other Christian bike ministries. I will always love and pray for the countless bikers to whom Mike and I sowed God's truth. To look at me now you would never believe that I know what it feels like to be dressed in leather, riding on the back of a Harley with the wind in my face, *but I do know, and I would not trade it for anything*! I continue to pray "one-line prayers" for every biker that passes me on the freeway!

In my current season, I most identify myself as a "praying missionary." My God-appointment in 2014 was to join the *United States National Prayer Council* (USNPC) as their International Director. The purpose of the USNPC is to "encourage the Christian Church throughout the world to be devoted to prayer and the fulfillment of the Great Commission." (www.usnationalprayercouncil.com). The USNPC is not a political organization. My focus with the USNPC is to help to appoint a national director in every nation as the Lord opens the doors and to maintain a relationship with them. We currently have 50 national directors!

At this writing in early 2017, and since my first mission trip in 2009, God has sent me on a total of 11 mission trips. I have visited eight different countries, including being on a mission prayer team first to the Comoro Islands in 2014, and Israel in 2015.

I would like to share a couple of insights from those two experiences.

After coming home from traveling and spending time in Kenya, Africa and then in the Comoro Islands at the end of 2014, I was at my home church worshipping with the congregation in song one Sunday morning. I was reeling from the culture shock of reentry into the States. My heart was still there in the Comoros, and it felt like lost luggage that had not yet found its way home.

As I prayed and worshiped, I shared my emotions with the Lord and asked Him, "When is my heart coming home?" I immediately heard Him answer back, "It's not."

I felt an ache and a sweeping love simultaneously rush through me. Of course, it wasn't coming back! The Holy Spirit had sent me there with a tent peg attached to my heart. This tent peg was stretched far across the continental United States, across the Atlantic Ocean, across the Continent of Africa and into the Indian Ocean where it was pounded into a tiny Island called The Comoros.

I had walked on their stony pathways following my friend, as she led me to visit the older woman who sat preparing vegetables, squatting on a tiny stool overlooking her village. I had made my way through the maze of ancient buildings in the capital city as we prayed and took spiritual territory for Jesus with every step. I learned how to say the traditional blessing in their native language that the older women gave to the younger children who would in great respect put out their hands to honor you. I sank my toes in their white sand beaches and felt the Indian Ocean sweep refreshingly over my feet with waves of welcome. I am aware now of their names and faces, their homes and the families who live in them, and their cultural lack of knowledge of who Jesus is.

A mission team has one main goal, and that is to share the gospel. When that is in the process, your heart is engaged at a heightened level. When you participate and then have to leave, you can't turn off the flow of the Spirit's call for them to come to salvation. Your heart stays connected through the tent peg, as your words spoken under the leading of the Holy Spirit travel across the miles to move obstacles of resistance and open hearts to the cross. My heart was aching for my body to go back, and my body was aching for their hearts to know their Messiah.

The second insight I would like to share came before my trip to Israel.

I was asked to join a prayer team going to Jerusalem the end of September 2015 under the leadership of Jerry and Margie Bowers, who, by the way, are currently representing Israel for the *United States National Prayer Council.* I was ecstatic to think I would be involved in praying for the harvest of nations, having a different continent focus each day, and that we would be there during the final of four blood moons which occurred within about a 17-month period. The fact that this one was to be a Super Moon made the trip even more appealing. To view this event from the night sky of Jerusalem would be super-amazing!

Another exciting element of our trip to Israel was that we would be there during the week of the Feast of Tabernacles, a major spiritual holiday, and not only added to the excitement on the streets, but also added a vast number of people in Jerusalem. This feast lasts for eight days and is a celebration of God's provision of bounty during harvest. It's another symbolic picture foreshadowing the coming Messiah (Jesus), as are all the Jewish feasts.

But, as I was announcing this trip, I began to hear some express concern about our safety in that part of the world. I asked God how to respond to those with these legitimate concerns. God directed me to the story of Peter walking on water in Matthew 14:22-33.

In the story, Jesus had directed his disciples to get into the boat and go ahead of him to the other side of the Sea of Galilee while He stayed back to pray. A storm came up and Jesus, concerned for His disciples, went out to join them — *walking on water!*

When the disciples saw Jesus, they were terrified. Jesus spoke to them from outside the boat, telling them who He was, and for them to be courageous and not to be afraid. Peter asked that if it were Jesus who was speaking to them, would He invite him to come to Him! Jesus told Peter to come, and Peter immediately climbed out of the boat and *walked on water toward Jesus!*

I was fully aware that God was giving me peace to travel. By discernment, I knew the water represented the world at large. In my mind, I was Peter in this story asking Jesus to bid me come (to Jerusalem). As He did to Peter, Jesus said, "Come!"

The truth of this story is that if we have God's direction, we can be courageous and without fear. I knew then that no matter what *could happen*, I was to go. Yes, later in the story Peter began to sink in the water, but as soon as He called upon the Name of Jesus, he was saved. If trouble should come when I am out "walking in the world," all I need to know is to call out to Jesus. My soul, if not my body, will be safe.

This trip to Jerusalem was a dream-come-true! I still get goosebumps to think of all that happened while we were there. I was able to invite a few others from my church: Kristy Rego, Linda Winsor and Sterling and Julie Sawyer. We joined the Bowers and our other team members: Liz Gibb from Scotland, Madeleine Bartley from the United Kingdom, Debbie Taylor with her young daughter, Bella, from Texas, and Mike and Dianne Fletcher from California, formerly from New Zealand. Our team bonded immediately, and we were in one accord to experience all that God had for us to accomplish in prayer and visiting historical biblical sites.

During the ten days we were in Israel, alongside the real purpose of our mission trip, God gave me a parallel personal spiritual journey that was a condensed picture of God at work in every human heart. Let me share this enriching last story with you!

Our first evening there we decided to meet for dinner at a restaurant with extended outdoor seating. I remember the thrill of taking our "selfie" picture to post on Facebook, feeling like I should pinch myself to see if we were eating on the streets of Jerusalem! After dinner, we decided to walk around and go through a few shops before trying to get some sleep amidst jetlag, and our extreme excitement to be there.

I came upon a little shop where I purchased a ring. I was intrigued by it and could not walk away without it on my finger! The ring, in style, was designed according to ancient Israel's High Priest's breastplate, as described in Exodus 28. There are even twelve tiny stones on it that represent the twelve tribes of Israel.

Back at our hotel, as I was doing a little research on the priest's breastplate, the Holy Spirit brought my attention to the date, and I realized that I had just purchased my ring *in Jerusalem on the actual day* of Yum Kippur, the Day of Atonement! This was the only day of the year that the high priest could enter the Holy of Holies to make atonement for the sins of the people, and speak out loud the Name of God! And, He would have worn his breastplate!

I remembered how for the few weeks prior, I had gone through a personal season of repentance. I wanted deep spiritual house cleaning to be accomplished in my soul before I came, so my heart was ready for my mission trip.

On my parallel personal spiritual journey, my ring became the first sign to me, a symbol of the atonement Jesus made for my sins and the sins of the world. I knew God was saying to me, "My Son was your sacrifice. Atonement has been made for your sin. *Today,* you are forgiven!"

It was amazing, in the next few days, to walk a portion of the Old Jerusalem Wall and to experience being a "prayer watchman on the wall" standing guard over the Israelites and the people of God throughout the world. We visited each point of the Via Dolorosa, lingering on one site that gave us the visual atmosphere to imagine Jesus carrying His cross for us. I touched Golgotha's Hill and stood inside Jesus' tomb where *resurrection power* brought Him up from the dead!

In a little shop, next to Herod's Palace in Jerusalem, which may be where Roman governor Pontius Pilate tried and condemned Jesus, Kristy Rego and I purchased Mite Necklaces. They are authentic mites (coins) excavated from the Jerusalem area and encased in silver.

We remembered the story in Luke 21:1-4 where Jesus observed the rich giving their offerings, then noticed a poor widow who put in two mites, which valued together a total

348

of about half a cent. He commented to His disciples that she gave more than all the others. She had given all she had!

My Mite Necklace became another sign on my parallel personal spiritual journey, a sign of total surrender. It was my symbol that represented that because Jesus gave His all for me, now I, like that widow, would give Jesus my all. I joked with Kristy that we each had one of the "original" mites this woman gave in her offering. Who knows? It *could* be!

Our team visited twice *Living Bread International Church*, overseen by Pastor Karen Dunham. Her message on that second visit was from Judges 16. She spoke of Samson and the "spirit of Dalila." She gave the word at the conclusion of her message of how the enemy had sent out his demons to target God's leaders, and to bring personal defeat to many in the Kingdom of God, to nullify our productivity through compromise and character failure.

Calling us all to a time of intercession, Pastor Karen instructed each of us to get a drum. There were several drums stacked against a wall in the room in which we were meeting. It was clear the drums had been used before. Though I had never participated in any prayer time like what followed, it was not weird or for show. Under her direction and lead, we began to beat the drums with our hands. We knew we were a part of God's war cry preparing for spiritual battle against the enemy. The beat of those drums was like hearing the very heartbeat of the Father wanting to liberate the nations. I think the enemy and his demonic forces trembled in their boots that day!

Pastor Karen prayed a *powerful* prayer of attack that resulted in an overwhelming sense of victory. Everyone in the room felt that our spiritual warfare had defeated the enemy on multiple levels across the globe.

Eternity will tell the lives God protected that morning from a tiny church in Jerusalem. One of them was mine. I felt a release from a spiritual attack that had lingered for months, and I felt generational bondages break off of me that day. *I had never felt freer.*

I came home and bought a drum myself. And, yes, I have used it in prayer. It reminds me no weapon formed against us or those we love can succeed. The spiritual forces of darkness are strong, but there are more in God's angel armies than in the camp of evil.

Once we have our sins forgiven and have given Jesus our all, His Name holds all authority to break off our strongholds and past failures. We are no longer slaves to sin or chained to addictions.

The third sign on my parallel personal spiritual journey in Jerusalem was found in that little church. A drum became the sign of spiritual warfare and the symbol that released freedom!

My next sign was for me to be baptized in the Jordan River. I liked to think that we may have been in the exact spot where Jesus walked into the water to be baptized by John the

Baptist! Though highly unlikely, I did have a profound experience there as God spoke to me prophetically through Jerry Bowers, that from that day forward God was giving me new eyes to see. God was removing the old, as you would remove a pair of sunglasses. The new vision meant revelation with clear spiritual insight.

I had been baptized in water when I was 11 years old, but this time, over 50 years later, I felt it was even more meaningful, more powerful than the first time.

It was here that I experienced my fourth parallel journey sign. A river became the sign of public commitment to Jesus; my baptism, the symbol of death, burial, and resurrection. Our eyes close in death to our old life of sin, and we are buried in baptism. Resurrection power brings us up and into a new life in Christ!

Our team visited two messianic churches, and three different houses of prayer, including one that was a secret house of prayer, *The City of David House of Prayer* in the City of David (Jerusalem). It is not unusual to feel a special presence of God there because the City of David is the place King David returned the Ark of the Covenant after conquering the city from the Jebusites. King David established his capital there, and the people of Israel were united under his rule.

The Ark of the Covenant is a gold-covered wooden chest, which contained the two stone tablets of the Ten Commandments, Aaron's rod that budded, and a pot of manna. The Ark represented God's holy presence guiding His people.

While praying at this house of prayer, I remembered it was the beginning of the Year of Jubilee, which occurs every 50 years and begins on the Day of Atonement. It was a year of great blessing where all land was returned to its original owner, and any who had been forced to sell themselves as slaves, because of extreme poverty, were set free.

God's presence that day was vibrant, and He revealed in my spirit some very encouraging words regarding my son and daughter. He said that a shofar would be blown to a generation declaring freedom and that a barren womb would give birth.

As I worshiped, I remembered Jesus' words to John the Baptist's disciples who, as John sat in prison, were sent to ask Jesus if He was the Messiah. Jesus sent them back to tell John that the blind see, the lame walk, the deaf hear and the dead are raised up. Yes, He is the Messiah and when He speaks supernatural things happen!

As we were about to leave, my eyes met with those of the woman who lives on site with her husband. Her looks and spirit of prayer reminded me of my mom. As she hugged me close, she whispered beautiful words of affirmation that God was pleased and would lead me in my journey after my visit to Israel.

This house of prayer in the City of David was my fifth journey sign. The Ark of the Covenant was the sign of

God's presence and the symbol that He is always with us bringing the miraculous!

As we began the last few days of our time in Jerusalem, we knew we must visit The Cenacle, or better known as *The Upper Room*. This is traditionally believed to be the site of the Last Supper and the coming of the Holy Spirit upon the apostles. I would try my best to envision both.

Walking up the stairs to its entrance was a holy moment. It is a beautiful room! We had communion as a team and then our leader, Jerry Bowers, asked me to step into the middle of our group as they encircled me. He covered my head and shoulders with a fire red shawl and had everyone come in close to take hold of the tassels on both ends. Jerry then prayed a descriptive and powerful prayer that commissioned me to go to the nations in the fire of the Holy Spirit!

Oh, my gracious! How does God do this? I was stunned speechless as I tried to grasp the reality of what had just happened. I had just been commissioned to the nations *in the Upper Room*! Even as I write this, I feel anew the *fire* of God's Holy Spirit *burning* in my heart.

The Upper Room was my sixth journey sign, and a firey red scarf became the sign and symbol of the Holy Spirit's fire. In Acts 2, in that same upper room I visited, tongues of fire came to rest on each of the 120 gathered there. They began to each speak a different language and went out in the power of the Holy Spirit, to fulfill the great commission Jesus had given them to go into all the world and make

353

disciples of all nations. Now, I was commissioned to do the same!

The last stop God gave me on my parallel personal spiritual journey was on our last full day there. First, we visited the Eastern Gate in the old walled City of Jerusalem. It faces the Mount of Olives and is the only gate of the city that leads directly onto the Temple Mount. This was the gate that Jesus entered Jerusalem through, riding on a donkey, on what we consider Palm Sunday. Jesus said in Matthew 23:37-39 that he would not be seen again there until Jerusalem acknowledges him as their Messiah. The Eastern Gate is sealed up and blocked off with Muslim tombs everywhere around it and is presently considered by the Arabs to be their exclusive property. But, one day, Jesus will return, and He will ride His white horse through that Eastern Gate, just as He said He would! Visiting this majestic and holy site stirred me deeply.

We left and headed toward the Five Protocols which included the Pool of Bethesda. In John 5:1-15 we are told about this pool; that when the waters of the pool were stirred, the first one into the water received their healing.

As we walked further away from the Eastern Gate and closer to the healing pool, I heard the Holy Spirit saying to me, "Ask for healing. Ask for the healing of the nations." When we arrived at the site, there was a huge fireman-type hose propped up, and water was pouring from it into the pool below. I heard the Holy Spirit speak to me again. He said, "Go put your hands in the water! I'm stirring the water!"

I left my group and headed directly to the hose! Putting my hands in the water, I prayed asking God for the healing of the nations with salvation! Each of our team members took their turn with their hands in the water as I explained what God had said to me. I was thankful for His voice that had stirred my heart to be as the first one in. That invitation is still open to us all!

Jerry Bowers said later that in all the times he had been there, he'd never seen water pouring into any of the pools. I believe the Holy Spirit provided that bubbling visual of healing through the water from that hose just for us!

Here at the Pool of Bethesda, I found my final and seventh sign on my parallel journey. A hose became a symbol of Living Water, and obedience became the symbol required to bring healing to the nations through salvation in Jesus Christ.

I left Jerusalem in awe of having walked where Jesus walked and having visited sites that made the Bible come alive to me as never before. As I put together the order of this parallel journey, I realized it shared a picture of the Christian life. If you haven't understood what it means to be a Christian, this is it! I think it's awesome that there were seven signs, God's perfect number.

1. Jesus came to make atonement and become the sacrificial payment for our sin.

2. Jesus wants us to *give* Him *our all* because we love Him.

3. We gain *freedom* from all bondages of sin and addictions if we ask Jesus to be our Deliverer.

4. As we make a *public commitment* to Jesus, our sin nature is buried. Resurrection power gives us grace, which includes what we need to live and obey God's Word.

5. *His Present Presence* promises us that nothing is too hard for God and that we are never alone.

6. He sent His *Holy Spirit* to empower us with fire to share the gospel with others.

7. Jesus is the *Living Water* for which we thirst, and longs to *heal* every heart. This healing immediately begins when we accept Him as our Lord and Savior.

After writing about my Jerusalem experience, I felt there was still one more insight I should share with you. The morning before we left Israel to return to the states, a few of us visited the Yad Vashem, the *World Holocaust Center*. We needed a full day to go through it properly, but we only had a couple of hours, so our visit and viewing were condensed, to say the least. However, I feel compelled to say that the persecution the Jewish people endured is by far the most horrific thing I have ever seen. God's chosen people were hated then, and they are hated by many in our world today.

Christians are also hated because we bear the name of Christ. The persecution of Christians has gone on for hundreds of years, but the number today is staggering. In an article by Paul Vallely, dated July 2014, entitled *Christians: The World's Most Persecuted People* states,

> *"The Centre for the Study of Global Christianity* in the United States estimates that 100,000 Christians now die every year, targeted because of their faith – that is 11 every hour."

People hate the name of Jesus. His claim to be the *only way* to the Father is violently rejected by many. They are so deceived, and they are in a rebellion against God's love and His perfect plan for their salvation from an eternity without Him.

When we give ourselves 100% to the cause of the cross, we become part of something we must be willing to live for; and if necessary, willing to die for. Having that type of a dedication brings honor and glory to the name of Jesus, and displays the true value of His priceless Kingdom.

Where do you stand in your life? Are you tired of sin? What is God saying to you these days? Are you a 100 % Christian? These are all questions only you can answer. God wants to write your name in the Book of Life. He wants to forgive your sin, and for you to hear His voice of love! He wants you to find your story in His Word. He wants to give you His best for now!

I want to close this last story with a verse I would ask you to think about. It is Romans 1:16:

"For I am not ashamed of the gospel because it is the power of God that brings salvation to everyone who believes: first to the Jew, then to the Gentile."

Let me explain one more time what the gospel is. *The gospel* includes believing in Jesus' virgin birth; His life lived to fulfill the Law of Moses; His voluntary dying in our place as payment for our sin; His resurrection that was witnessed by many; and His ascension to heaven with the promise that He will come again. To believe the gospel ignites the *power* of God that brings your salvation.

However, *believing is* just the *beginning*! If we truly believe, we will also *follow* Him. If we follow Him, we will act like Him and talk like Him. If we hold back when it's time to be identified as a Christian, or feel embarrassed to use the name of Jesus; if our pride keeps us from speaking of the cross or of the promise of healing to those who are hurting, then we are of those with little faith.

Believing is the start. Being awakened in our hearts and active in our lives is what makes us a part. So, let's be strong and courageous *together*! Let's be bold and rise with love, *as one*! Let's embrace the name of Jesus, and be 100% committed to Him. Let's take our stand in *unity* and go out to draw a line with our lives in every nation! *Let's become His bold "blue" signs!*

Conclusion:
Goodbye for Now

Ending my book is bitter-sweet. It has been an incredible journey for me all the way through. From my heart, I want to say thank you for walking with me to the end! I feel as if I am saying goodbye to a special friend; as my neighbor who lived next door and that we did life together. I hope you feel that way, too. Some of you I know personally and others, I do not. I sincerely *hope* our paths will cross someday! Please feel free to contact me on Facebook under *God Writes in Blue* or you can visit my blog page at www.godwritesinblue.com.

It also feels like I am saying goodbye to a part of myself as well. Revisiting all the different stages of my life, I became reacquainted with the "younger Sherri," and saw her strengths, weaknesses, and struggles as I would see them in a friend. I feel like I watched her grow up before my eyes. There were times I wanted to give her counsel so she might make different choices. There were times when I wanted to encourage her to keep trusting God, and times I wished I could hug her during those days that she felt so lost and alone.

Owning my choices, writing down my thought process during each season, reliving in detail my most cherished moments and my most difficult of days, have given me a fresh perspective on my life. Writing my stories brought me both laughter and tears, remembering the countless expressions of God's faithfulness at every turn. I discovered that if I did not understand "why" something happened, I just might find the answer, as a hidden treasure, in the next story! I can confidently track God's blue love across each story's page.

I wrote this Facebook post on September 5, 2011. I'd like to share it with you now:

> "God doesn't tell us if the journey is going to last months or years because that's not the issue. The issue is *His* invaluable *truths* that we are given the opportunity to process, to painfully apply and to empower our lives. It is in our willingness to forsake our roles and goals forever that opens the deep places of God's heart holding His treasures of darkness and hidden riches in secret places."

My life verse from the Bible is found in Isaiah 45:2-3 (NIV). God first gave it to me when I was 19 years old as I was sitting in a little closet remade into a "war room" at the Bible school I attended in Vancouver, British Columbia, Canada. It shares what God will do that we will know He is the LORD! I would like for it to be the last Scripture I leave with you.

> "I will go before you and will level the mountains; I will break down gates of bronze and cut through bars of iron. I will give you

hidden treasures, riches stored in secret place, so that you may know that I am the LORD, the God of Israel, who summons you by name."

The LORD will move Heaven and earth so that we will know Him! He, who knows *your* name, just wants you to call on His.

For we who call on the name of Jesus, as our LORD and Savior, one of the hidden treasures we are given is His peace deep in our heart, even when our world seems out of control. With His peace, we have great hope for our future and are full of anticipation, knowing that the best is yet to come.

I look forward to the day we will all sit together in heaven and tell each other of Jesus in our earth lives! I can't wait to hear you tell how God wrote in blue to change your stories, too. We will all be thankful that we chose to be unbending in our faith because, then, we will be living in *His story that is unending*!

To contact author Sherri Sumstine, or to invite her to minister at your church or ministry, email her at:

Sherri@GodsBestForNow.org

Made in the USA
San Bernardino, CA
20 November 2017